HAMLINE UNIVERSITY
A History

HAMLINE UNIVERSITY
A History

by David W. Johnson

Printed in the United States of America
at the North Central Publishing Company, St. Paul

FOR GERRI

CONTENTS

LIST OF ILLUSTRATIONS

PREFACE

HAMLINE UNIVERSITY, founded in 1854, is Minnesota's oldest college. For 125 years it has been a representative example of private liberal arts education in America, and in more recent years has typified the struggle waged by urban universities confronted with critical socioeconomic challenges. Once essentially an academy with a curriculum tailored to the expectations of an undereducated rural Methodist constituency, Hamline has evolved into a sophisticated, cosmopolitan institution with mature ties to its founding denomination. Thousands of alumni, including five Rhodes Scholars, have preserved and publicized its influence. Today, the University's recently modernized campus testifies to Hamline's leadership in preserving a transitional urban neighborhood only recently threatened with decay.

Yet no comprehensive history of this significant institution has ever been published. In 1907, alumni brought together a brief account of the University's Red Wing years. In 1939, Charles Nelson Pace edited a collection of alumni and faculty reminiscences. In 1924 and again in 1966, the University published alumni directories containing brief historical sketches. Manuscripts and published essays provide topical information on aspects of University life. No work, however, examines the institution in its totality.

What follows is an interpretive history of Hamline. It is not a chronicle; it is not a filiopietistic rendering of the past; and it will not be of antiquarian interest. Rather, it is an effort to place the University squarely within its cultural context, examine themes unique to the Hamline experience, and investigate questions bearing upon the nature of private higher education in the United States.

Many individuals have played a part in the preparation of this history. They deserve mention.

C. S. Griffin of the University of Kansas, then at work on what was to become his magnificent history of that institution, once cautioned in seminar that an individual had to be out of his mind to write institutional history. Thus forewarned, I ignored him.

Phil Nordquist of Pacific Lutheran University once asked me whether anyone had ever sought to explain a particularly fascinating aspect of Hamline's past. I replied that nobody had ever sought to explain much of anything about Hamline, a typically brash assertion which was not exactly correct, given what I would soon learn about — and from — Grace Lee Nute's groundbreaking effort of the early 1950s. But my curiosity was aroused.

Jim Halseth, also of Pacific Lutheran, and like myself a product of the Midwest, understood banality and counseled against it. After living on the frontier, one acquires a certain vigor, and hates to see it disappear.

Several former colleagues at Pacific Lutheran read and commented on portions of the manuscript. Chris Browning not only managed to understand what I was trying to say in Chapter 1, but in his gracious manner assured me that I could get away with relegating the entire early history of Methodism, along with the first twenty-five years of Hamline's history, to twenty pages. Dan Van Tassel, MLA Style Sheet at his fingertips, provided humorous and insightful critiques of Chapters 2 and 3. Morty Rozanski was of invaluable assistance in my effort to discard half the material contained in what finally became Chapter 4. And Phil Nordquist, drawing upon his athletic prowess as well as his historian's training, made many helpful suggestions regarding Chapter 10, in the process sparing me certain embarrassment.

Others, too, deserve thanks. Robert Holliday and David LaBerge read Chapter 8 and raised important questions. Paul Giddens, Hurst Anderson, Lynn Beyer, and Carlyle Beyer provided detailed written responses to my inquiries. Shortly before his death in December, 1977, Richard Bailey granted an extensive interview. University Archivist Muriel McEachern, whose successful effort to organize and catalog a significant portion of the material now housed in the archives can only be regarded as heroic, accommodated my every need and request, listened to my complaints, and made intelligent responses to my speculations.

Librarian Jack King and his capable staff made working in the Bush Memorial Library a pleasure. Director of Publications Carol Lindahl guided segments of the manuscript to publication in the *Bulletin*. President Jerry Hudson, Academic Dean Kenneth Janzen, Registrar Stewart Shaw, and Vice President for Development Thomas Ruddy regularly made the resources of their respective offices available and offered words of encouragement. Grace Lee Nute reflected upon aspects of her own research and shared ideas about some of the personalities who dominated the institution's past. In Duluth, Rudolph Johnson, David Gaynon, and Judy Trolander provided access to the Nute Papers. And Ralph Olmsted of the University of Evansville kindly allowed me to borrow portions of the Alfred Hughes Papers.

Research was made possible in part by a sabbatical leave of absence from Pacific Lutheran University, by a Faculty Travel Award from the Center for the Study of Public Policy, and by a Faculty Growth Award from the American Lutheran Church.

On a more personal level, I owe particular debts of gratitude to several other individuals. Each, I trust, will understand what I have in mind. They are Bill and Joanne Archerd, Dennis Boom, Roger Reiling, and Marvin Schilling.

Finally, I am indebted to my family. My parents sacrificed in untold ways to make my education possible. My children, Elizabeth and Jeffrey, have lifted my spirits with their love and good humor. My ultimate and altogether inexpressible debt is to my wife. Her patience, wisdom, sensitivity, and grace have brought this history to fruition.

CHAPTER 1

RED WING

IN THE YEARS between 1815 and the outbreak of the Civil War, a spirit of almost indiscriminate optimism pervaded life on the American frontier. When the War of 1812 ended and the British gradually began withdrawing from the vast territory that lay between the crest of the Appalachians and the Mississippi River, Americans who possessed the necessary daring began to move almost literally overnight into that great expanse. There they hoped to carve out new and more independent lives for themselves and their families. Thousands of settlers invaded the New West in the years after 1815, migrating like a tide across western Pennsylvania, across Ohio, Indiana, and Illinois to Wisconsin and Minnesota. And with them moved American Methodism, which had first sent itinerant circuit-riders across the Alleghenies in 1782. Methodist preachers were present in Michigan by 1823, in Minnesota by 1824, and in Wisconsin by 1826. By 1840, the Church had organized fifteen annual conferences west of the Alleghenies — including the Ohio in 1812, the Illinois in 1824, the Indiana in 1832, and the Michigan in 1836.[1]

The period which witnessed this expansion was one that embraced a comprehensive, democratic idealism. Proclaiming the importance of the "common man" and seeking in various ways to meet his needs, Americans in the decades before the Civil War promoted such concepts as universal suffrage, free tax-supported public schools, workingmen's and women's rights, the abolition of slavery, and — especially significant with respect to the founding of frontier colleges — the idea that higher education should become

1

more accessible to all. While the Methodist Church had previously displayed little interest in the establishment of colleges and universities, its attitude toward higher education and its conception of the proper relationship between faith and learning gradually underwent a fundamental change during the early part of the nineteenth century. The end product of that barely discernible transition, which culminated in a resolution enacted by the General Conference of 1820, was the Church's sudden decision aggressively to promote the founding of educational institutions. That Methodists had established only one permanent college on the frontier prior to 1830 owed largely to their historic mistrust of learning — their conviction that "bookishness," especially in ministers, was suspect. Faith and physical fortitude, not knowledge of Greek and Hebrew, reasoned the Methodists, were the qualities most suited to spreading the faith on the frontier. They sincerely believed that college and university graduates would lack both the will and the stamina to function effectively in a crude environment. But as the rigors of life in the sparsely-settled West diminished, the need for stouthearted circuit riders also dwindled, and there arose an increasing respect for the benefits of education. The impact of that transition, in terms of Methodism's willingness to invest in educational pursuits, was sudden and profound.[2]

Still, it is not altogether surprising that early nineteenth-century Methodists gradually matured in their attitudes toward learning. The Church's roots, after all, were in a university. Both John and Charles Wesley were graduates of Oxford colleges, as was George Whitefield, and the first Methodists were Oxford students. Wesley's concept of education and learning admittedly differed from that which Methodists of the antebellum period later embraced. But intellectual interests and concerns were nonetheless integral to the Evangelical Revival which produced the Wesleyan movement in England. Thus, while some of Wesley's beliefs and attitudes conflicted with contemporary scientific developments, and while a decided anti-intellectualism inhered in some of his religious proclamations, the Wesleyan movement also spawned a great array of philanthropic and humanitarian endeavors which by their very nature did much to educate the untutored masses. And the latter circumstance found its counterpart in the activities of the Church in America from the third decade of the nineteenth century onward.[3]

Once American Methodists had decided to abandon the anachronistic notion that ministers were more effective servants when left uneducated, they soon made up for lost time. At the 1820 General Conference, held in Baltimore, delegates approved a recommendation that annual conferences establish literary institutions under their control as soon as practicable. The recommendation was a pragmatic response to two significant developments. In the first place, Methodist young people were going to college in ever-increasing numbers. And in the second, the colleges and universities available to them were chiefly controlled by Congregationalists and Presbyterians. Incited to action by the Conference's resolution, the Methodists quickly demonstrated their new commitment to higher education. They chartered Randolph-Macon College in Virginia in 1830 and Wesleyan University in Connecticut in 1831. They assumed control of Dickinson and Allegheny Colleges — both former Presbyterian institutions — in 1833. They established McKendree College in Illinois in 1835, Indiana Asbury University (subsequently DePauw) in 1837, Ohio Wesleyan in 1842, and Iowa Wesleyan in 1844. They founded Baldwin-Wallace in 1845, Lawrence and Taylor in 1847, and Albion in 1850. Northwestern came into existence in 1851 and Illinois Wesleyan in 1853. By 1854, when the Wisconsin Conference sought and received a charter to establish Hamline, the Church was operating no fewer than twenty-three permanent western colleges.[4]

Like their counterparts in other denominations, the Methodists' interest in establishing frontier colleges was clear and logical. Persons living on the frontier were poor. It was quite impossible for them even to consider sending their sons or daughters to the established colleges and universities of the Atlantic seaboard. Therefore, the Church would bring education to the frontier. Consistently, the charters of colleges established under Methodist auspices corresponded chronologically to the advance of that frontier. The incorporation of Hamline University under the Laws of Minnesota in 1854 was no exception.[5]

It was Chauncey Hobart, who became pastor at St. Paul in 1849 and who was a member of the Wisconsin Conference which then included the west bank of the Mississippi in its jurisdiction, who took the lead in agitating for a Methodist institution in Minnesota Territory. Corresponding with friends in New England and Illinois in the hope of securing enough money to build an academy — that is, a preparatory school — he met initially with a discouraging response. Subsequent efforts to locate and establish the school on land available at what was then the head of Jackson and Robert Streets in St. Paul proved similarly fruitless. But in January, 1854, Wisconsin Conference ministers led by the Rev. David Brooks applied to the territorial legislature for a seminary or academy charter. Urged by the Hon. William Pitt Murray, a St. Paul Methodist and a member of the legislature, to set more ambitious sights, the group agreed that Murray should introduce a substitute bill calling for the establishment of a "university." Minnesota Methodists, Murray felt, should not content themselves with creating a preparatory school which would subsequently send its graduates to other parts of the country for their college education. They should assume patronage of a full-fledged university or nothing at all. Murray's rewritten bill, approved by the legislature, received the signature of Territorial Governor Willis A. Gorman on March 3, 1854.[6]

Creation of the yet-hypothetical institution, which bore the name "Hamline University of Minnesota," was a remarkable yet altogether typical act of faith consistent with frontier optimism. There were, after all, only 32,000 white settlers living in Minnesota Territory in 1854, and fewer than 800 of those were Methodists. Most were desperately poor. There was no public school system and there were no high schools. Brooks, Murray, and their associates must have known that the mortality rate for frontier institutions of learning was discouragingly high. Undeterred, the new trustees, adhering to the charter provision that they should locate Hamline "at some point on the Mississippi between St. Paul and Lake Pepin," and apparently influenced by the strong urgings of Red Wing freeholder and real estate speculator William Freeborn, decided to establish the fledgling institution in that hamlet. Trustee Freeborn's speculative interests in Red Wing, which had begun two years earlier, led him to claim the "prophetic vision" typical of the age that the tiny village would one day become "a city that would rank high in intelligence, wealth, and population among the cities of Minnesota." Nor was Red Wing itself, then but 300 strong and with a total real and personal property valuation of less than $70,000, averse to welcoming the college. Pledging about $10,000 to enable construction of a building and the beginning of an endowment, and donating a tract of land on the hillside overlooking the Mississippi, the residents of the community testified to their enthusiasm. But it remained unarguably the case that despite those civic inducements, Hamline University took root in Red Wing primarily because Freeborn and two other trustees — ex-Governor Alexander Ramsey and B. F. Hoyt — were among the proprietors of the townsite.[7]

Although the trustees held pledges from the residents of Red Wing, they proceeded during 1854 and 1855 to erect a college building largely in anticipation of receiving approximately $12,000 from the sale of six New York City lots, located just west of Fifth Avenue on Forty-fourth Street, which formed part of Bishop Leonidas L. Hamline's gift to the university which bore his name. Hamline, a wealthy member of the Methodist hierarchy living in retirement at Sharon Springs, New York, had long been interested in the progress of education on the frontier. In 1852 he had made the acquaintance of William Pitt Murray at a reception in Cincinnati and in the course of his conversation with the young Minnesotan had sought to learn everything he could about the recently established territory. Subsequent to his visit, Hamline corresponded with Murray, who was flattered both by the Bishop's personal interest and his inquisitiveness regarding Minnesota. For those reasons, Murray quite logically attached the Bishop's name to the bill which he introduced into the territorial legislature. Complimented by the fact that his Western admirers had named the new institution after him, the Bishop in turn gave the University $25,000 worth of real estate, including the New York City lots and several more in Chicago. He gave an equivalent sum to the trustees of Cornell College, founded at Mount Vernon, Iowa, the same year. Together, Hamline's contributions to the cause of Methodist higher education in the West constituted approximately one-half of his estate.[8]

The unpretentious but utilitarian brick structure which the trustees erected at Red Wing contained a chapel, recitation rooms, a school room, a library and a laboratory, reading rooms, and dormitory quarters. When the building opened in January, 1855, the University was already in its second term, having conducted classes during the autumn of 1854 in rooms housed on the second floor of the village general store. Viewing as unrealistic the immediate establishment of a full-fledged university in a thinly-populated territory without high schools, the trustees had decided to begin with a Preparatory Department, which the charter had also authorized. Then, when enough students had received sufficient training, it would be appropriate to introduce collegiate classes. Presiding over the endeavor was the Rev. Jabez Brooks, son of the clergyman who had initially approached William Pitt Murray.[9]

Although the trustees' decision to begin the college course in 1857 presented the appearance of stability, Hamline had in fact been financially distressed from the outset. The New York City lots donated by Bishop Hamline — supposedly worth $12,000 in 1854 — plummeted so rapidly in value thereafter that when the trustees sold them in order to help pay for the college building, they realized only $7,000. The Panic of 1857, which adversely affected the economy of the entire country, had a devastating effect upon the financial fortunes of a sparsely-settled agricultural region. President Brooks, exhausted and health failing from overwork, resigned in 1857, leaving to his successor, the Rev. Benjamin F. Crary, the task of rectifying what would to a disinterested bystander have appeared an almost hopeless situation. Following a common and almost invariably misguided practice of the age, the trustees had also sold perpetual scholarships for $100 each and ten-year scholarships for $50 apiece as one means of financing the institution, a scheme which soon proved self-defeating. As early as 1857 it had also become apparent that the Methodists of Minnesota, in their enthusiasm for advancing the cause of higher education and in their intense local pride, might not settle for the maintenance of one institution alone. For in that year, the Conference Committee on Education noted with anxiety its fear "that the earnest desire for the education of the youth and the intense spirit of enterprise of the people" might lead to the establishment of rival institutions and the consequent weakening of the

Hamline University, Red Wing, 1854 to 1869.

Jabez Brooks. (From the collections of the Minnesota Historical Society.)

whole effort. By 1860, the committee reported that Hamline had become "very much crippled in its operations" and that its very existence was in danger because of its financial embarrassments. And it again pointed out the danger of succumbing to the temptation of chartering rival Methodist institutions within the state.[10]

The competitors, whose sinister presence just around the corner brought perennial warnings from the Committee on Education, never materialized. But the University's financial condition showed little sign of improvement during the ensuing decade. When the Civil War severely reduced the college's male population, the propriety of continuing to conduct classes seemed even more questionable. Annual statements of the institution's assets and liabilities proved especially disconcerting. Although the 1866 report showed assets totalling $42,604, including the five Chicago lots (optimistically valued at $20,000), the college building and grounds ($18,000), library books, apparatus, and other equipment ($4,000), and outstanding accounts ($604), the liabilities amounted to $8,717. Of this figure, $4,770 consisted of a mortgage on the building and just under $3,947 consisted of payments "due to various individuals." Thus, while the University with technical accuracy reported an excess of assets over liabilities amounting to $33,887, the cold fact remained that there was no money available with which to make a mortgage payment, and that the college owed almost $4,000 in unpaid bills, including $1,482 in faculty salaries.[11]

By the time of the Board's annual meeting in 1867, the University's debts had increased to $6,604, exclusive of the mortgage. Of this amount, $3,478 consisted of unpaid faculty salaries. The only assets immediately available appeared to be $794 in "cash on hand." The Chicago lots, now listed as worth only $15,000 were in the strict sense worth nothing at all, for Bishop Hamline had given them in perpetuity as income-producing property, and they could therefore not be sold. The University building and grounds, now heavily mortgaged, had declined in value to $11,000, while another $1,000 worth of books, apparatus, and other equipment could obviously not be sold either. Real estate with a book value of $1,065, given primarily in payment of subscriptions to the endowment, was of inferior quality and of little or no market value. Finally, the college could only expect to collect $325 in unpaid tuition when the students who owed it had first managed to find jobs, and jobs were anything but plentiful.[12]

When the Conference met at St. Anthony in 1868, the University's financial condition had seemingly improved to a degree. The treasurer was able to report that only the mortgage and $1,100 in salaries remained unpaid — an improvement of almost $9,000. But despite those positive signs the Committee on Education felt compelled to suggest that a radical change in attitude on the part of the Conference was long overdue. "The question is simply this," the members stated bluntly, "— will the 10,000 Methodists of Minnesota sustain their school . . . or will they through inaction . . . write up its history in the simple word, a synonym at once for defeat and disgrace, a failure?" But even as the committee sought to impress upon the Conference the necessity of renewed attention to Hamline's financial fortunes, it successfully secured the appointment of a Commission on Removal which was to study the entire Red Wing situation relative to other possibilities, reporting its recommendations one year later.[13]

During the ensuing year, the Commission pursued its investigation, and presented its report at the 1869 session in Minneapolis. Several communities, it indicated, had made financial proposals relative to removal and relocation. Faribault had offered to issue $25,000 worth of municipal bonds in order to secure the University for that community. Former trustee Ira Bidwell of West St. Paul had offered to donate a 25-acre site. Parties representing Rochester, Winona, and Minneapolis had also submitted statements, and Red Wing had later added its name to the list. But the Commission, whose chairman was former trustee J. F. Chaffee, went on to inform the Conference that it had made no decision and favored leaving the matter open for further study. Hearing this, the members resolved that "owing to financial embarrassments," and since the question of removal "continued to be agitated," it would be necessary to suspend college operations temporarily. Vowing to reopen the University as soon as the matter of location was settled and the endowment had increased, the Committee on Education recommended that the Conference convene an Educational Convention at Faribault the following spring. At that session, the Commission on Removal would once again discuss all relocation proposals, and would have authority to make a final recommendation on disposition of the matter.[14]

In deciding to close the University for the time being, the Conference was acquiescing in a judgment already made by the trustees. After discussing whether to abandon the enterprise altogether or merely suspend operation until it had paid existing debts, the Board had initially agreed simply to dispense with the spring term and to resume a full schedule of classes in the fall. But on July 6, 1869, it resolved instead that "in the present state of the finances of the institution, we find it impossible to employ a faculty for the coming year." Yet while the University's perennial "financial embarrassments" seemed on the surface to explain the Board's action, the treasurer's report for 1869 actually showed that the institution had never been better situated financially. Total immediate liabilities were only $895, while liquid assets were relatively substantial. The trustees had recently received $500 from the sale of stock, $1,265 from scholarship payments, and $2,250 from the sale of an estate. Most of this $4,015 was already invested in securities.[15] Why, therefore, just when Hamline's fortunes seemed for the first time in fifteen years to rest on a reasonably secure footing, did Board and Conference alike decide to give up the struggle?

In fact, money had little to do with the decision. If the friends of the University had managed to secure a charter, select a site for the campus, issue a construction contract, and open the University for classes in 1854 — all this on nothing more than the unrealistic promise of $10,000 from Red Wing citizens and confidence in the superior marketability of Bishop Hamline's New York City lots — why should they have decided to suspend operations fifteen years later when the institution's financial prospects had never looked more promising? Two factors in particular bore upon the decision. In the first place, Minnesota Methodists had increasingly questioned the wisdom of retaining the Red Wing site, where the building was inadequate and the tract of land too limited to allow room for expansion. Hardly a metropolis in 1854, sleepy Red Wing was rapidly losing ground to St. Paul and Minneapolis, both of which were developing into major centers of population and commerce. With the arrival of the railroad, moreover, the Twin Cities threatened to eclipse not only Red Wing but every other outpost which had depended upon the Mississippi for its existence and its survival. Sentiment for removal had been present within the Conference for more than a decade, as had the desire to establish other Church-sponsored institutions of higher learning. The second principal ingredient was the Board itself. Between 1866 and 1869 eight new men had become trustees, leaving only one of the original number — David Brooks.[16] There was no assurance that the earlier Board, had its personnel remained essentially unaltered, would have chosen to ignore the agitation for removal. But the relationship between the institution and the original Board was quite unlike that which pertained by 1869 when the new trustees opted for closure. The former members identified themselves and their fortunes with the institution and with Red Wing in a way that the new members could not. Thus, the trustees who met in 1869 to consider the institution's fate were less prepared to question — or better able to accept — the prospect of closure, which contained within it the unstated but obvious implication that if Hamline were in fact to reopen, it would not be at Red Wing.

The Educational Convention and Commission on Removal met in Faribault according to plan on May 5, 1870. Rochester, Red Wing and Faribault again presented propositions, Rochester alone avoiding any mention of tax-supported municipal bonds. Although the 42 ministerial and 32 lay delegates questioned the propriety of financing a sectarian institution by means of public support — the essence of the Red Wing and Faribault proposals — they rejected none of the plans outright, preferring instead to leave the decision in abeyance once more. Thus, when the Annual Conference met at Owatonna in October of that year, the Commission on Removal requested and received continuance. It also sought and received an enlargement of powers which in retrospect proved crucially significant. For in securing from the Conference "entire authority to handle our present educational interests, either to organize a new Board of Trustees with a view of commencing *de novo*, or to reorganize and enlarge the Board of Trustees of Hamline University if it should be thought best to continue our educational interests under that name and charter,'' the Commission, led by the increasingly influential Chaffee, now had the power to alter the original charter in order to relocate the University wherever it wished. It wasted no time in making a choice. On March 6, 1871, the legislature approved a charter amendment which enlarged the size of the Board from fifteen to twenty-one members and, of immediate importance, allowed relocation wherever the trustees and Conference wished.[17]

When the Conference convened at Mankato in September, 1871, Rochester seemed to have won the relocation war. Part of the reason was the delegates' continued reluctance to accept tax dollars for sectarian purposes. In addition, a Rochester layman had promised to secure $50,000 in building pledges, payable in ten equal annual installments. Enthusiastically approving the Commission's recommendation that the University relocate at Rochester, the Conference at the same session appointed Chaffee college financial agent.[18] If it believed that the first of its decisions was the more important of the two, it was mistaken. For when it entrusted to the shrewd and aggressive Minneapolis pastor ultimate responsibility for all recommendations which pertained to the raising of capital gifts, the Conference unwittingly gave Chaffee *carte blanche* to re-establish the University wherever he wished. As subsequent events quickly demonstrated, that was precisely what he did.

Although Chaffee did not immediately publicize his preference for a site within or near Minneapolis or St. Paul, he soon scuttled the Rochester effort. When a committee of citizens from that community confessed in November, 1871, that it could not guarantee the full $50,000 previously pledged, Chaffee bluntly recommended abandoning the Rochester option, and the Board dutifully agreed. Indicating that the location of the University was still open for consideration, it resolved that Chaffee, Professor H. B. Wilson (a former Red Wing faculty member and currently State Superintendent of Public Instruction), and Board members residing in St. Paul, Minneapolis, and St. Anthony ''be constituted a committee to receive propositions and report to this board,'' and gave them power to convene special Board meetings if necessary. Thus, at a single stroke, the trustees had illegally concentrated sole decision-making authority regarding the future of the University in the hands of a committee which was naturally predisposed toward relocating Hamline in the general neighborhood of St. Paul and Minneapolis, and which had as its principal spokesman an individual who was determined to relocate it there. Within less than a week, Chaffee had written a letter to the Rochester promoters informing them that the Conference no longer felt certain their city offered the best future prospects for the college. Everyone realized, he boldly asserted, that support for the move came not from the community at large, but only from a few individuals. Rochester, he concluded, "was not a better town for a college than Red Wing, and it was not more central."[19]

Thus the search for a new home continued. By the time the Conference met at Winona in September, 1872, the hard-working Chaffee had managed to raise about $100,000 in endowment pledges. He had also worked diligently to promote relocation in the Twin Cities. Largely as a result of his efforts, the Board on September 24, 1872, received from St. Paul residents Girart Hewitt and E. F. Drake a proposal to sell to the University the southwest quarter of Section 27, Township 29, Range 23, in Ramsey County — which included the future Snelling Avenue location — for $54,000. After weeks of complex negotiations, the trustees and the Commission on Removal finally decided, on December 11, 1872, to accept the proffered tract under terms which now specified that Hewitt and his associates would in effect donate half the site, with title to be transferred when Hamline completed construction of a University building to "the walls of the first story." If the Board wished, the donors would repurchase half the land for $20,000 on July 1, 1873. The trustees combined their acceptance of the offer with a resolution that Hennepin and Ramsey counties raise $50,000 to erect the necessary buildings.[20]

It was hardly surprising, given Chaffee's desires and the presence of several influential Twin City businessmen on the Board, that the University's new location was a 77-acre prairie plot midway between the two largest cities in the state. Nor were the trustees and Chaffee alone in their desire to secure a more urban location. As Chaffee's successor, Financial Agent J. R. Creighton, later reported, several bishops and many "distinguished and experienced educators of the church'' had implored the trustees to situate Hamline "at or near the great commercial centre of the state." No matter how great the financial inducements held out from other quarters, they argued, "the question of locality should have precedence over and outrank all others." When Hewitt and his business partners held out their several inducements, the choice of the Midway site was virtually assured.[21]

For his singleminded efforts to secure a new home for the college, Chaffee ultimately earned the rebuke of his congregation and trial before the Conference in 1874, where he defended himself against charges of "imprudent conduct," "falsehood," dishonest and wrongful business behavior, "unchristian and unministerial conduct," and finally, "stirring up strife among the brethren, and fomenting and promoting dissension in the church;" while "continually and persistently interfering with the interests and business matters of Centenary Church in an illegitimate and unwarranted manner." Of the five, the Conference sustained only those specifying "imprudent conduct" and "unchristian and unministerial conduct." The members, it seemed, felt obliged to slap Chaffee's hand for reasons which pertained to his more offensive personal qualities and not his sound, if overly aggressive, business acumen.[22]

Meanwhile Chaffee found himself and the institution confronted by a new round of financial difficulties. Hardly was work on University Hall underway when, precipitated by the collapse of the New York City banking house of Jay Cooke and Company, financial panic swept the nation in October, 1873. The effect at Hamline, where the trustees were already struggling to raise the $13,840 required to purchase the 37 acres not donated by Girart Hewitt and his associates, was immediate and profound. By 1874, the Board had managed to raise only $6,748, although there were in hand pledges amounting to an additional $2,933. Of the $104,000 which Chaffee had secured in pledges between 1872 and 1874, the college had actually collected only $2,400. Hennepin and Ramsey counties, having pledged only $44,000 of the $50,000 requested by the trustees, had delivered but $10,500. In addition, there was an immediate need for $4,400 to meet construction costs on University Hall. While the college held $5,100 worth of real estate as building fund assets, none of this was immediately available to apply to the indebtedness. Nor did the Chicago lots return more than the amount necessary to meet mandatory municipal improvements. The story was the same elsewhere. In short, most of the University's assets were nonproductive — just as they always had been.[23]

And then there were the grasshoppers! From 1873 until 1877 Minnesota suffered from successive invasions of the insects, which wrought their havoc upon an agricultural economy already plagued by constricted credit and low prices. So great was the devastation produced by the unrelenting locusts that when they finally disappeared, the Conference felt compelled to pass a resolution of Thanksgiving.[24]

Still, reported J. R. Creighton, who had recently succeeded Chaffee as agent, the trustees had recently set aside 60 acres located east of the main campus as endowment, and had arranged to plat and lay out this area into streets, blocks, and lots. The remaining 17 acres would become the campus proper.[25] Thus, in the early 1870s as in 1854, the individuals most responsible for the University's well-being had chosen to risk its future by speculating in real estate. Their decision was hardly unique. For given the venturesome temperament which prevailed nationwide between the end of the Civil War and the Panic of 1873, it was only natural for the Board to decide that real estate provided a small, struggling college with the best means of assuring an adequate endowment. The cause of Christian education in Minnesota was at stake, they believed, and what better way was there to establish Hamline on a sound financial footing, thereby avoiding repetition of the Red Wing difficulties. To their credit, they were willing to take risks. To their detriment, the Panic soon dashed their hopes.

Through the worst of the troubles, Creighton labored heroically onward, managing to accomplish without breeding resentment far more than Chaffee had ever pretended to achieve. He not only worked tirelessly to raise money, but regularly provided the trustees with competent and thorough financial advice. One of his first efforts concerned the Chicago property, which had long suffered from bad management. Creighton quickly discovered that four of the lots showed an indebtedness of $617 for unpaid taxes and other assessments. After a comprehensive investigation, he placed the total value of the lots at $30,000, with an estimated annual yield of $1,188. He drew up a list of all University assets and liabilities, and presented it in his 1875 Annual Report. Undoubtedly referring to the hard feelings engendered by Chaffee's high-handed tactics, Creighton explained that he had ''used every endeavor to remove misunderstandings,'' and judged it ''important that these matters be fully discussed, clearly understood, and thoroughly settled in the minds of the members of this Conference, to the end that the confidence of the entire Church may be secured in the faithful management of the affairs and interests of the University.'' Although he found accounts correct in every detail, he was shocked to discover that irregularly-preserved memoranda constituted the entirety of the University's financial records. Creighton soon remedied that frightening situation by instituting double-entry bookkeeping and by posting all accounts from the beginning of endowment collections in 1871. A man of temperance, he also sought to preserve the health and morals of future generations by securing in 1876 an amendment to the charter which forbade the sale of intoxicating beverages within one-half mile of the campus.[26]

Predictably, he was loathe to reopen the institution prematurely. Despite the advances which Hamline enjoyed under his leadership, there was good reason for Creighton to remain concerned about the University's economic fortunes. It bothered him, for example, that in order to enclose University Hall, it had become necessary in 1875 to place an $8,000 mortgage on the structure and on 40 of the 60 acres which adjoined the campus proper. Chaffee criticized him for allowing the transfer to the building fund of Minneapolis and St. Paul pledges obtained earlier as endowment subscriptions, although the Board undoubtedly rationalized the move on the grounds that the 60 surveyed acres were themselves allocated to endowment. Creighton made the extent of the problem clear in his 1875 report. Building fund assets were certainly available, he admitted, but completion of the structure, along with mortgage payments and incidental expenses, would necessitate raising an additional $30,000. The source of that substantial sum was problematic, for the Twin

Cities had already proven their inability to make good on pledges. Now that the University had actually committed itself to the Midway site, it was no longer possible to hang the relocation carrot from a string when soliciting funds. Within the Church, there existed a widespread and not inaccurate understanding that St. Paul and Minneapolis had agreed to finance the building. Therefore, until funds previously pledged by other sources materialized, the Methodists of the state were also unlikely to empty their pockets. Still, Creighton resolutely urged the Conference to allocate $10,000 per year for three years — an average of one dollar per member per year — to raise the required capital. The delegates refused to authorize the allocation, but magnanimously promised to welcome Creighton as he made his rounds.[27]

By the summer of 1876, the Agent was able to report that total receipts for the year were $20,375, including $864 collected on endowment subscriptions, $17,484 paid on the building fund, $1,645 income from the Chicago property, and $382 in trustee donations to help meet the Chicago taxes. But again he cautioned against succumbing improvidently to the temptation to reopen the college. "The country is passing through a very severe financial crisis," he told the Board in a special report submitted in July. "There can possibly be no improvement in money matters the coming fall and winter." It would be quite impossible to raise any significant amount of money in cash during the next six months, and would be equally unwise to borrow money simply to allow an early reopening. Rather, it was time "to trim our sails and hug the shore all the closer," until prosperity had returned, current debts were paid, and conditions in general looked more promising. He concluded his statement by tendering his resignation, explaining that there was not much point in continuing to collect a salary, given the institution's financial condition. But he volunteered to remain on as an "office agent," and suggested that in order to create an image of stability, the trustees appoint the Rev. David Clarke John, Principal of the Mankato State Normal School, as both president and agent. The Board accepted Creighton's recommendations, and in September the Conference approved John's election — an appointment that looked to the future, for the new president remained at Mankato until 1880. Creighton became both "office agent" and Presiding Elder of the Mankato District.[28]

While Creighton was busy with the books, Chaffee was again busy with the charter. Persuaded that his earlier attempt to modernize the Board by enlarging it had not wholly resolved the troublesome matter of electing suitable trustees, he now determined to make the governing agency self-perpetuating. Whereas the charter specified that the Conference *elect* individuals annually to fill vacancies on the Board, Chaffee now proposed that the Board *nominate* the individuals and the Conference then elect them. Chaffee later bragged that he had personally "engineered" the change, and that only "after a pretty sharp fight on the Conference floor" had the delegates seen fit to authorize the amendment. The legislature approved the new provision on February 14, 1877. "It is safe to say," Chaffee wrote many years later in a self-serving but informative document, "that ever since that change was made, we have had a much more influential and effective Board of Trustees than we had had, or ever could have had under the old plan. . . ." The new procedure was open to abuse, he acknowledged, but the original procedure "was all abuse. . . ." Thus, the Board became a closed corporation and the Church found itself one step further removed from immediate influence over the University's affairs. Parenthetically, the change also legalized Chaffee's 1870 request that the Conference give the Commission on Removal extraordinary authority.[29]

Although the prolonged depression regularly defeated the trustees' efforts to complete University Hall, the Board and the Conference in 1878 renewed their efforts to raise the necessary funds. In that year the Committee on Education recommended that Hamline reopen in 1879 and that the Conference raise $20,000 to pay the institution's indebtedness and complete construction. The Church would raise $4,000 immediately, and would apportion the remaining $16,000 among the districts and charges. Confident that the recent nationwide financial upswing signalled a positive economic impact on Hamline, the delegates adopted the report. Selected to become the new agent was the Rev. John Stafford, who had studied at Hamline during its Red Wing days and who had been associated with Minnesota Methodism since the early 1860s.[30]

Stafford pursued his work vigorously, but by the autumn of 1879 had managed to secure only $13,000 in pledges, of which $9,000 was actually in hand. Accordingly, the Conference again voted to delay reopening for a year, and to levy another $10,000 assessment. But by the summer of 1880 Stafford had managed to collect an additional $8,900, the institution's financial condition seemed secure, and work on University Hall was essentially complete. On July 20, 1880, over 1,000 persons attended its formal dedication. President John, who had formally taken office the previous May, was on hand to participate in the gala event.[31] At long last, the University stood ready to welcome its students once more. Hamline's eleven-year hiatus had ended.

CHAPTER 2

BEGINNING ANEW
IN ST. PAUL

HAMLINE UNIVERSITY "stood grim and bare, like a monument in a desert with nothing between it and the North Pole," when the first term of the college year began on September 22, 1880. Stubble from a recently-harvested wheat crop surrounded the four-story brick and limestone building which loomed up from the treeless prairie, while a lone stack of straw situated directly in front of the mansard-roofed structure greeted the sixty students and five faculty who arrived to take up their preparatory and collegiate work together. Immediately adjacent to the north and, apart from the real estate deal struck eight years earlier with Girart Hewitt, a major reason for the University's otherwise inexplicably bleak and barren location were the short line tracks of James J. Hill's St. Paul, Minneapolis, and Manitoba railroad. One mile to the south, beyond the Territorial Road which ran diagonally from St. Paul to St. Anthony, and University Avenue which ran rough and ungraded from the capital to Minneapolis, lay the Chicago, Milwaukee, and St. Paul railroad. A solitary house stood just west of Snelling Avenue, five others in process of completion nearby. What could be said for amenities? No graded streets, no sidewalks, no street cars, no water pipes, and no fire protection. If the University's Fathers had consciously sought to select a more desolate and depressing setting for the rejuvenated college, they could not have done a better job.[1]

But while disinterested observers may well have scoffed at the trustees' choice of so seemingly unpromising a site, President John enthusiastically took up the task of publicizing the University's virtues. To the former normal school president, Hamline's "long looked for hour" as a coeducational liberal arts institution had finally arrived, while "the reproach of Minnesota Methodism" had at last disappeared. In its "elegant and commodious" home, the college once again presented "the opportunity for Christian culture" which for eleven years it had found itself forced by circumstance to deny. As for its location, John declared, "a more beautiful, eligible and healthful" site existed nowhere in North America. "In the center of a population of one hundred thousand intelligent, industrious and highly cultured people," he went on, "it combines the advantage of rural quiet and urban refinement; and no pupil can long be in contact with such surroundings without catching . . . inspiration and awakening to a new life, such as he never dreamed of before." For books alone did not constitute an education; "moral, industrial and esthetic surroundings contribute powerfully, though unconsciously, to the general development of the pupil." Other institutions, older but "less fortunate in their location," were unable to provide these opportunities.[2]

Although the advantages which Hamline's suburban location would one day offer were in fact foreseen with considerable accuracy by John, they were not immediately apparent to the students who picked their way through the stubble that autumn. "In those early years," recalled Leonard J. Dobner of the Class of 1884, "we were a little world by ourselves. The winters were long and exceedingly cold. We were, in a way," he remembered with essential if chilling accuracy, "snowed in from December to May." Women students housed on the upper floors of University Hall suffered constantly from lack of adequate heat, and the classrooms below were no better shielded against the northern blasts which howled unmercifully and unrelentingly. Diphtheria, probably the result of the community's primitive sanitation system, overtook the University in November, 1881, forcing closure of the college for the duration of the autumn term. Far more serious was the fire which swept through University Hall in February, 1883, burning the structure to the ground. Apparently caused by defective flues and chimney, the fire had gutted the building by the time the horse-drawn engines of the St. Paul fire department arrived.[3]

Fortunately, President John had earlier seen the need for a more satisfactory dormitory arrangement than that which existed initially, and it was therefore possible to transfer all college operations to the recently-completed ''Ladies' Home.'' Constructed during the summer and autumn of 1882 and architecturally similar to the ill-fated structure next door, the three-story brick veneer building contained rooms for women on the upper floors. On the first floor were parlors, music rooms, and quarters for lady teachers and the college Matron. In the basement were kitchen, dining rooms, store room, laundry room and servants' quarters. Groundbreaking ceremonies took place on May 27, 1882. J. F. Chaffee presided over the cornerstone laying on July 27, and the dormitory, originally scheduled for fall occupancy, opened late in December. Within little more than a month, as a consequence of the University Hall fire, the building had become a home not only for the women but for the entire college.[4]

Meanwhile, college officials quickly made plans to reconstruct the destroyed structure. The Executive Committee of the Board met at once and decided to rebuild, and on March 8, the trustees authorized building plans. They also personally subscribed more than $10,000 toward the estimated $61,000 needed to clear debris, rebuild and refurnish, construct a separate heating plant (thereby hopefully avoiding repetition of the earlier disaster), and pay architect's fees. By October, 1883, the Church had contributed an additional $26,572, with the bulk of that sum, about $21,000, coming from Mr. and Mrs. Thomas A. Harrison and H. G. Harrison of Minneapolis and the Norton family of Winona. Constructed on the same foundation but with only three stories above the basement instead of four, the new structure was dedicated, debt-free, on January 4, 1884. Although the original University Hall had contained quarters for women, Ladies' Hall now provided ample space for female students, and the third floor of the rebuilt structure accordingly became a dormitory for men. In October, 1884, Presiding Elder Samuel G. Smith of the St. Paul District was able to tell the Conference that the two buildings and the campus were estimated to be worth $90,000 and that the endowment, both productive and unproductive, totaled about $145,000.[5]

By the time Smith gave his report, John was no longer president, for in the spring of 1883 he had submitted his resignation. While he gave no specific reasons for the decision, it was obvious that the strains of the presidency had finally worn him down. Shortage of funds and no plenitude of students were fast becoming perennial problems, and John, of serious demeanor and stern countenance, was neither skilled promoter nor effective solicitor. More familiar with normal school methods than with those of the liberal arts college, he tried but failed to introduce the former at Hamline to his ultimate discredit. His wife, who died of cancer in February, 1885, had been ill during the closing months of his Hamline tenure. Nor did John get along especially well either with certain more progressive members of the Board or with many residents of the community nearby. The University Hall fire seemed to discourage him more than ever, and in the aftermath of that episode he apparently decided to call it quits. Leaving St. Paul, John accepted appointment as pastor of the First Methodist Episcopal Church of Winona.[6]

His successor as president, and the individual destined to preside over Hamline's fortunes for the next twenty-nine years, was the Rev. George Henry Bridgman. A Canadian by birth and most recently principal of Genesee Wesleyan Seminary at Lima, New York, Bridgman received the Hamline invitation largely because Minnesota's Bishop Cyrus D. Foss, who was also president of the Board, knew a good deal about his skill as an academic administrator. Foss had been president of Wesleyan University in Connecticut prior to coming to Minnesota, and in that capacity had watched and admired Bridgman's work at relatively close range. When President John announced his resignation, Foss immediately thought of the Genesee principal as a suitable replacement. Although Bridgman knew nothing about Hamline, he accepted the proffered position after corresponding with the Bishop, and the trustees gave their unanimous stamp of approval.[7]

The scene which greeted Bridgman when he alighted from the train at the grandiosely named College Place station in June, 1883, was not markedly different from that which had presented itself to students and faculty three years earlier. To be sure, a small red brick building standing at the end of Simpson Street had replaced the tiny

clapboard shack which had served previously as the Hamline station, and two buildings, one of them only partly completed, now
graced the pasture. A narrow plank which ran diagonally from the
station toward the ungraded campus through fields of goldenrod and
ragweed partially eliminated the indignity of the trek. Endowment,
however, remained small and was still almost wholly unproductive.
Only 119 students had attended classes during the preceding year,
down fourteen from the second year and virtually identical with the
first, and liberals and conservatives on the Board had not even
pretended to patch up their differences. With few exceptions, the
faculty which awaited its new president was devoted but academically weak. There was no library and there were no science
laboratories. Overall, the situation appeared very nearly hopeless,
and Bridgman was almost beside himself with depression. ''I found
everything at Hamline so new and crude and disappointing and
discouraging,'' he wrote many years later, ''that I was homesick
from the outset and keenly regretted having left Lima where I
greatly enjoyed my work and where my position was secure as long
as I cared to hold it.'' Sensing from her husband's letters that he was
thoroughly discouraged, Mrs. Bridgman advanced her own travel
plans and arrived in St. Paul that August. In later years Bridgman
personally credited his wife with instilling in him the will to continue in his new position and the capacity to foresee with optimism
Hamline's potential for advancement in the midst of a rapidly developing agricultural, industrial, and commercial region.[8]

Once the President had managed to shake his depression, he
moved with the same vigor, talent, and devotion that had marked his
previous tenure to cultivate broadly based support, to strengthen the
faculty and augment the curriculum, to secure students and enlarge
the physical plant, and to build a substantial and productive endowment. Through Foss and Chaffee, both of whom lived in Minneapolis, he began to meet citizens who were financially capable of
assisting the young institution. Within one year of his arrival, the
college was free from debt. Within five years, Bridgman was able to
report a $90,000 increase in the endowment. Between 1884 and
1889, the Treasurer registered only one instance of a deficit, which a
special $22,000 subscription largely eliminated. By 1888, the value

George H. Bridgman in 1916. (From the collections of the Minnesota Historical Society. Photo by Lee Bros., Minneapolis.)

of the physical plant stood at $198,000, largely the result of the doubling in size of Ladies' Hall in 1886 and the completion of a science building in 1887.[9]

The massive three-story red brick Science Hall, which was Bridgman's first major development project, stood between Ladies' Hall and University Hall. Dedicated on January 5, 1888, it contained recitation and lecture rooms; a biological laboratory, lecture rooms, and store room; and on the third floor a Museum of Natural History. Professor H. N. Winchell, State Geologist and a member of the faculty at the University of Minnesota, had already presented a collection of valuable mineralogical and geological specimens as the Museum's first gift. Soon Henry L. Osborn, whom Bridgman hired in 1887 as professor of biology and geology, had augmented Winchell's gift of rocks and Palaeozoic fossils with some one hundred zoological specimens, a synoptical collection from the Smithsonian Institution of invertebrates from the New England coastal region, approximately 150 lithographs from the Boston Society of Natural History, a small collection of dried plants, specimens from his own highly sophisticated collection, and many lesser additions.[10]

Although Bridgman managed during his first years in office to stabilize Hamline's finances, to hire several talented faculty members, and to increase the size of the student body (enrollment grew from 80 preparatory and 24 college students in 1883–84 to 124 preparatory and 126 college enrollees in 1893–94) the good times ended temporarily with the onset of depression in 1893. Faculty members loyally accepted salary cuts, and by the summer of 1893 the trustees had begun to borrow large sums of money in order to pay the corporation's indebtedness. In August, the Executive Committee authorized the trustees to mortgage the campus and adjacent real estate and to borrow up to $27,000 to pay University debts. In December, the Board empowered itself to borrow up to $30,000 properly secured and, obviously troubled by the drift of events, appointed a special committee "to consider the outlook and prospects of the University." By the following June, in addition to having mortgaged University Hall, it had become necessary to borrow an additional $2,000 to pay faculty salaries for April and May, and to defer the June and July payments until the receipt of fall tuition income. Chaffee, by then president of the Board, was having his own difficulties. In October, 1894, he reported that he could no longer pay interest to the University on $51,000 worth of mortgages which it held against him. Accordingly, he submitted both a proposal to surrender property which he owned in Minneapolis in payment of the debt and his resignation as president, but the trustees deferred action on each. Between 1895 and 1897, the Executive Committee empowered the Board to borrow still another $11,000. In June, 1896, Treasurer E. F. Mearkle reported that indebtedness for the preceding year was $7,000.[11]

Both Bridgman and the trustees were of course hard at work on remedies. In the process, Chaffee, never one to overlook himself, managed to extricate himself from his financial plight. The manner in which he did so was complex but effective. It traced its origin to an earlier bequest by Minneapolis businessman Thomas A. Harrison, who had served as a trustee from 1873 until his death in 1888. Harrison had stipulated that the University should use the bequest, amounting to $50,000, to endow the Rebecca M. Harrison Chair of Mathematics in memory of his wife and the Carrie A. Widstrand Chair of Chemistry in memory of his daughter. This the trustees had faithfully done, and in 1889 Loren H. Batchelder succeeded to the Widstrand Chair, while E. F. Mearkle became Harrison Professor of Mathematics. Simultaneous with the creation of the two endowed chairs, however, the Board loaned Chaffee the entire $50,000, taking from him five promissory notes. Subsequently, they loaned him an additional $500.[12]

On March 20, 1896, Chaffee proposed to convey to the trustees immediately, subject to a $35,000 mortgage, the east ½ of Block 17, Snyder and Company's Addition to Minneapolis in full discharge of his $51,500 obligation to the University. The plat in question was the half-block fronting on the west side of Marquette Avenue (then First Avenue South) between Eleventh and Twelfth Streets. Chaffee assumed it would soon become profitable business property. Meanwhile, in December, 1895, Mrs. Anna Harrison Goheen, sister of Thomas A. Harrison, had loaned the University $5,000 at 5 per cent interest, payable by January 11, 1898, and had mortgaged her homestead, the east half of Lot 8, Block 25, Town of Minneapolis, which lay on the south side of North First Street between Second and Third Avenue North, as collateral. She now offered, in a document dated March 3, 1896, to give the University an additional $25,000 at 5 per cent per annum, payable in the fall of 1897, if it decided to accept Chaffee's proposal. The Board could use the money to defray better than two-thirds of Chaffee's $35,000 mortgage. Mrs. Goheen promised to surrender the trustees' 1895 note for the original $5,000 if they accepted her proposition, and stipulated that if they were to repay the full $30,000, she would use it to endow a professorship in memory of her brother. Next, she pledged to give the University $10,000 of Security Bank of Minneapolis stock. Finally, she indicated that she would bequeath the property where she lived, namely, 110 feet square on the northeast corner of Nicollet Avenue and Twelfth Streets. She expressed her desire that the trustees erect "a business property" on the plat and use the revenues derived from it, together with interest on the bank stock, to endow a divinity school which the Board had for some months hoped to establish.[13]

In effect, Mrs. Goheen proposed that the trustees use additional money from the Harrison estate, along with money of her own, to divest themselves of the better part of a $35,000 mortgage which they would acquire by virtue of their decision to reinvest the original Harrison bequest in a second mortgage on the Chaffee property! Treasurer E. F. Mearkle argued vehemently against acceptance of Mrs. Goheen's offer and, by implication, against Chaffee's proposal. To agree to this complex and dubious scheme, he explained, would unnecessarily jeopardize the Harrison bequest during a period of great economic uncertainty. Instead, he suggested, the trustees should consider arranging to retain the Harrison securities, and to accept Mrs. Goheen's gift "as soon as the funds from it are realized to pay off the mortgage," thus avoiding "the risk of total loss." Not one element of the entire proposal was certain, he contended, except that there was a $35,000 mortgage on Chaffee's property.[14]

But Mearkle failed to convince his colleagues. The trustees voted tentatively to accept the two propositions, appointing a five-member committee to investigate the matter and, if they saw fit, effectuate it.

After postponing action for a year and a half, the committee recommended unanimously that the Board accept the plan. On June 8, 1898, by which time market conditions had improved considerably, the trustees ratified the arrangement. According to the terms of the agreement, Chaffee deeded to Hamline 330 front feet on First Avenue South in full payment of his obligation to the University. He estimated the half block to be worth $66,000. Mrs. Goheen gave the trustees $30,000, including $25,000 in cash and the $5,000 note, to apply to the $35,000 mortgage. Since Chaffee owed $2,000 in back taxes, the trustees paid that sum, made a $23,000 mortgage payment, and placed a new $12,000 mortgage on the property. Finally, the Board agreed to pay Mrs. Goheen a $1,500 annuity for life, which was 6 per cent per annum on $25,000. Assuming the accuracy of Chaffee's estimate on the market value of his property, the trustees had accepted $96,000 worth of real and personal property, had cancelled $51,500 worth of interest-bearing notes, had assumed a $12,000 mortgage at 6 per cent interest, and had agreed to the Goheen annuity. But this was not enough to suit Chaffee. For on December 28, 1898, he informed the Board that when surrendering the First Avenue units, he had forgotten to remove a small heater which belonged to his son-in-law. The trustees promptly authorized a $25 payment.[15]

Meanwhile, President Bridgman had made great strides toward eliminating the University's debt. Early in 1898, he had secured from rail magnate James J. Hill a $20,000 pledge, contingent upon the college identifying an additional $15,000. By June of that year, the President had raised the requisite amount, seven-eighths of which was pledged by individuals outside the Methodist Church. After years of financial stress, the University was able to burn the $35,000 mortgage on its property.[16]

In the years that followed, Bridgman continued to demonstrate his talent as an aggressive fund raiser. In June, 1899, he announced that he had embarked upon an effort to add $250,000 to the University's endowment. By the end of 1902 he had procured the full amount, including $80,000 from Matthew and James Norton, $50,000 from James J. Hill, and $9,500 from the two Minnesota Methodist conferences. By June, 1903, the President was able to

announce the endowment of four new chairs: the James J. Hill Chair
of Ethics and Christian Evidences, the Matthew G. Norton, Jr.
Chair of Latin Languages and Literature, the Herbert H. Norton
Chair of English Literature, and the James L. Norton Chair of
Modern Languages and Greek. These joined the Widstrand Chair in
Chemistry and Physics, the Harrison Chair (now Political
Economy), the James McLaughlin Chair of Mathematics, and the
Joseph Dean Chair of Biology and Geology, endowed by the sale of
$26,817 worth of agricultural property in Nobles, Wright, and Mille
Lacs counties. By 1907, Joseph M. Hackney had endowed the Chair
of History. Campus beautification and physical plant renovation
also followed completion of the successful $250,000 endowment
campaign.[17]

If steady growth in the University's endowment fund provided
one means of assessing the calibre of Bridgman's leadership, expansion of the physical plant provided another. In 1905, Matthew G.
Norton, who had succeeded Chaffee as president of the Board three
years earlier, gave $1,500 to construct a new athletic field. Norton,
who had been a member of the Board since 1878, agreed with
Bridgman that the time had come to remove the football field from
the south campus in order to open that area for academic development. The new athletic facility, located east of the campus on a site
which lay south of Hewitt Avenue between Pascal and Holton
Streets, opened in the autumn of 1905. In March, 1906, although
pressured by both students and alumni to build a gymnasium first,
Bridgman made his priorities clear by securing from Andrew Carnegie a $30,000 pledge to build a library, on the condition that the
trustees raise a like sum to endow the facility. Work on the building,
designed by St. Paul architect Clarence H. Johnson, began that
autumn, and on May 13, 1907, Governor John A. Johnson spoke at
cornerstone-laying ceremonies. Dedication of the $28,000 struc-
ture, which was located just west of University Hall facing Hewitt
Avenue, took place on October 9. Meanwhile Bridgman had secured authorization from the trustees to add a second story to the
rear wing of Science Hall. Constructed at a cost of approximately
$8,000, the addition housed a biological laboratory and freed former

Matthew G. Norton.

Hamline University about 1885: Ladies Hall, University Hall, and a boardwalk grace the prairie. (From the collections of the Minnesota Historical Society.)

laboratory space in the front of the main building for two badly needed classrooms.[18]

The President next turned his attention to the gymnasium, which remained a source of alumni discontent. Furthermore, absence of a modern athletic facility was making it increasingly difficult to compete for promising high school athletes and to maintain a position of equal footing within the Minnesota-Dakota Athletic Conference. In October, 1906, the *Alumni Quarterly* had published an article by Coach Lewis Drill noting that plans for the building, also drawn by Clarence Johnson, were at last in hand. Calling attention to the "far-reaching consequences" which the structure would have, Drill predicted that it would "engender a universal athletic feeling in the college and very probably inaugurate a new athletic era." But before the plans could become reality, it was necessary to raise $35,000. In an effort to secure those funds, President Bridgman turned to the General Education Board, founded in 1902 by John D. Rockefeller for the purpose of promoting education in the United States. The President had as his objective the raising of $300,000 as an addition to the endowment, and in December, 1908, met in New York with representatives of the Rockefeller agency. He proposed that the General Education Board grant Hamline $75,000, and that the University procure the remainder. On January 26, 1909, the Board agreed to Bridgman's request, providing that Hamline raise its share by June 15, 1910. Of the total, $90,000 was earmarked for buildings and equipment, while $210,000 would become part of the permanent endowment. It was undoubtedly no coincidence that on February 13, 1909, President Charles Eliot of Harvard, a member of the General Education Board, spoke at Hamline in what was perhaps Bridgman's greatest coup. Three days after Eliot's visit, the trustees accepted the Rockefeller offer, and Bridgman announced that he had already secured $23,000 in pledges.[19]

In an editorial published on February 4, 1909, the St. Paul *Dispatch* discussed the significance of the General Education Board's decision to assist Hamline. The Board, noted the paper, included such men as Eliot, President Harry Pratt Judson of the University of Chicago, President E. Benjamin Andrews of the University of Nebraska, Dr. Albert Shaw, editor of the *Review of Re-*

views, and Andrew Carnegie — a distinguished body by anyone's reckoning. With its decision to provide $75,000 it had made Hamline "a member of the large educational scheme of the country," partly through the gift, "but largely through a recognition of its own unaided effort in the past. These gifts from the fund," the *Dispatch* continued, providing a commentary on Bridgman's overall leadership, "are not made unless the college has demonstrated its capacity, its ability in its own field, its high requirements and its good faith, both in education and in finance. An endorsement by this board places an institution in the ranks of the strong." Bridgman had evidenced superb leadership for a quarter of a century, the paper concluded, "and no finer monument to his life work could be secured than this fit endowment of Hamline."[20]

Groundbreaking ceremonies for the gym, held April 14, 1909, were of a most unusual nature. With President Bridgman as referee, Athletic Director Fred Burgan in charge of arrangements, and Professor Thomas Beyer of the Department of English at the helm, three hundred students hitched themselves to a plow and "at a given signal, proceeded at breakneck speed to turn over the turf." Drawn by the frenzied horses — damsels in the lead, males of modest physique next in line, behemoths borrowed from athletic workouts closest to the plow, the instrument "skimmed through the sod to the tune of yells, shouts and merry laughter," while Athletic Committee chairman Beyer "did some extraordinarily quick sidestepping in a futile effort to keep the nose of the plow in the ground and at the same time maintain some degree of dignity." The easiest part of the job, reported the *Alumni Quarterly,* was in the tennis court, where the team "scarcely slackened the pace going around the curves." Cornerstone-laying ceremonies for the building, which fronted on Simpson Street directly south of Ladies' Hall (recently renamed Goheen Hall in memory of Hamline's great benefactor), took place on June 8, 1909, and University officials dedicated the structure on November 30. The gymnasium proper measured 55 by 80 feet, contained a regulation running track nine feet above the floor, and was fully outfitted with the latest equipment. Adjoining it was a handball court, while directly underneath was a dirt-floored basement, excavated for a future swimming pool. Located on the main floor of the building's west wing were a kitchen and serving room, and on the floor above were a reception room and banquet hall. With four hundred lockers for men and one hundred for women, the building testified silently to an age-old inequity. Raymond P. Kaighn, who had served from 1893 to 1898 as Hamline's first physical director, returned to St. Paul for the November ceremonies. Kaighn concluded that he had not seen a "better arranged, more attractively finished, and better adapted" facility. The gymnasium complete, President Bridgman announced that his next project was a magnificent chapel, which would rise adjacent to the physical facility on a site facing Capitol Avenue (Englewood), directly opposite the Hamline Methodist Episcopal Church.[21]

But as events would soon prove, the gym and the $300,000 endowment campaign were the President's last major contributions to the physical expansion and financial development of the University. For Bridgman had already begun to experience pressures demanding his removal. Although he continued to serve in office until June, 1912, his time and energy were increasingly dissipated by the necessity of responding to charges brought against him by a variety of parties.

That Bridgman should have closed his Hamline career on a negative note appears puzzling in retrospect, in light of his many achievements while in office and the veneration which he enjoyed in the two decades following his retirement. Almost singlehandedly he had managed, by means of two major capital campaigns and an unrelenting effort to secure lesser gifts, to provide for the University an endowment of more than $400,000. By 1911, the college held over $500,000 worth of income-bearing securities in the Twin Cities alone, not including real estate. The original Chicago donation was generating $4,000 income per year. Together with securities in other cities and real estate, the corporation's total estimated capital valuation was more than $1 million. Bridgman had raised funds for the construction of three major buildings and had enlarged two others at a total approximate cost of $163,000. He had presided over the debt-free dedication of University Hall; built a president's house (1886); secured money for the grading and construction of the University's first athletic field; and, at a cost of about $2,500, made it possible to grade, seed, and landscape the campus in the 1890s. He had doubled the size of the student body; hired almost fifty members of the faculty, many of whom remained to give years of dedicated and talented service; secured the funds necessary to endow nine faculty chairs; and made impressive contributions to curricular development. His catholic spirit and his humane, liberal character were known not only within the Twin Cities but regionally and nationally as well. Why should Bridgman, "heartily greeted by friends and students" following his return from a European excursion in 1888, "beloved" for loyally painting his house red and gray in 1895, applauded prior to another Continental holiday in 1903, prominent in Methodist educational circles, respected within the Twin City business and professional community, have found himself gradually engulfed by a critical tide which eventually achieved his removal? What were the circumstances under which this enlightened and benevolent president fell from grace?[22]

Signs of trouble had long been apparent. As early as May, 1908, the Executive Committee of the Board had met to hear student complaints against Bridgman, but had concluded that there was no evidence "to sustain a charge of improper conduct" on the president's part. "In our opinion," they declared, "the so-called charges are trivial and puerile and have no foundation in fact and we find no reason in the evidence submitted to pursue the matter further." For more than two years, opposition to Bridgman remained relatively dormant. Then, in October, 1910, a second wave of criticism broke loose which continued without remission until the President submitted his resignation in the spring of the following year. Although the trustees did not record the incident in their minutes, three of their number, the Rev. W. I. Kern, the Hon. W. H. Eustis, then Mayor of Minneapolis, and E. F. Mearkle, appeared unannounced in order to corral and cross-examine students about their anti-Bridgman sentiments. The students quite properly "resented the method of investigation and refused to state charges" against the President.[23]

Meanwhile, student editor R. T. Hambleton called attention to the low enrollment — 251 that autumn, down from 288 the year before and a high of 301 during 1908–1909 — and blamed it more on administrative indifference than "poor crops." Many of Hamline's competitors were growing, he observed, and were doing so with less endowment and fewer resources. The editor also attacked Bridgman for taking up residence in Minneapolis, where he had lived for some months in a suite at the Leamington Hotel. During the following week, a culprit defaced a portrait of the President which had hung since 1898 in the college chapel. When Dean Loren H. Batchelder ordered Hambleton to cease airing the University's dirty linen in public or submit his resignation to the Literary Board, the editor promptly chose the latter course. In turn the Literary Board, chaired by Thomas Beyer, made its attitude toward freedom of the press clear when it refused to accept the resignation.[24]

Late in October, two students journeyed to Winona to confer with Board president Matthew Norton and trustees Frank Doran and William McKinley. Norton, while conceding that the situation was "very serious," preferred to attribute Bridgman's difficulties and the sagging enrollment to "trivial causes." While he and his associates "admitted that Hamline was going backward by comparision with Macalester and Carleton," he suggested that the situation would not improve "without the vigorous support of the students and alumni. . . ." The next weekend, several students attended a special meeting called by St. Paul Methodist laymen to discuss the situation. There, trustee Joseph M. Hackney spoke on behalf of the Board in support of the President, whose situation he compared with the recent effort by 600 University of Minnesota students to oust President Cyrus W. Northrup. It would be "foolhardy," Hackney pontificated, in words which would have rankled a later generation of undergraduates, for the trustees to take any more seriously than had the University of Minnesota Regents "the talk of students in all matters and especially in the government of educational institutions." On the following Monday, students, trustees, and faculty held a mass meeting to discuss the growing crisis.[25]

As the controversy raged, the Minneapolis *Journal* published a report which declared that "open war" had broken out against Bridgman. It indicated that in addition to the charge of nonresidence, opposition centered in the fact that "Hamline, although a St. Paul institution, is controlled by Minneapolis trustees, who see that most of the funds of the University are deposited in a Minneapolis bank and wish to keep control of the . . . endowment for certain financial institutions.'' The St. Paul *Dispatch* called upon the trustees to put Hamline's house in order so that the ''demoralizing controversy'' might pass. By now, the crisis was taking its toll, for in November, Bridgman revealed to the Executive Committee that he had found it necessary to renegotiate the University's contract with the General Education Board. The agreement, he explained, allowed a one-year extension in the deadline, a clear indication that the President was having difficulty raising the required $225,000. Subsequently, the Board once again modified its original offer, and provided $50,000 toward a total sum of $200,000, which Bridgman managed to secure.[26] With gymnasium construction costs paid, the endowment grew by $165,000, a figure $45,000 short of the amount originally sought.

Far more revealing of the source of the difficulty than the vague accusations and innuendos of students was the increasingly visible anti-University scheming within the Conference. Although reports compiled by the district superintendents revealed no overt displeasure with Bridgman's leadership in particular or with University matters in general as late as 1908, things took a turn for the worse the next year. For at its 1909 session, the Conference appointed a special commission to study the University's charter, and to report ''relative to the rights of the Conference to nominate and elect the Trustees of Hamline University.''[27]

The Conference *had* no right to nominate trustees, of course; J. W. Chaffee had neatly taken care of that matter in 1877 when he secured the amendment which gave the Board the sole right to name its own replacements. Increasingly the Church had chafed over this restriction, as had the alumni, who won from a grudging Board in 1906 the right to nominate some of their own colleagues for consideration. Failing in their attempts to secure greater influence by other means — to complain about a diminishing interest in religion among the students, for example, when such interest was in fact substantial; or to deplore President Bridgman's secular tendencies when his solicitation of businessmen was consistently successful — members of the Conference who wished to get rid of the President had obviously decided by 1910 to employ more extreme measures.[28]

When the charter commission, headed by the Rev. F. M. Rule of St. Paul, presented its report to an executive session of the Conference on September 29, 1910, it was hardly surprising that the document indicted Chaffee's "closed corporation" amendment. The delegates adopted the report and empowered Bishop John W. Hamilton to appoint a seven-member commission "with legal knowledge" to study the matter further and to report back the following year. Appearances to the contrary, Conference opposition to Bridgman was not universal. St. Paul District Superintendent Benjamin Longley implored the members "to appreciate more fully the work of Hamline University and to do more to promote it." The President, Longley told the assembly in words which must have incensed some of his colleagues but given assurance to the beleaguered Bridgman, had "been doing more than his share of that work which is most difficult and ofttimes most thankless of all — the work of money-getting." Amid "almost insuperable" obstacles, he added, Hamline had made great gains. Meeting at Faribault in 1911, the Conference heard the commission's most recent estimate of the situation, again read by Rule, and again recommending legal action through charter revision. But after twice postponing consideration, the members voted to defer action for another year.[29] The reason for their sudden lack of interest was unstated but obvious: Bridgman had resigned the previous June. Amending the charter might well prove to be the ultimate answer to grievances voiced by certain members of the Conference, but with a lame duck chief executive, the issue of charter reform was academic.

The ministers' discontent understandably focused upon the bothersome fact that neither within the Board in general nor on the Executive Committee in particular did the Conference wield any measurable degree of authority. President Norton and First Vice-President Benjamin F. Nelson were lumber barons; Second Vice-President J. T. Wyman was a prominent Minneapolis manufacturer, banker, state legislator and president of the University of Minnesota Board of Regents; Secretary S. S. Thorpe was another Minneapolis businessman; and Treasurer E. F. Mearkle was an officer of the Minneapolis Security Bank. Other members included Redwood Falls lumberman and banker W. H. Gold; Alexandria merchant and banker William Moses; Minneapolis Mayor Eustis; F. A. Chamberlain, another officer of the Security Bank; James Quirk, a Mill City lawyer, banker, miller, and insurance man; Joseph Hackney, who was a St. Paul realtor, investor, and state legislator; Judge Hascal R. Brill of St. Paul; Crookston banker J. W. Wheeler; and of course, President Bridgman himself.[30]

In fact, there were five clergymen in addition to Bridgman, one more than the minimum specified both in the charter and in the 1871 amendment which also permitted relocation. But none served on the Executive Committee, which possessed almost complete authority in its own right, and the few ministers who sat on the Board found themselves wholly outnumbered by "men of action, wealth, influence, culture, and humanism" who dominated the University's affairs. Nowhere in the charter nor in its amendments had the Church received wholesale authority to govern the institution. Its powers were solely those of "patronage," although clergymen who served as trustees obviously had the right to help "prescribe and regulate the course of studies to be pursued" within the University, and to assist with other administrative matters. Still, the degree to which the Church had lost control over the internal affairs of the college was substantial. When Bridgman arrived in 1883, Bishop Foss was president of the Board, and two other ministers — Chaffee and the Rev. Robert Forbes of Duluth — were vice-president and secretary, respectively, although Chaffee was hardly a typical midwestern Methodist clergyman. Three other members of the Conference also held seats on the Board, including former President John, whose conservative ways had perturbed students as well as trustees of more progressive stripe and had contributed to his resignation. By comparison, business influence in 1883 had been relatively slight. It was true that Thomas A. Harrison, B. F. Nelson, Matthew Norton, H. G. Harrison, and other men of commerce and industry sat on the board, but the day of their pre-eminence was still well in the future. But by the middle of the 1890s, the balance had shifted, and it was inevitable that Bridgman would eventually feel the repercussions, for he had participated intimately and enthusiastically in the Board's reconstruction.[31]

It was also clear that Bridgman's personal relationship to the

Conference had grown increasingly more distant. From the outset of his administration, the President realized that it would be impossible to maintain and strengthen the institution solely on the basis of financial aid from the Church. Both Jabez Brooks and Benjamin Crary had learned that fact at Red Wing, and Bridgman himself remembered it from his years at Genesee. This the members of the Conference recognized and acknowledged. But what they could not accept was Bridgman's increasing preference for the progressive forces of the age, and his willingness to voice attitudes and convictions acquired through years of experience which had included broad and extensive contacts throughout the United States, Canada, England, and the Continent. Bridgman had chosen to substitute prominent men of business and industry in place of the trustees who served before them not merely to enhance the financial prospects of the University. He had taken such action because he was more at home with these individuals than he was with their predecessors. The President's "ability to enthrall a cultivated audience, play superbly the role of dinner and home library guest of millionaire art collectors, and impress successful lumber barons, railroad empire builders, and other influential citizens," wrote Grace Lee Nute in her unpublished history of the University, "led him little by little to grow with his era, away from the confining walls of pietistic chapels and small parsonages."[32]

A prominent and perceptive member of Bridgman's faculty, who would demonstrate during more than forty years of service to the institution that his analyses were almost never misplaced, blamed the alumni for part of the difficulty. Writing in the *Alumni Quarterly* in October, 1910, before the crisis had come to a head, Thomas Beyer delivered an uncompromising indictment. "The alumni are either in a state of coma, quiescence or violent eruption all the time," he charged. "The violent eruption is never pro-Hamline. There are no rabid fanatics for Hamline among the alumni — at least none has gladdened us by his presence for many a day." The faculty were quite accustomed "to see periodically some foaming, ranting, gesticulating lunatics of '77 or '88 or '99 in sheer ecstasy" around their own *alma matres,* "not knowing 'whether in the body or out of the body.' Alas, no alumni go crazy over Hamline.'' They were active, he acknowledged, but they were active "on the wrong side. I have heard many rumors and know of some specific instances where alumni have actually discouraged prospective students from coming to Hamline. Faults and foibles of many members of the faculty have been italicized and magnified so that he who runs may read.'' Beyer urged the alumni to work toward closer relationships with the faculty and with the students, that they might together restore sanity and work toward "a better, more vital Hamline.''[33] But it was obvious that he sensed accurately the drift of events, and that he was deeply concerned about the fate of the President, whose academic leadership he trusted and respected.

In accepting Bridgman's resignation "with great regret,'' the Executive Committee promised to begin immediately the search for a "worthy successor.'' Having previously refused to accept the President's offer to resign, preferring to retain him in office until he had raised sufficient funds to meet the General Education Board's challenge, the trustees now indicated that the resignation would become effective one year later, on June 5, 1912. Commenting upon the event, the St. Paul *Dispatch* remembered the University over which Bridgman had taken charge in 1883. "That was the day of small things for Hamline,'' the paper observed. "It was financially in distress. With no money and no resources of any kind to work with it was an unpromising proposition. But Dr. Bridgman took hold of it with courage and what there is of Hamline today . . . is his work. This is a sufficient testimonial of what men of affairs and friends of education have thought of his work and of the aims and purposes and standards he stood for in higher education.''[34]

The editor's closing observation was a perceptive one. Alumni, trustees and others might well choose to remember Bridgman as the President who established the University on a sound financial basis and secured for it the physical facilities requisite to its existence. But Bridgman knew that no educational institution could hope to achieve academic excellence on the strength of superstructure and finances alone. A strong and dedicated faculty, a rational and academically defensible curriculum, a broadly-based commitment to the liberal arts — these were the ingredients out of which greatness arose. George Henry Bridgman understood this, and the manner in which he presided for twenty-nine years over the academic affairs of the University made that understanding clear.

CHAPTER 3

ACADEMICS AND
ACADEMICIANS

THE CHARTER WHICH the territorial legislature granted to
the trustees of Hamline University on March 3, 1854, specified that
the Board should establish the institution "on a plan sufficiently
extensive to afford ample facilities to perfect the scholar." Although neither the trustees nor the original Red Wing faculty
bothered to define what they meant by "perfecting the scholar,"
there was no need to do so. A common phrase in college and
university charters of the era, it meant, simply, that the University
would have the obligation to raise students to the highest possible
intellectual, spiritual, and social levels, that they might be broadly-
educated and effective citizens. "It ought always to be remembered," observed President Joseph McKeen of Bowdoin College in
1802, "that literary institutions are founded and endowed for the
common good, and not for the private advantage of those who resort
to them for education. It is not that they may be able to pass through
life in an easy or reputable manner," he explained, "but that their
mental powers may be cultivated and improved for the benefit of
society. If it be true no man should live for himself alone," McKeen
added, "we may safely assert that every man who has been aided by
a public institution to acquire an education and to qualify himself for
usefulness, is under peculiar obligations to exert his talents for the
public good."[1]

While Hamline was not a "public" institution in the mid-
nineteenth-century sense of the term, the charge to its faculty and
administration was nonetheless essentially the same. In its 1860

report to the Minnesota Annual Conference, the Committee on Education unknowingly echoed President McKeen's thoughts. Calling attention to "the indispensable necessity" of maintaining a "first class literary institution" in the state, "where our sons and our daughters may receive the very finest intellectual finish of which they are capable," the committee noted that such an institution should provide its students with "moral and religious influences as will most certainly and most successfully fit them to attain the great end of their being." It was especially significant, in light of the charter's stipulations, that the trustees should have decided to appoint the Rev. Jabez Brooks, son of David Brooks, to head the institution when it opened at Red Wing in 1854. For Brooks was himself a scholar of considerable achievement. Born in England in 1823, he came with his parents to the United States in 1840 and lived for several years in Kenosha, Wisconsin. Completing his preparatory course at Rock River Seminary, Mount Morris, Illinois, in 1847, he enrolled as a sophomore at Wesleyan University in the same year and took his A.B. in 1850. Although eagerly sought by several eastern educational establishments, the young Phi Beta Kappa graduate preferred to return to the Midwest, and thus accepted the position of principal at the Watertown, Wisconsin, Seminary. One year later he moved to Lawrence College at Appleton to become professor of Greek and mathematics, the post he held when contacted by the Hamline trustees. When a group of clergymen met at Hamline on August 7, 1856, to organize the Minnesota Annual Conference, the extent of Brooks' academic achievements became clear. For among the members of that session Brooks, who had entered the ministry himself in 1852, was the only college graduate.[2]

For three years, the classicist presided over an institution which, despite its formidable name, was nothing more than a preparatory school divided into four classes. Students in the primary class, or section, received elementary instruction in reading, writing, spelling, arithmetic, geography, and grammar. Those in the junior section studied composition, declamation, "analysis," American history, natural philosophy, and astronomy in addition to the primary subjects. In the middle and senior sections, students had an opportunity to choose between either the Collegiate Preparatory Course or, for those unable to go on to college, the Academic Course. Each of these was in turn subdivided into Classical Studies and English Studies, with students pursuing Greek and Latin in the former. In the latter, those enrolled in the Collegiate Preparatory Courses studied Greek and Roman history, while those enrolled in the Academic Course studied a broad range of liberal arts subjects, including natural science, mathematics, natural history, rhetoric, logic, the United States constitution, political economy, science of government, "Evidences of Christianity," and "Universal History." In the senior section, Academic Course, students could also opt for instruction in music, painting, drawing, "ornamental work," and modern languages. The division of labor among the faculty during that first academic year was unclear. In addition to Brooks, who served as librarian, the catalog listed only two other faculty: Louisa Sherman, who taught modern languages, painting, and drawing; and Frances L. Dunning, who taught music and "ornamental work."[3] Undoubtedly Brooks, with his broad background and with his intensive training in the classics and mathematics, was busy tending to far more than the virtually nonexistent library.

By the time the Rev. Benjamin F. Crary replaced the ailing and grossly overworked Brooks in 1857, the University had begun to offer collegiate work on a regular basis. Hence, the new executive assumed the title of "president." Unlike Brooks, who was a scholar, Crary was primarily an evangelist. Born in Indiana in 1821, he received his early education in Cincinnati and in 1842 graduated from Pleasant Hill Academy, later to become Belmont College. Successively thereafter, he taught school, read the law and was admitted to the bar, and became a Methodist itinerant preacher in the Indiana conference. Elected president of Hamline in 1857 at the urging of former Hoosier Ezra Lathrop, Crary had by that December taken up his duties with vigor.[4]

Under Crary's leadership, the collegiate course of study soon broadened to allow three avenues to the degree. The first was the classical program, which led to the B.A. and emphasized Greek, Latin, English language and literature, and mathematics. In addition, it included work in Hebrew or German grammar, history,

civics, ethics, philosophy, and chemistry. The scientific course led
to the B.S. and included all of the classical studies with the exception of Greek and Latin, for which it substituted German. Finally, a
separate course for women, the "Lady Baccalaureate of Arts,"
made a host of mid-nineteenth-century assumptions about the role of
women in society as well as their capacity for education. It offered
abridged work in Latin and mathematics, omitted Greek, and introduced French, German, and the fine arts. Of the three degrees, the
first proved by far the most popular. Between 1859 and 1869, seventeen students earned the B.A., one the B.S., and four the L.B.A.
Nor did the University appear interested in promoting the quaint
Lady Baccalaureate. For as early as 1858 the catalog stated that
women were "admitted to all the classes, and may gain all the
honors of the University." By 1858, as well, the Academic Course
within the Preparatory Department had become, less euphemistically, the Business Course. A Normal Department now combined
the Business Preparatory Course "with special instruction . . .
upon subjects relating to the Teachers' vocation," and an opportunity to do practice teaching. A Commercial Department offered a
scaled-down business course, and a Biblical Department afforded
candidates for the ministry a three-year program. By 1865, the
entire curriculum had been simplified — no doubt the result of the
Civil War and the loss of almost the entire male population within
the Collegiate Department. The catalog for 1865–66 listed and described a Collegiate Course, a two-year Preparatory Course, and a
Normal Department. During the years from 1857 until the beginning
of the War, the University also had a Law School.[5]

Twenty-one individuals, including Brooks and Crary, are known
to have served on the faculty during the University's Red Wing
years. Of these, eight were clergymen. Six, including five of the
ministers, held the M.A., while four others had earned the B.A.,
and one was a medical doctor. In addition, six women, including
four Hamline graduates, served in the position of preceptress, which
combined the functions of dean of women and head resident. Be-
sides Brooks, only Frederick Merrick, professor of Latin and Greek,
served for more than three years; while in addition to Crary, only
H. B. Wilson and Salem Town, both of whom taught mathematics,

served for more than two. Of the entire faculty and preceptorial staff, only half remained at the institution beyond one year. When Crary resigned in 1861 for the same reasons given earlier by Brooks, he assumed the position of state superintendent of public instruction. Brooks then returned to the University, remaining until it closed in 1869. He thereafter accepted an appointment as professor of Greek at the University of Minnesota, a position which he held until 1909. He also wrote during this later stage of his professional career a widely-used and respected introductory Greek textbook.[6]

By the time the University reopened in 1880, the Lady Baccalaureate degree, anachronistic even in the Red Wing years, had disappeared. In both Preparatory and Collegiate Departments, students were permitted to choose between the Classical Course and the Latin Scientific Course. Additional work in mathematics and natural science replaced Greek in the latter, and at the collegiate level, students pursuing the Latin Scientific Course received the B.S. degree. But before the University had actually awarded any B.S. degrees, the faculty had substituted in its place the Bachelor of Philosophy (Ph.B.). As might be expected, the absence of Greek from its specifications made it by far the more popular. Long before the faculty dropped the Ph.B. and restored the B.S. in 1915, the Bachelor of Philosophy had come to account for the overwhelming majority of degrees granted.[7]

President John early took note of the fact that Hamline, along with dozens of other colleges and universities of the era, was gradually moving away from the classical education with which earlier generations of Americans had been familiar. "The curriculum is a compromise between the extremes of linguistic and scientific courses of study," he explained in 1881. "Though we regard a knowledge of Latin and Greek — certainly of Latin — as essential to a liberal education, yet it is neither possible nor desirable to devote as much time to them as was customary formerly." Rapid developments in the physical sciences, in literature and in philology made it mandatory to require additional work in these disciplines. Since "the spoken languages of civilized nations" had become "the sole vehicles" of classical literature, there was "no longer any occasion to study Latin and Greek with sufficient thoroughness to write and speak them as was customary three centuries ago.'' Because it was possible at Hamline to acquire sufficient expertise in the classics within six years, he added, ''the study of Latin and Greek terminates with the Sophomore year.''[8]

Minor curricular changes occurred at the collegiate level throughout the 1880s, but the first major development took place in 1891, when the faculty voted to inaugurate a limited system of electives. The catalog of that year indicated that sophomores, along with taking the required subjects in mathematics and modern languages, might elect to enroll in an equal number of courses chosen from among Latin, Greek, calculus, surveying, and history. Juniors were allowed to omit one course of their own choosing from spring term studies, and seniors were permitted to omit one course each term. Students warmly supported the innovation. The faculty had made the curricular changes, noted the student editor in the autumn of 1891, ''in accordance with the dictates of experience and in obedience to the general tendency toward a larger number of electives and more exhaustive work in history;'' the changes, he added, were ''in harmony with the most advanced ideas in the college world and the improvement is only acquiescence to a demand which has been respected by the leading colleges in the East.'' Another student editor of the period had a more realistic view. ''The fact is,'' wrote John Lathrop in January, 1891, ''that the average student with several options before him in making up his year's work will select those branches which are easy for him. It is by no means demonstrated,'' he noted accurately, ''that the present system of electives in existence in many of the schools has secured the best results.'' The objective point, Lathrop urged late that spring, was ''to secure a course of study which covers a wide range of subjects, and those the best in classics, literature and sciences, and at the same time requires hard, honest labor on the part of the student.'' The editor's argument was hardly new, for it was part of a debate that had raged with little remission since 1869, when President Charles W. Eliot introduced the elective principle at Harvard. By the 1890s, Columbia, Cornell, Indiana, Chicago, and Stanford had also adopted the new view. From its inception at Harvard, the objective of the elective principle had been to broaden the curriculum without at the same time subtracting essential ingredients from it, and to recognize and accept the fact that individual differences posed significant problems of academic motivation. Opponents of the new system, including the faculties of such distinguished institutions as Princeton, Amherst, Williams, and Yale, held firmly to the belief "that every student must pursue certain clearly defined fields of knowledge deemed either indispensable in disciplinary value or essential to a liberal education." John Henry Newman and Matthew Arnold carried on a similar curricular debate in England with Herbert Spencer and T. H. Huxley. When the Hamline faculty decided to move with the times and introduce a degree of choice, they took a step wholly in keeping with almost a quarter century of curricular development and discussion on both sides of the Atlantic.[9]

Although the faculty inaugurated a much more limited elective system than that in force at Harvard and elsewhere, their decision indicated that the institution's academic growth since 1880 had been considerable. When President Bridgman arrived in 1883, the faculty were not, by and large, sufficiently well-trained to possess the depth or breadth of expertise requisite to a system which relied upon a degree of student initiative, and which demanded a more diverse group of curricular offerings than those which characterized systems that afforded no opportunity for choice. Nor were the faculty's numbers great enough to staff the additional courses. During the 1883–84 academic year, for example, there were still only five full-time members, not counting the President — hardly enough to launch even the most cautious curricular diversification. The academicians who chose to implement the elective principle in 1891 were not substantially greater in numbers. But they were much better trained, for in hiring faculty, Bridgman had consistently focused upon strength of academic preparation.

When the former Genesee principal arrived in St. Paul to begin his twenty-nine year tenure, there were six departments in the College of Liberal Arts: Mental and Moral Science, Latin Language and Literature, Greek Language and Literature, Chemistry and Physics, History and English, and Mathematics. Conforming to current practice, the President himself taught mental and moral science. Of the five full-time faculty, Bridgman regarded three as academically competent. The first of this chosen triumvirate was Professor of Mathematics Erastus F. Mearkle. A transplanted Pennsylvanian who had taken both the Normal Course and the Scientific Course at the Pennsylvania State Normal School, Mearkle had been a member of the original St. Paul faculty in 1880. After teaching for a number of years in his native state as well as in New Jersey and Illinois, he had studied both medicine and law at the University of Michigan, where in 1877 he received both the A.B. and the L.L.B. Leaving Ann Arbor, he opened a law office in Minneapolis, but soon accepted the chair of science and mathematics at Hamline. In 1881, as well, he began forty-one uninterrupted years as trustee, during all but five of which he served as Treasurer. Mearkle left the faculty briefly between 1882 and 1884, but thereafter served continuously until 1906 — first in mathematics, then in political economy, and finally in social science.[10]

The second individual who, in Bridgman's view, was capable at his task was Joseph R. Taylor, Professor of Greek Language and Literature. Taylor, who had replaced Mearkle in 1882 as professor of mathematics but had soon moved over to the classics, was, in the President's mind, "a thorough scholar and a splendid teacher of Greek." But in 1886 he left Hamline to become professor of Greek at Boston University.[11]

The third was Loren H. Batchelder, who arrived the same year as Bridgman to become professor of chemistry and physics, and remained until his retirement thirty-five years later. Born in Montpelier, Vermont, in 1846, he was a graduate of Middlebury College, where he had taken the A.B. in 1874 and the A.M. in 1877. He had taught mathematics and physics from 1874 until 1881 at Centenary Collegiate Institute in New Jersey, and had also studied law. He became a member of the New Jersey bar in 1882, and joined the Minnesota bar the following year. Batchelder made his principal contributions to the University not in the arena of scholarship, although he was apparently a competent chemist, but as an academic administrator. It was he who revised and strengthened the various courses of study at Bridgman's request even before becoming academic dean in 1895. As dean, he stood squarely for thorough scholarship, and because of his attitude, caused many Hamline faculty to become better teachers. An incisive and constructive critic, he often noted shortcomings in faculty efforts to legislate on curricular matters, and interjected his comments in a manner calculated to win support for his point of view without alienating those who disagreed. Batchelder was also a notable figure in the development of secondary education in Minnesota, and was chiefly responsible for the fact that during his tenure as dean, the institution enjoyed an excellent reputation with regard to the training and placement of teachers.[12]

Beyond these three, the President was willing to admit that there existed sufficient devotion but little in the way of scholarly ability. Surely the most notable of the remaining group was the Rev. George Swan Innis, whom President John had hired in 1881 as professor of natural science. But Innis never had a chance to test his wings in the laboratory, for John decided instead to separate the disciplines of Greek and Latin, transferring the latter to Innis and leaving the former with the Rev. C. F. Bradley. Innis was born in Columbus, Ohio, in 1850, and had graduated from the public high school there in 1869. He took his B.A. with Phi Beta Kappa honors from Ohio Wesleyan University in 1872, received the S.T.B. from Boston University School of Theology in 1876, and became a member of the Minnesota Methodist Conference in 1877. Between 1877 and the time of his Hamline appointment, he had served as a pastor in the Winona and Mankato Districts. That President John should have contemplated placing Innis in charge of natural science instruction doubtless reveals more about John's attitude toward science than it does about Innis's academic expertise. Innis was no desultory scholar, but his training had hardly prepared him to offer coursework in biology, chemistry, and physics. Rather, he was the prototypical nineteenth-century small denominational college faculty member: preacher, devoted servant, beloved friend of student and alumnus alike, and obliging to a fault. Hired to teach natural science, he successively held chairs in Latin (1881–89), history (1889–1916), and education (1915–21). He was librarian from 1883 until 1898, when President Bridgman finally placed that position on a full-time basis with the appointment of Anna M. Davis. And from

1916 until his retirement in 1921, he also served as dean of men. When Innis died in 1947 at the age of 97, he left a legacy of nearly seven decades of service to the college.[13]

Innis brought his pastoral training with him to Hamline in 1881 and never abandoned it. Passionate in his social concern, he possessed a deep feeling of responsibility for the welfare of his students, and often showed this concern by battling against what he perceived to be the lowering of spiritual standards within the University. He regarded education not as "an end, but an aim, a method and a means." It was "not an adornment or accessory of life," he told students in 1893, but rather "the only foundation of any life worthy the name." Innis felt that good students tended to get "too much rather than too little information" in the process of becoming educated, and urged them not to be content merely to absorb facts, but to make them "the basis of intellectual activity." He also applauded science for its insistence upon precision and methodology, and urged teachers to develop sound educational methods based upon precision and commitment to practical purpose. So seriously did Innis treat each new responsibility that when Bridgman moved him from Latin to history in the late 1880s, he spent two years in Europe studying informally and traveling in order to prepare for the new enterprise.[14]

In 1886, the President made the first in a series of notable appointments designed to strengthen the Hamline faculty and move the institution toward educational excellence. With an eye toward maintaining the quality of instruction in Greek which J. R. Taylor had offered prior to his resignation, the President hired Milton J. Griffin as professor of Greek language and literature. And in an effort to strengthen curricular offerings in English while at the same time aiding Innis in Latin, he appointed Arthur Z. Drew as instructor of Latin and English. Drew, who had taken his B.A. from Hamline that spring, technically replaced the Rev. Sylvanus Gale, who had taught history and English. A native of New York, Drew had moved with his family to Le Sueur County, Minnesota, in 1875, and after teaching and holding various other jobs had entered the Hamline Preparatory Department in 1881. By 1889, he had also received his M.A. from the college. In 1890, Drew moved to the Mathematics

Department to assist Mearkle, who was by that time chiefly occupied as an officer of the Security Bank of Minneapolis. Griffin,
the other 1886 appointee, was born in Michigan and grew up in
Pennsylvania. He had taken his preparatory work and much of his
collegiate course at Genesee Seminary and College, had twice
taught in the Seminary, and had received from Syracuse University
both the A.B. (1874) and the A.M. (1876). Between 1873 and
1886, he taught the classics at various institutions in western New
York, and in the process came to know Bridgman, who was then at
Lima. Griffin left Hamline in 1898 to accept a position on the
faculty of Dakota Wesleyan University.[15]

With the arrival of Henry Leslie Osborn, who became professor
of biology and geology in 1887, the University science curriculum
at last became fully developed, and the college acquired its first
scholar. A native of Newark, New Jersey, where he was born on
July 5, 1857, Osborn had attended the Preparatory Department of
Drew Theological Seminary from 1872 to 1875, and had graduated
from Wesleyan University with Phi Beta Kappa honors in 1878.
Moving on to the Johns Hopkins University after a brief period of
service as assistant in zoology at Wesleyan and as an employee of
the U.S. Fish and Game Commission, he took his Ph.D. in 1884,
specializing in marine biology. From 1884 until 1887, he was a
professor of zoology at Purdue University, which undoubtedly
helped to ease the pain of transit from New Jersey and Maryland to
the prairies of Minnesota, but which came nowhere near eliminating
the shock completely, as the letters of Mrs. Osborn made clear. But
once settled into his new position, Osborn ended up serving the
institution for more than fifty years — as faculty member, dean,
three times acting president, and in his last years historian of the
University. He retired in 1933 at the age of 76. A published scholar
of national renown, he was also an accomplished musician and
artist, a connoisseur of the fine arts, interested in painting, sculpture,
architecture, and literature. He was in fact almost singlehandedly
responsible for interjecting the fine arts into the curriculum. As a
supplement to his biological specialty and growing devotion to the
geology of the North American West, he supplied the energy and
direction for developing two academic departments and the Museum

of Natural History. Dr. Osborn, an inveterate letter writer, more
than any other individual maintained contact with the alumni. Mrs.
Osborn, too, gave her life to the University, not merely as the supportive wife of a devoted and prolific scholar, which then as now
became the fate of many women in her position, but as a teacher of
music and a devotee of the arts. Together, the Osborns' influence
was enormous, and the personal and scholarly contributions of Professor Osborn himself were, in the words of Grace Lee Nute, "beyond all calculating." [16]

By the time the young biologist and budding Renaissance man
arrived at Hamline, he had already begun to carve out a scholarly
career which would eventually make a name both for himself and
for Hamline. His specialty was the trematode, or flatworm, and
between 1901 and 1911 he published a series of scholarly articles in
professional journals on the structure and distribution of several
fresh-water parasites of that class. Discussing representative examples studied during extensive research conducted primarily in the
Lake Chautauqua region of western New York, Osborn earned a
reputation for careful and thorough scholarship such that he could
easily have secured appointment to almost any prestigious faculty.
In 1895, he published his first textbook, *Invertebrate Dissections*,
and followed it with three others: *Studies in Elementary Biology*
(1896), *Studies in the Elements of the Anatomy of the Lower Vertebrates* (1897), and a laboratory guide for the study of smelt (1909). In
addition to many other scholarly articles, notes, and communica-
tions, he wrote an account of Hamline's contributions to the war
effort in 1917–18, and in 1924, largely as a result of efforts to
collect data for a Phi Beta Kappa application, edited a comprehensive college alumni directory. With E. F. Mearkle he co-authored a
brief history of education in Minnesota for the U.S. Bureau of
Education. His lecture "The Mission of the Public Park with Reference to the Preservation of Our Native Animals and Plants," first
delivered in 1896, revealed an understanding of ecological considerations so acute that it could as easily have been delivered
seventy-five years later. In it, Osborn discussed man's individual
and collective relationships, the nature and purpose of public institutions, the antagonism between public and private interests, and the

public park as a means of counteracting past injuries to nature. He also warned against the careless overuse of public lands, and with a scholar's eye for detail and analysis, explained the implications of heedless human behavior on plant and animal wildlife. Honorable, scholarly, and cultivated, Osborn was a man of dignity, respected by all who knew him.[17]

President Bridgman's second major appointment to the faculty, William E. Thompson, became professor of Latin in 1889. A native of Bristol, Rhode Island, Thompson was a graduate of Bristol High School and of the Wilbraham and Phillips Exeter Academies. He studied, as well, at the Rhode Island State Normal School, and taught briefly in the public schools of his native state. At Brown University, where he took his A.B. in 1873 and his A.M. in 1876, he was accorded membership in Phi Beta Kappa. Joining the faculty of Genesee Seminary in 1873 as professor of classical studies, he worked with Bridgman during the entirety of the latter's career in Lima. He also served as faculty secretary there, and when he arrived in St. Paul, Bridgman again appointed him to that post. He held it continuously until his unexpected death in 1918.[18]

With Thompson's arrival to fill the chair of Latin, Innis moved to history. In turn, this set the pace for a noticeable expansion in social science offerings during the closing years of the century. By 1896, the catalog contained descriptions of coursework in education, mental and moral philosophy, and American constitutional and common law. Sociology appeared in the 1897 spring schedule of courses, although without an instructor's name. By 1901, the sociologists, still without an instructor who was willing or able to be identified, journeyed to Stillwater in order "to get new ideas in the problems of the day" from inmates and administrators of the State Prison. In 1898, the faculty approved and sent to the Board a long-sought change which established a Department of Physical Culture, and which required that every student enroll in at least two hours of physical exercise each week. The trustees, no doubt impressed by rapid advances made in the field of physical education during the recent tenure of Raymond P. Kaighn as Physical Director, approved the request.[19]

In 1899, another significant curricular advance occurred with the

The University's first scholar:
Henry L. Osborn in 1900.

One of the small band of
campus liberals: Thomas P.
Beyer in 1937. (From the col-
lections of the Minnesota His-
torical Society. Photo by Lee
Bros., Minneapolis.)

arrival of R. Watson Cooper to fill the chair of English literature. The University had required a limited amount of work in the discipline since 1881, but Bridgman's decision to create a separate department, and to hire a full-time instructor, represented the first real expansion of that curriculum. Cooper, like so many of the Hamline faculty in those years, had taken his A.B. from Wesleyan University. He had taught literature at Wesleyan Academy, Wilbraham-son, Massachusetts, for eight years prior to accepting the Hamline appointment. For ten years thereafter, until his departure in 1909 to become president of Upper Iowa University, Cooper gave skilled service and brought the college additional prestige. When Thomas P. Beyer joined the faculty in 1906 as professor of the English language, that prestige was further enhanced.[20]

Beyer was yet another Wesleyan alumnus, having graduated with Phi Beta Kappa honors in 1903. A Pennsylvanian by birth, he had done his preparatory work at Williamsport Dickinson Seminary, and had taught English literature and history at Tarkio College from 1904 until his Hamline appointment. In 1907, he took his M.A. degree from the University of Minnesota. His forty-year career, like that of Osborn, was truly noteworthy. In addition to his curricular responsibilities, he served for twelve years (1908–20) as chairman of the Athletic Board and, though they may appear to be strange bedfellows, for twenty-five years (1921–46) as chairman of the Literary Board. He edited the *Bulletin* for nineteen years, coached track and tennis, and was primarily responsible for the organization and growth of both the Faculty Club and the student Quill Club. Largely at his urging, students began in 1908 to publish a literary magazine, the *Maga*, which survived with several changes of name until the late 1960s.

Nor did Beyer confine his involvements solely to the campus. During the last year of the First World War, he was an administrator for the War Labor Board, which managed to secure innumerable settlements favorable to workers. With the swift return of anti-labor attitudes following the war, he was instrumental in establishing the St. Paul Labor College, which he hoped would ease strains in labor-management relations by providing elementary, non-political education. Beyer was the author of verse, essays, and book reviews which appeared regularly in the pages of the *Forum*, the *Dial* and other literary journals of the day. Liberal in temperament, he was a fearless, uncompromising, and vocal advocate of the carefully-chosen causes in which he believed and to which he committed himself unswervingly.[21]

Even a brief glance at the essays which Beyer published in early twentieth-century literary periodicals reveals his unequivocal allegiance to freedom of mind and spirit. In "The Unpragmatic Truth," which appeared in the *Forum* in 1912, he observed that "the earliest and most transparent of the white lies concerning Truth is that Truth is simple." Time and again, he pointed out, mankind had encountered creeds and doctrines packaged as truth which were nothing more than expedients. The following year, he argued in another *Forum* essay that in "religion, politics and ordinary intercourse," men and women were "engaged in the work of traduction, not education; instead of teachers and learners," he charged, "we have evolved by our fundamental axioms of thought a world of proselytizers and proselytes. Any assumption not our own we regard as eccentric, and make no effort to understand it sympathetically."[22]

In this regard, Beyer saw the Church, despite its foundation "upon the tolerant gospel of Jesus," as a prime offender. An autobiographical reminiscence served to illustrate the point, and he drove it home in picturesque fashion. "As a boy of eleven I had a season of sleeplessness induced by the horrible pictures stamped upon my imagination by a minister of the gospel," he recalled. "It was the Last Day in the final conflagration of the world; and I saw myself, a little charred, blackened imp, running to and fro over the shrivelled earth, stumbling against seared, overtaken sinners, and striving vainly to hide from the wrath of God." Perhaps, he acknowledged, "that was the only way to stop my shooting sparrows with my air gun, or to secure an ungrumbling attendance at three Sunday services," but it was all the same an inexcusable "usurpation of the vivid and nascent imagination of youth." Nor did the effects of religious preachments go unnoticed among college and university faculties, especially "in schools and colleges of pronounced religious bent," for here altogether too many students developed what Beyer termed with timeless accuracy "a flippant cynicism or even something like a small pretentious atheism." Rebels against evangelicalism and orthodoxy, their skepticism resulted directly from excessive preachments and "cant phrases," both from the pulpit and from the home.[23]

Had Beyer stood on the stage a half century later he could have delivered precisely the same injunctions. His essay, "A Discord in the Sweet Orchestra of Optimism," warned against becoming engulfed by "unthinking goodness," which was perennially "the graveyard of optimists." Principal philosophers of this destructive creed, he contended, were "the Editorial Writer on the prosperous daily," and "the Pastor of the Contented Flock." The former, who typically equated unflattering criticism with economic disloyalty and who saw such critiques as "bad for business," was "a retail purveyor in wholesale quantities of the most reliable optimistic opiates." The latter provided an equally disquieting example of intellectual repression. For the cleric whose flock had never known hard times; had never suffered indignities arising out of race or class or creed; had never struggled against seemingly hopeless odds; had never, in short, looked in on the system from the outside — this pastor stood in danger of treading another shameful and dishonest path. Such a clergyman, who weekly assured his parishioners that "If we whisper 'credo' to an intellectual fossil, say our prayers and give to the poor, we may safely leave the conduct of the political, social and economic order in the hands of God," was the other advocate of "soporific balm." Optimists, he concluded irreverently but perhaps rightly, might well have given the world more pleasure, but pessimists had done it more good.[24]

Contemporaneous with the appointments of Beyer and Cooper were others which also demonstrated President Bridgman's commitment to the quest for a faculty of exceptional ability, and his capacity to corral such individuals when he found them. In 1901, he hired James Sherman King to replace Samuel J. Pease as professor of Greek and Modern languages. King was a 1901 graduate of Northwestern University, where he had been elected to Phi Beta Kappa. He took his master's degree from Northwestern in 1910, and in later years did additional graduate work at the University of

Berlin and the University of Minnesota. During his fifty-one-year period of service at Hamline, King was twice dean of the University and on another occasion acting dean, and held the post of faculty secretary from the death of William E. Thompson in 1918 until 1933. When William J. Keller arrived in 1903 to become professor of Greek languages and literature, the first full-time instructor in that discipline since Professor Griffin's departure five years earlier, King ceased instructing in the classics, thenceforth devoting all of his academic energies to modern languages, which became, organizationally, a separate entity. And when that department subdivided into Romance Languages and German in 1916 during a period of expansion and further reorganization urged by President Samuel F. Kerfoot, King became professor of German, holding that chair until his retirement in 1952.[25]

With R. Watson Cooper's departure in 1909, Bridgman found himself confronted with the formidable task of hiring a replacement who would continue the standard of excellence established and maintained for a decade in the Department of English Literature. He located such an individual in the person of M. LeRoy Arnold, who held the B.A. from Minnesota (1904), the A.M. from Harvard (1905), and was completing his doctoral work at Columbia. Arnold's area of specialization was the theatre, and his dissertation, completed in 1911 and published the following year, examined the soliloquies of Shakespeare from the standpoint of their technique. During his years at Hamline Arnold was a prolific writer of reviews on subjects related to the theatre, and frequently lectured on drama to Twin City audiences. Almost annually he made a pilgrimage to New York City in order to remain abreast of developments in the American theatre, and in 1915 wrote and published, under the auspices of the prestigious London drama publisher Samuel French, a comedy in three acts which he entitled *Hurry, Hurry, Hurry*. Arnold was a popular teacher who had served the University faithfully for almost thirty-five years until his resignation in the autumn of 1943.[26]

As with Arnold in English Literature, Bridgman was also fortunate to locate a suitable replacement for Arthur Z. Drew, who resigned his mathematics post in 1908. Hired the following year was George W. Hartwell, a 1903 graduate of Wesleyan, where he had

The library rooms on the second floor of University Hall, about 1890.

RARY, HAMLIN UNIVERSETY,
ST. PAUL MINNESOTA.

Carnegie Library in 1908.

been a classmate and close friend of Thomas Beyer, and where he had, with Beyer, been elected to Phi Beta Kappa. Hartwell held the A.M. and Ph.D. degrees from Columbia. He had taught at the University of Colorado, the University of Kansas, and Michigan Agricultural College prior to his Hamline appointment, and was a member of several professional societies and a scholar of rank in his field. In addition to his work as professor of mathematics, Hartwell became the University's first registrar in 1910, and continued in that post until his untimely death in the summer of 1917. "He has left a large and lonesome place in Hamline University," Beyer wrote sadly that autumn. Like William E. Thompson, Hartwell was a quiet and reserved individual who was not given to self-aggrandizement, but who bore knowing.[27]

With the appointment of Erville B. Woods as professor of political and social science in 1906, the expansion of the social science curriculum which had begun with Innis' 1891 move to history reached another milestone. Woods was a graduate of Beloit College and had taken his Ph.D. from the University of Chicago in 1906, writing a thesis which examined progress as a sociological concept. In the dissertation, published by the *American Journal of Sociology* in 1907, Woods acknowledged that the idea of progress was one of the more "elusive notions," but that precisely for this reason, sociologists should join those attempting to explain it. Cataloging and discussing in turn theories of progress which rested upon Divine and Natural law, economic determinism, Hegel's notion of metaphysical necessity, and Darwinian theory, Woods concluded that "the center of gravity of the notion of progress" was situated in none of these. Rather, it was found "in the expanding content of the human life-interests whose increasing realization constitutes progress." Woods took a leave of absence during the academic year 1908–09 to become an examiner for the U.S. Commission on Immigration. Two years after that he resigned, taking both himself and his liberal sociological dispositions to Hanover, New Hampshire, where he became professor of sociology at Dartmouth.[28]

Woods' successor, and without question an equally capable appointment, was Don D. Lescohier, a specialist in labor relations. Lescohier held both the B.A. (1905) and the M.A. (1907) from

Albion College, and had done further graduate work at the University of Wisconsin. Like his predecessor, he was a liberal in politics and economics and an ardent practitioner of his craft. Prior to accepting the Hamline appointment in 1911, he had worked on the staff of the Wisconsin Bureau of Labor and had also been a special agent for the Minnesota Bureau of Labor, Industry, and Commerce. An experienced analyst of labor-management relations and of industrial conditions, Lescohier, a zealous champion of the workingman, published a stream of articles and monographs in the reform-oriented periodicals of his day. Together with progressives across the land, he lamented the deplorable conditions endured by the working class and the failure of the American industrial system to keep pace with the negative implications of economic expansion. Along with such progressive contemporaries as Jane Addams, Ray Stannard Baker, Ida Tarbell, and Lincoln Steffens, Lescohier publicized and exposed what he understood to be the shortcomings of that system. It relied, he contended with considerable accuracy, upon the continued servility of the working class, which in its ignorance and lack of organization suffered not merely indignity but danger in the course of its employment. His study of industrial accidents in Minnesota, published as the Twelfth Biennial Report of the Bureau of Labor Industries and Commerce in 1911, was the most comprehensive statistical study of job-related accidents which had appeared anywhere up to that time. It was also a good example of the fashion in which early twentieth-century social scientists sought to apply their academic training to the elimination of social, political, and economic injustice. In an editorial entitled ''Minnesota Leads,'' published in March, 1911, the most famous reform organ of the day, the *Survey*, called attention to the report, praised it, and urged progressives everywhere to read it.[29]

Yet another Bridgman appointment deserves notice, not merely because it was one more example of the President's remarkable good fortune and insight in choosing talented academicians to serve on the faculty, but because it eventually became a *cause célèbre* which in the end proved a brutal illustration of the drift from academic principle that followed Bridgman's departure. In 1907, the President decided to inaugurate a chair of psychology and philosophy, doing so by hiring Gregory Dexter Walcott, a Phi Beta Kappa graduate of Brown University, Class of 1897. Walcott, another fearless spokesman for liberal causes, held the B.D. from Union Theological Seminary (1900) and the Ph.D. (1904) from Columbia. He had studied in Berlin during 1900 and 1901, and had served a Congregational pastorate for two years following his return to the United States. When elected to the Hamline post, he was professor of philosophy and the classics and dean of Blackburn College at Carlinville, Illinois. During a tenure which lasted until he was summarily fired by President Alfred F. Hughes in 1928, Walcott published several essays in professional journals, lectured regularly, and received a $10,000 Carnegie Corporation grant to edit a series of source books in the history of the sciences. He and Thomas Beyer also made plans to co-author a textbook in the field of ethics, but the idea never materialized. For by the time the two colleagues had managed to lay the foundation for their work, pressure from within the Conference had caused Hughes to desert Walcott.[30]

That virtually all of Bridgman's later major appointments reflected the President's own growing liberalism and respect for social activism spoke well for the trustees. They were, after all, of generally conservative disposition, and those whose professional interests were tied to the business and industrial communities were not likely to appreciate or give overt support to the social and economic concerns voiced so articulately by individuals like Lescohier, Woods, Walcott, Beyer, and Hartwell. Yet they were totally open-minded in their reliance upon Bridgman's good judgment and in their response to his challenge to improve the University by upgrading its faculty. Nor was it necessary to look merely to the last years of Bridgman's own tenure in order to detect the manner and extent to which he placed his personal stamp upon the nature and quality of Hamline's faculty. For while most of Bridgman's successors demonstrated that they too understood the need for making quality academic appointments, it would be more than forty years before another would work conscientiously and with such consistency to locate, hire, and retain the finest academic talent available.

During twenty-nine years as president of the University, Bridgman made twenty-eight full-time academic appointments, and roughly twenty appointments that were either part-time positions, replacements for faculty on leave, or posts whose responsibilities were essentially administrative in nature. Of the twenty-eight, fully nineteen, or 68 per cent, remained at Hamline at least six years, and twelve were still on the faculty after ten years. Seven gave more than a quarter-century of service, and their combined period of tenure was two hundred sixty-two years, or an average of just under forty years each. Beyer and King outlasted four more administrations, and Arnold came within five years of doing the same.

Viewed with regard to academic preparation and professional competence, the record was just as remarkable and said even more about Bridgman's efforts to build a faculty of exceptional talent. Whether judged from the standpoint of earned degrees, the institutional sources of those degrees, the record of scholarly publication and professional commitment, membership in Phi Beta Kappa, or involvement in matters of social, political, and economic concern, the individuals brought to Hamline by Bridgman demonstrated professional competence and commitment, skill as teachers, and interests which ranged far beyond their specific academic assignments. There was every reason to suppose, given their several records of scholarly achievement, that many of Bridgman's appointees could have sought and gained far more prestigious academic appointments. Some did, of course — Woods, for example; Lescohier for another. But in many instances Bridgman never again had to concern himself about staffing a particular department once he had made the initial appointment. Henry L. Osborn was the only person ever appointed by Bridgman to fill the chairs of biology and geology. The same was true of William E. Thompson in Latin, James S. King in modern languages, Thomas Beyer in English language, Gregory Walcott in philosophy and psychology, George Hartwell in mathematics, and Anna M. Davis, who became University librarian in 1898 and remained on the faculty until her retirement (she was the first individual to collect a pension) in 1923. This was a formidable list of achievements on Bridgman's part, and says much about his faculty's loyalty, not merely to Methodist liberal arts education, but to the President himself.

CHAPTER 4

DIVERSIONS AND FRUSTRATIONS

THE PERIOD WHICH began with the retirement of President Bridgman in 1912 and ended with the formal inauguration of Charles Nelson Pace in June, 1935, was an exceedingly difficult one for Hamline University. To be sure, the era began on a positive note with the welcome selection of Samuel Fletcher Kerfoot as Bridgman's successor, and in the years that followed there was often good reason to remain optimistic about the future of the college. Between 1912 and 1927, endowment grew from $634,000 to more than $2,000,000 and the value of the physical plant almost tripled, increasing from $240,000 to $680,000. As public high schools continued to increase in number and size, the need for the Preparatory Department had diminished, and in 1911 the University had closed it permanently, enabling resources to flow exclusively to the collegiate division. The full-time faculty, numbering 14 in 1912, stood at 42 in 1927, and by 1926 the student enrollment had reached an all-time high of 639. But despite these and other seemingly encouraging facts and figures, much that happened within the University during that era proved discouraging and frustrating. For it was a period marked all too frequently by financial stress, academic and philosophic indecision, administrative tension, and problems with important segments of the constituency.[1]

In considerable measure, the source of the difficulties was external. There was no way, for example, to control completely the effects which the European War would have upon colleges and universities, and particularly upon those the size of Hamline where the impact of conscription and economic retrenchment was bound to be severe. Nor was it possible for the most part to counter the effect which the prolonged agricultural depression of the 1920s was certain to have upon institutions like Hamline which depended so heavily upon a rural economy for their student body and financial support. Then too, the profound social and economic changes and resultant stress which characterized the decade following the war posed significant intellectual challenges to all institutions, especially those which, like Hamline, had their roots in a conservative and evangelical past. Finally, the University was relatively helpless when confronted by the worldwide economic collapse of 1929, which bankrupted and forced closure of many institutions of higher learning. But Hamline's problems during the fourth and fifth decades of its reincarnation went much deeper than war and depression, which, after all, adversely affected people and institutions everywhere. At the heart of the matter lay explicit and implicit disagreement over the essence of the University, and the failure of Hamline's many devoted supporters to reach a working consensus regarding what its nature and purpose were.

The charter, which spoke of perfecting the scholar and placed Hamline "under the patronage" of the Methodist Church, was of little use when it came to such efforts at definition. Indeed, its broad and liberal provisions and its lack of specificity with regard to such qualities as goals and attributes were more hindrance than help. In stipulating that "no religious tenet shall be required of any person to entitle him or her to all the privileges of the institution," and in guaranteeing freedom of worship, the charter legally prohibited sectarian or bigoted behavior. Thus it was legally impossible to regard the institution as in any sense narrowly Methodist in its teachings. Furthermore, while the trustees received authority "to prescribe and regulate the course of studies" which students were to pursue, the charter wisely made no attempt to give advice on the subject. Since the document specified that only four of the fifteen trustees need be members of the Conference, it was clear that the founders had no desire legally to bestow upon the Church permanent discretionary authority over matters pertaining to institutional policy, academic or otherwise. That there would obviously be a friendly and supportive relationship between Church and college was evident, and that the institution would bear the Wesleyan rather than the Puritan stamp was just as apparent. But it was beyond dispute that the Methodist Church did not *own* Hamline University; the trustees did. Moreover, the Church from 1877 onward could not even argue that its power of patronage extended to that of controlling nominations, for the "closed corporation" amendment engineered by J. F. Chaffee had eliminated that right. In sum, the charter stipulated that the trustees were "a body politic and corporate," and were thus the sole legal custodians of the institution's destiny. They alone could "sue and be sued;" "plead and be impleaded;" "acquire, hold and convey property, real, personal and mixed, in all lawful ways." In one sense, therefore, the nature and purpose of the University were beyond the power of the Church either to determine or control.[2]

But legal documents cannot define essence. They can only provide an organizational framework or at best suggest philosophic texture. Myths and perceptions, not charters or constitutions, ultimately determine such things as nature and purpose, and as those factors change, so do the goals and workings of the institution affected. At Hamline, it became clear within relatively short order following President Bridgman's retirement that the balance had begun to shift toward a more sectarian point of view. Although evangelicalism did not entirely displace the more liberal currents favored by Bridgman and many of his associates, the tendency was decidedly in that direction.

George Bridgman's view of his role as chief executive, and of the institution he believed Hamline might become, was unmistakably clear. He wanted the University to become not merely a reasonably respectable college of the Methodist Church, but a very good liberal arts college indeed, and one that enjoyed diverse support. Because he was a typical late nineteenth-century small college president — possessed of enormous discretionary authority and both the physical energy and ego to accompany it — he caused Hamline to conform, in no small measure, to that view. While Hamline had not become, by 1912, anything more than a regional institution in terms of its student clientele, president and faculty alike had made it well known in educational and business circles nationwide. Just as important,

Bridgman consciously sought to build a faculty which looked, not to Minnesota and the Midwest for its attitudes and predispositions, but to the eastern seaboard, where Victorianism had long since ceased to flourish, where cultural admixture and a constant immigrant influx had for decades precluded the dominance of an insidious isolationism, and where liberal attitudes tended to hold sway in matters of religious and educational policy. These were faculty born and raised in New England and New York, in New Jersey and Pennsylvania; and they had taken their advanced degrees at such prestigious institutions as Johns Hopkins, Brown, and Columbia; at Chicago, Wisconsin, and Northwestern. When they traveled, they frequently journeyed to New York City and to the Continent, and their words and actions made their cosmopolitanism clear. To a considerable extent, Bridgman himself became immersed in his later difficulties because a growing body of alumni and clergymen, born and raised in Minnesota and the Upper Midwest, could not understand, and therefore found it impossible to countenance, much that they sensed was happening within the University.

Thus it was no accident that Bridgman's successor was an alumnus, a clergyman, and a midwesterner. Although born in Canada, Samuel Kerfoot had grown up in Dakota Territory. He had entered the Hamline Preparatory Department in 1883, and had taken his A.B. from the University in 1889. He had received his B.D. from Drew Theological Seminary in 1892, and had then become a member of the Minnesota Conference. From 1908 until his election to the Hamline post he was president of Dakota Wesleyan University, where he had proven to be a highly capable fund raiser. Commenting on Kerfoot's election, the editor of the *Alumni Quarterly* captured the essential nature of the executive transition which had just occurred. "From the program as outlined by Dr. Kerfoot," he observed, "it would seem that he proposes to enter into a partnership with friends of Christian Education, ministers of the Methodist Church in Minnesota, students and Alumni of Hamline, to work for 'A Greater Hamline,' and a large freshman class."[3] Whether or not the new president had made all of this clear was open to question, but the editor's perceptions and implicit judgments of both Kerfoot and Bridgman were not.

In his inaugural address the President presented his views on the role of the church-related college. Discussing the development of higher education in Western Europe and the United States, and taking note of the impact of evolutionary theory and the growth of the natural sciences on college curricula, Kerfoot reflected upon the survival of such colleges. To do so, he believed, they must have "intrinsic worth," which in turn meant the facility to develop "Christian personality" in their students. To achieve that end, the Christian college must attend to several ingredients. The physical plant should be adequate. The curriculum should stress the liberal arts while remaining open to the possibility of vocational training. Methodology should take current educational theory into account. The faculty must be "imbued with the principles of evangelical Christianity." The trustees must be men of influence, "business sagacity and balanced judgment," economic means and generosity, public spirit, and cooperation. And the University's administrators must hold and express their convictions courageously.[4]

The President concluded his address with two caveats. He warned first against succumbing either to sectarianism or secularism. The former could easily interfere with the pursuit of truth, while the latter too frequently emphasized "science and scholarship rather than native standards of character and service." In the second warning, he called attention to the negative consequences of differing ideals within college and Church, "whereby the church is given the evangelical aim and the college the educational task." Often this artificial division of purpose had led to situations wherein the Church criticized the college for its intellectual honesty, while the college belittled the Church for its evangelical aims and sat in judgment of those aims by subjecting them to "analytical processes of criticism." Pastor and professor should supplement rather than make war upon each other, Kerfoot declared, for only under such conditions would students be most likely to grow both intellectually and spiritually.[5]

If Kerfoot's references to evangelical Christianity disturbed the more liberal members of the community, his endorsement of curricular modernization righted the balance. Within short order he had made clear his willingness to support the introduction of "a scheme of major and minor studies,'' and by the beginning of 1914 the faculty had approved such a plan. Freshmen who enrolled that autumn came under the requirement, and the University awarded its first degrees specifying majors in the spring of 1917. At Hamline as elsewhere, the new system, along with the entire concept of concentration and distribution, owed much to the earlier appearance of the elective principle. For if that principle had, in the words of President Eliot, made "scholarship possible, not only among undergraduates, but among graduate students and college teachers,'' it had also imposed new schemes of curricular organization upon the nation's colleges and universities.[6]

One result of this nationwide tendency toward more rational pursuit of curricular freedom was the growing predisposition of educational foundations, accrediting agencies, and honorary societies such as Phi Beta Kappa to extend and intensify their own standards. Accordingly, educational institutions found it increasingly necessary to gather and to submit data bearing upon such matters as faculty teaching loads, faculty academic preparation, student-faculty ratios, endowment, library holdings, classroom space and its utilization, laboratory facilities and equipment, and statistics on alumni. At Hamline, the need to produce such data and to present it convincingly became apparent at least as early as 1914, when Carleton became the first four-year college in Minnesota to secure a Phi Beta Kappa chapter. From that year onward until 1931, Hamline faculty who were members of Phi Beta Kappa engaged continually in the quest for a chapter. Consistently the national organization turned down their applications, citing teaching overloads and the fact that too many faculty were teaching too many subjects to assure comprehensive treatment — in short, urging the college to hire more faculty, and particularly more faculty sufficiently well trained to offer advanced courses. It was therefore no accident that during Kerfoot's presidency the faculty tripled in size, or that there was constantly underway a process of departmental organization and reorganization designed to promote curricular depth as well as breadth.[7]

Nor was it surprising that the University's efforts to strengthen itself academically corresponded closely to the policies of the General Education Board, which between 1902 and 1914 alone had given Hamline and other colleges and universities more than $10 million to advance their respective educational interests along lines specified by the Board. Regularly, the Rockefeller-funded agency issued policy statements which reflected upon current conditions within American higher education, and upon the Board's perception of its relationship to those conditions. In the process, colleges and universities frequently took their cues not from internal study and discussion, but from external offers of assistance provided by the Board as it sought to reshape American higher education according to its own values. From its founding in 1902 until 1919, the Board had confined its efforts to assisting "promising institutions" by means of challenge grants designed to stimulate endowment giving; Hamline three times received such grants. Between 1919 and 1924, the Board redirected its focus so as to concentrate upon the improvement of teachers' salaries; Hamline sought and received a $250,000 grant for that purpose. From 1924 onward, it chose to focus upon "raising the standards of scholarship, such as the development of honors courses, research fellowships, more adequate facilities and opportunities for fundamental research and training in the physical and biological sciences, and special encouragement in the humanities;" and a proposed program of renewal designed in 1930 by President Alfred F. Hughes took that focus into account.[8]

Finally, there was the matter of academic accreditation. By 1915, the North Central Association of Colleges and Secondary Schools had placed its seal of approval upon the University. In 1920, the Association of American Universities likewise granted accreditation. In 1925, the University of Illinois recognized Hamline as a "Class A" institution. And by the 1920s, both the American Association of University Women and the Minnesota State Department of Education had also awarded full accreditation. Each of these instances of accreditation meant not simply that Hamline graduates received full credit for work completed at the college when enrolling in graduate schools, or that Hamline credits in general transferred with ease, but that the University had satisfied the respective agencies and associations of its academic legitimacy.[9]

The effects of these external stimuli were conspicuous and significant. When Samuel Kerfoot took office, not a department in the University had more than one faculty member, and several were jointly staffed with part-time personnel. Loren Batchelder taught every course in both chemistry and physics, while James King did the same in German and French. George Innis found his energies spread across education, history and Bible. Henry Osborn presided, as he had since 1887, over both geology and biology, and both LeRoy Arnold and Don Lescohier helped Innis in Bible while tending to their primary responsibilities in English literature and social science. Of the full-time faculty, only William E. Thompson in Latin, Thomas Beyer in English language, and Roy Towne in Greek taught exclusively within their respective fields.[10]

Within short order, Kerfoot made sweeping changes. In 1913 he separated the Romance Language Department from the German Department, and in 1914 separated Physics from Chemistry. Next, he organized a Biblical Literature Department, reorganized the History Department, and gave Innis full-time responsibility for the Education Department. Then in 1917, he separated Political Science from Social Science, and reorganized the latter by establishing Departments of Economics and Sociology. In 1920 he established the Religious Education Department. And he was constantly enlarging the faculty as well. To keep pace with these developments, he appointed almost 100 individuals to the faculty between 1912 and 1922, and by the time of his retirement in 1927 had appointed more than 130. While many came and went within a year or two, and while a good number were undistinguished in training or ability, there were several important exceptions.[11]

Perhaps the foremost example of Kerfoot's occasional good fortune in securing faculty of exceptional talent and promise was John D. Hicks, whom the President hired in 1916 to staff the History Department. Hicks, who had done his undergraduate and master's work at Northwestern, and who had written his doctoral dissertation under the direction of Frederic Logan Paxson at Wisconsin, was a brilliant young scholar who would soon become a noted authority on populism. During his six years at Hamline, he delivered two major papers before professional associations and wrote another, revised his dissertation for publication, and published several articles. By the time he left Hamline in 1922, he had become sufficiently well known within the profession to have attracted the favorable attention of the eminent historian Frederick Jackson Turner. In the afterglow of a long and productive scholarly career which included nine years at the University of Nebraska, ten at Wisconsin, and fifteen at Berkeley, Hicks wrote a moving and informative essay about his years at Hamline which at one point provided whimsical insight into the degree of intimacy which characterized Hamline in 1916. "Since I was the entire history department," Hicks noted, "decisions were easy to reach — I could have a department meeting standing on a corner waiting for a streetcar, and often did."[12]

Hicks brought high professional ideals to a department which was, at the time of his arrival, the weakest in the college. Moreover, his primary role in the recruitment and selection of faculty contrasted sharply with customary routine, in which the President made hiring decisions with only minimal advice from others. In fashioning a comprehensive history curriculum, Hicks soon concluded that it was impossible for one individual to teach all the history courses listed in the catalog. Thus, in 1917, he persuaded the President to hire Hamline alumnus Harold S. Quigley as professor of political science. Quigley, who in 1911 had become Hamline's first Rhodes Scholar, had taken a Diploma in Political Science and Economics as well as a B.A. in Modern History from Oxford, and thus was eminently qualified to assist in history as well. He had received his doctorate in 1916 from the University of Wisconsin, where he had met Hicks, and had taught for one year at Princeton before accepting his *alma mater's* call. Quigley was a specialist in international relations, and was fast becoming an authority on the Far East. By 1920, his research interests as well as salary considerations had influenced him to accept a position at the University of Minnesota, where he remained for the rest of his professional career.[13]

Hicks next turned for assistance to the University of Minnesota. There, he located and hired Theodore C. Blegen, who was an Americanist like himself. Blegen's specialty was Minnesota history, and he was particularly interested in Norwegian immigration, regarding which subject he published profusely. During his seven-year association with Hamline, he worked zealously to promote interest in state and local history, and was a prolific writer of scholarly articles. In 1922 he became assistant superintendent of the Minnesota Historical Society, and in 1931, superintendent. Blegen left Hamline in 1927 to become professor of history at the University of Minnesota, where he remained until his retirement.[14]

Together with Blegen, Hicks secured the appointments of Clarence W. Rife and Arthur S. Williamson in 1922. Rife, who was then completing his doctoral dissertation at Yale, and who succeeded Blegen as departmental chairman in 1927, remained at Hamline until his retirement in 1956. Williamson, who had studied under Hicks as a Hamline undergraduate, and who had followed his mentor's lead by taking his M.A. from Wisconsin, was destined for an even longer relationship with the University. Except for a brief period between 1925 and 1927, during which time he completed his doctoral work at Iowa, Williamson remained active on the faculty until 1963 in a formal capacity, and continued to serve the University informally for several years thereafter. And when Grace Lee Nute succeeded Blegen as professor of Minnesota history in 1927, the chain of continuity was again replenished. Like Blegen, Nute was a scholar; she was a Radcliffe Ph.D. interested in research and publication, and during her thirty-three-year association with the University, published dozens of articles and several books. Most notable was *Caesars of the Wilderness*, a definitive study of Médart Chouart, Sieur des Groseilliers, and his brother-in-law, Pierre Esprit Radisson.[15]

Although the History Department under Hicks' sensitive and professional leadership made by far the greatest academic gains during Kerfoot's presidency, other departments grew in stature as well. Arriving in 1919 to become professor of Latin and Greek was H. Osborn Ryder, who held his Ph.D. from Boston University and was interested not only in the classics, but in philosophy and archaeology. Osborn was a prolific contributor to educational publications and the author of a Latin text. In the Romance Languages Department, Kerfoot appointed Louis R. Herrick in 1913, Solomon M. Delson in 1920, Dorothy M. McGhee in 1923, and Hays P. Archerd in 1925. Herrick, who had taken his Ph.D. at Wisconsin, divided his talents among French, Spanish, and Italian until 1918, when the

President finally saw fit to hire an assistant. Delson taught French, and remained at the University until 1931, when he resigned to accept a position at the City College of New York. McGhee, who had graduated with Phi Beta Kappa honors from Minnesota, was a student of seventeenth- and eighteenth-century French literature, and wrote her dissertation at Ohio State in 1930 on the *conte philosophique*, a literary form which attacked serious subjects humorously. Like Herrick, she contributed frequently to professional journals. Archerd, a Hamline alumnus and a Methodist clergyman, had spent fifteen years in Peru as Superintendent of the Coast District before returning to the United States in 1924. He received his M.A. from Minnesota in 1925, and served his *alma mater* for twenty-seven years thereafter with distinction.[16]

For several years following creation of the Economics Department in 1917, Kerfoot searched in vain for a competent instructor. In 1922, he finally succeeded with the appointment of Charles B. Kuhlmann, who was then working on his doctorate at Minnesota. In 1929, Kuhlmann published an important study, *The Development of the Flour-Milling Industry in the United States*, which took the city of Minneapolis as its point of reference. Although ignoring labor relations, problems associated with prices and costs, and for the most part the interaction between government and industry, he provided a broad historic account which served as a foundation for subsequent studies. Kuhlmann gave many years of service to Hamline, retiring in 1952.[17]

In the Natural Sciences, Kerfoot made several important appointments. One was Jens M. Rysgaard, who arrived in 1914 to head the newly-created Physics Department and remained until his retirement in 1941. Rysgaard was a teacher rather than a scholar, and for several years was able to exploit his talents to the utmost, for until 1920 he was responsible for the entire physics curriculum. In Chemistry, the President hired George W. Muhleman to succeed Loren Batchelder. Muhleman was chiefly interested in teaching methods, and during his twenty-three-year association with the college published several articles and manuals describing laboratory equipment and procedures.[18]

With the appointment of Walter A. Kenyon to the Department of

Biology in 1924, Kerfoot ended his halfhearted eleven-year effort to aid Henry Osborn. Kenyon held his Ph.D. from Wisconsin, and had also taught high school biology in that state. Although he became increasingly interested in the study of human genetics, his earliest research concerned digestive enzymes in fish. He was particularly interested in determining whether differences in such enzymes had occurred in the course of biological evolution, and in a paper published during his first year at Hamline, sought to establish one base for such a comparative study by investigating the rate of digestion in representative fishes, amphibians, and reptiles. In subsequent articles, Kenyon presented the results of additional studies made on fish, and in 1940, published a much-discussed article entitled, "Who Shall Inherit the Earth?" which discussed aspects of population control, and focused particularly upon the eugenics programs of Nazi Germany.[19]

Yet another Kerfoot appointment, and one which ultimately had far-reaching consequences, was that of Charles Horswell to the Chair of Biblical Literature in 1917. Horswell held undergraduate and master's degrees from Northwestern, his B.D. from Garrett Biblical Institute and his Ph.D. from Yale. Ardently devoted to intellectual freedom and committed to modern Biblical scholarship, Horswell was a serious scholar of gentle demeanor who urged his students to delve beneath surface appearances in order to discover reality, and who warned frequently against threats to academic integrity. But his liberal theological views, which he consistently expressed straightforwardly, were at odds not only with the fundamentalist attitudes which many Hamline students brought with them from their homes, but more importantly with the views held by many alumni and members of the Conference. Confronted by expressions of disapproval regarding Horswell, the President suddenly seemed to capitulate. In December, 1924, he announced Horswell's "withdrawal" from the University, effective the following spring.[20]

Although at first glance puzzling, Kerfoot's decision was not difficult to explain. For Hamline was then in the final phase of a lagging $1.5 million capital campaign begun earlier that year. Worried about the success of the development effort, plagued for years by ill health, concerned that Minnesota Methodists in considerable number had not made good on pledges to a $500,000 campaign conducted in 1916, and distressed by the absence of support from the faculty, the President succumbed to conservative external pressure.[21]

Alumnus and former faculty member Harold Quigley was irate. In a stinging attack published in the *Alumni Quarterly*, the perceptive and candid political scientist unleashed his wrath. A college such as Hamline should maintain "interest in another's welfare, intensity of earnestness for personal attainment," he urged. It should display "high and generous sportsmanship, loyalty to the point of sacrifice, reverence for learning, love of the good." And such qualities could only live and grow "in an atmosphere of freedom." Supremely offensive were attacks upon intellectual freedom within the arena of the social sciences, which he defined as including politics, economics, and religion. "One may mention the Constitution or the Bible only in the tones of the Vicar of Bray," Quigley charged, "lest he run the risk of the supreme penalty — for that is what dismissal involves for most college professors. . . . Is it not a tremendous pity that colleges should prolong this period of bitter social and religious antagonism by failing to teach what they know or believe to be the truth?" One could perhaps allow the older generation its biases, he conceded, for to disturb long-sustained and nurtured convictions might well not be worth the effort. "But why, in the name of a happy, well-articulated society, if not of truth," he inquired, "refuse the saving fruits of scientific investigation and thinking to the young, whose aspirations and tentative conclusions have not hardened into indissoluble prejudices?"[22]

These were brave and uncompromising words, which tore with a vengeance at the intellectual repression that had become so much a part of the national atmosphere in the postwar period. Born of fear and ignorance, and stimulated by the sometimes painful social and economic readjustments which had followed in the war's wake, it was a pervasive repression that affected all of society's ranks, and found its way to the most remote geographic quarter. At its base lay the conviction, seldom consciously articulated, that deep-seated social, religious, and economic values were in process of displacement by forces alien to America's past. That past, as seen by Protestants possessed of middle-class convictions and virtues, appeared superior to the values held by certain other religious and ethnic groups, who were identified, in turn, with social and economic forces at odds with the prevailing mentality. In short, it seemed that insidious influences, led by members of minority groups, were undermining capitalism and the work ethic, evangelical Christianity, and the prevalence of English and North European social and cultural values which had guided the nation from its inception.

Thus, when Attorney General A. Mitchell Palmer, without first consulting the ailing President Woodrow Wilson, led a coordinated series of raids on dozens of labor union headquarters in January, 1920, he did so because he believed that unions in general were run by radicals, Bolsheviks in particular, and that the government must swiftly dissipate their strength before they destroyed the American economic system. When Italian anarchists Nicola Sacco and Bartolomeo Vanzetti, accused of the murder of two payroll guards in Massachusetts, were tried, found guilty, and eventually put to death in 1927 — all without full presentation of the evidence — it was because they were convenient ethnic scapegoats, and not because anyone ever convincingly proved their responsibility for the crimes. When members of the Ku Klux Klan ran rampant through the night during the early years of the 1920s, seeking out and dealing violently with blacks, Jews, Roman Catholics, and all others whom they regarded as threats to their own well-being, they did so because they found group support for their ignorant and irrational prejudices. And when the state of Tennessee tried and convicted high school biology teacher John Thomas Scopes in 1925 on the charge that he had taught evolutionary theory to his classes, it did so because religious fundamentalists in Tennessee and elsewhere had temporarily won out in their battle against science, which they regarded as evil and at odds with Scripture.[23]

All of this meant, at Hamline University in the winter of 1924, that the forces of conjunction and not those of coincidence were at work when President Kerfoot decided to send Charles Horswell packing to his Michigan retreat, there to spend the rest of his days in reflection and writing. Kerfoot himself had done what he undoubtedly regarded as his best to resist external pressures of the sort which led to Horswell's downfall. He had voiced open disapproval of a bill, pending before the state legislature, which would have forbidden the teaching of evolutionary theory in public schools. He had sympathized with Methodist clergymen who opposed dancing, but had attempted to explain that, since more than 80 per cent of all freshmen who enrolled at the University knew how to dance when they arrived, it was difficult to take a hard line on the matter. He had tiptoed over the issue of the relationship between classroom instruction and the faculty's obligation to provide witness to its Christian faith, noting on one occasion that while few were "evangelists in the ordinary meaning of the term," contemporary academic conditions made that virtually impossible. Hamline's faculty, he indicated, was "so largely academic" in its training that it inclined naturally to stress "the gradual growth of knowledge and development of character" rather than to cultivate "the warmth of an appeal" which would lead to Christian conversion. Some of the latter work went on, he pointed out, "and all our men are ready to testify to their faith, but after their own academic fashion." When it became clear in the aftermath of the Horswell episode that much ill-feeling existed both within the Conference and within the University regarding the matter, the President took the lead in urging that Hamline sponsor a conference to consider the college's proper relationship to the Methodist Church.[24]

The Conference, which convened in April, 1925, opened with a keynote address by the Rev. R. B. Tibbetts of Albert Lea. Speaking on the "Obligations of the University to the Constituency," Tibbetts contended that the Christian college had four principal functions. First, it must demonstrate that scholarship and faith should be mutually supportive and beneficial. Second, the college should enhance the student's critical abilities and stimulate "a broad spirit of appreciation." Third, it must "maintain the integrity of God's word." Finally, it must provide students with "a reverent, consecrated teaching influence and atmosphere."[25]

Following Tibbetts' remarks, the session moved directly to an address by James S. King, who examined the obligations of the constituency to the college. Although Professor King defined a constituency as "any body of persons whose interests are merged or concentrated around a common project or enterprise,'' he chose, significantly, to address most of his remarks to the clergy. There was hardly any limit to what they could do to further Hamline's interests, he declared, but without their wholehearted support, the college could not hope to prosper. To King, ministers were ''shock absorbers'' who, supposedly imbued with ''the free air, the breadth, liberality and Christian atmosphere'' of the colleges and seminaries in which they had received their training, stood between college and constituency, interpreting one to the other. King reminded his listeners that as recently as the autumn of 1924, Minnesota's presiding bishop, Charles Locke, had strongly urged pastors under his jurisdiction to spend half of each working day in solid and uninterrupted study. That was wise advice, the veteran teacher observed. For in doing so, the clergy would ''insure a revitalized church constituency and an enlightened and understanding college constituency.''[26]

King then tackled the controversy between religion and science, an issue highlighted at Hamline by Charles Horswell's recent ''withdrawal.'' A church headed by a pastor who was a ''thorough student of the Old and New Testament,'' and was in touch with modern Biblical scholarship, he proposed, would hear ''few if any complaints regarding distinctive and dangerous teachings in Christian colleges.'' Ministers should have free and open minds. They should understand that growth and progress were fundamental laws of life and that the facts of science remained the same both within the denominational college and outside it. Students who came to Hamline from churches guided by pastors thus enlightened, he contended, would not wind up ''writing home after the first week that Christianity is being undermined and God Almighty dethroned.'' He concluded his remarks by reminding his listeners that neither Hamline nor any other church-related college was ''a hospital, sanatorium, cold storage warehouse, cloister, or house of correction.'' Nor could it ever become any of these, for it lay perpetually open ''to the great, wonderful, heaving, surging, noisy, naughty, and distracted world.''[27]

King's cunning observations were a clear and unequivocal indictment of what he regarded as destructive forces within the Conference — forces which in his view proclaimed with unquestioned sincerity but little intelligence that the University should be a prose-lytizer rather than an agent of education. Moreover, he regarded those ministers, in their fundamentalist zeal, as so thoroughly at odds with science, Biblical scholarship, and the whole thrust of contemporary thought in the humanities and social sciences, that they threatened the continued viability of the Church. Accordingly, he shrewdly chose to stress not the more obvious opportunities for service to the University — pledging money, for example — but the clergy's obligation to cultivate and renew its own scholarly abilities. In doing so, he quite properly believed, ministers would become better educated to the world which so many of them seemed to fear, better servants of their flocks, and better stewards of their trust as spokesmen for the Church Universal. No member of the college community had ever delivered a more pointed yet loving indict-ment. None had ever sought, with greater care, to indicate shortcomings while at the same time providing the basis for renewed and more collegial association between Church and University.

In the midst of the Horswell controversy, and as plans for the 1925 Conference were getting underway, yet another grievance came to a head. At issue was the calibre of the faculty. On this point, many alumni were persuaded that a steady regression had taken place since President Bridgman's retirement. As early as 1921, Alumni Association President Charles R. Richardson had pleaded with the administration to improve the faculty's overall quality. "There is at Hamline a little group of choice men whom she must cling to, for they are the salt of the earth," he wrote, undoubt-edly referring to Horswell among others. "But there is also a group, whom the exigencies of the times have forced upon her, who must be replaced. Their teaching is utterly inadequate. They lack personality, vision, and an understanding of the problems that Ham-line must meet." Since the college was neither wealthy nor re-nowned, only the faculty's "compelling personality" could win and hold students, and the administration must understand and act upon the implications of that fact. Quigley, writing in 1924, saw salaries as the key. Hamline could not afford merely to hire "earnest" and "high-minded" faculty, he argued. Above all else, the institution must seek to employ individuals who possessed superior credentials and were both academically alert and professionally involved. Having secured such individuals, the University must then make certain that when other institutions sought to lure them away by offering higher salaries, there would be money available to induce them to remain. Quigley noted that Carleton College at Northfield and Reed College at Portland, Oregon, were nationally known not because they had better physical facilities "but because they have recognized that the only way to maintain a faculty of superior excellence is to recognize its worth tangibly every month." Hamline's $3,000 maximum salary was a pitiful and revealing expression of the University's tendency to place its emphasis upon devotion and community rather than upon professional commitment and academic worth.[28]

The data tended to support the critics' concerns, although clearly it could provide only quantitative assistance. Of the faculty whom President Kerfoot hired, only twenty-one — about 17 per cent — held the Ph.D. at the time of their appointment, although two others completed doctoral work later. More than sixty — roughly 50 per cent — had done no advanced work whatsoever, and several possessed no academic credentials at all. Furthermore, continuity of service was a problem, for only nine of the Ph.D.'s whom the President appointed remained at the University more than three years. Allowing for the enormous pressure which Kerfoot must have felt as he sought to satisfy Phi Beta Kappa, the alumni, the students, the Conference, and a handful of accrediting agencies, the fact remained that George Henry Bridgman, many years earlier, had done a better job of upholding academic standards while at the same time securing the services of excellent teachers.[29]

At the height of the University's painful process of self-examination, *Oracle* Assistant Editor Ingvald Talsness published an editorial which indicated that observant students understood perfectly the origins of the dilemma. "It is hard to name a more dissimilar, a more heterogeneous group anywhere than that upon which a small denominational college must depend for its success, for its very existence," Talsness wrote in December, 1924. Constantly the several elements were "competing and quarreling for the opportunity to dictate the policies of the institution, often down to the minutest detail." While all labored honestly according to their own notions of what was best for the University, the diversity of viewpoints was truly staggering. Certain "staid, conservative, well-meaning, small-town pastors and church members" thought it should be "a theological seminary and a training school for deaconesses." Some felt it should attempt to compete with the University of Minnesota by establishing professional programs. Others believed that it should spend most of its energy promoting scholarship. "An athletic Sophomore in a red sweater," Talsness went on, conjuring up an image familiar to all generations of college students everywhere, "says that what we need at 'this here' college is better buildings to attract more athletes 'so as to make us conference champs.'" One element within the student body thought that Hamline's future lay in "its increasing liberalism in every line," while "some of the stand-pat conservatives on the Board of Trustees shudder at the mention of anything with a progressive tinge."[30]

Talsness was equally realistic and candid in his advance assessment of the Conference on "Our College," which he quite accurately predicted would settle Hamline's problems "about as much as one of our editorials can settle them." For in the end, the Board and the administration would make the decisions — "if they haven't already decided pretty well." But by convening such a conference, clergy and laity alike would have a chance to vent their frustrations, thereby perhaps feeling that they had participated personally in determining the nature and future direction of the college. "It will tend to make them more loyal toward Hamline," he wrote optimistically. "There is much advantage in that."[31]

Compounding the University's problems were the conspicuous deterioration of the physical plant and the limited potential for developing and expanding the Midway site. Image was important, President Kerfoot told the trustees, citing the case of a prospective student who had refused even to leave the streetcar when confronted by his first glimpse of the grounds. After a series of stopgap measures, including halfhearted efforts at beautification and $15,000 worth of improvements to Goheen Hall, the Board agreed in December, 1915, to launch a half-million-dollar endowment campaign, with proceeds to be divided equally between construction and endowment. With major contributions from the General Education Board, Matthew G. Norton, and trustee Watson S. Moore of Duluth, plus $300,000 from Minnesota Methodists, the 1916 Advance achieved its goal in pledges. But collecting them proved difficult.[32]

In urging the trustees to authorize the campaign, Kerfoot had sometimes compared Hamline with its principal rivals. Carleton had approximately the same enrollment, he noted, yet had many more buildings and was in the midst of an extensive program of physical expansion. This had created an image of progress and prosperity, although few realized that the Northfield institution had financed the construction through a policy of deficit spending. Macalester, too, was moving forward, seeking $400,000 for new facilities. A capital campaign would provide Hamline not only with significant material gains, but with a much-needed psychological boost as well. "My only desire," he explained, "is that we shall realize the need sufficiently and believe in the enterprise so thoroughly that we shall put the most aggressive enthusiasm into the movement and be impelled to move forward and cooperate by planning to interview or reach others who might be able to assist."[33]

By the spring of 1917, Kerfoot's position had hardened. While Hamline in its present location was "not entirely unattractive," and while it was conveniently situated, spatial and environmental considerations posed significant problems. Railroads to the west and north, a new coke plant to the northeast, and the fact that the entire area was rapidly becoming industrialized made the campus "somewhat less desirable as a place of attractiveness and appeal, especially to cultured people." Calling for a comprehensive study before authorizing any new construction at the Snelling site, Kerfoot declared himself unreservedly in favor of relocation.[34]

For three years the question remained in abeyance, with trustee indecision and the European War combining to preclude speedy resolution. Patriotic enlistments in an ambulance unit which ultimately saw service in France, compulsory enrollment for males in military science and drill, and the presence on campus of a Students' Army Training Corps unit combined to cause attention to drift momentarily from problems on the home front. Then, in the summer of 1919, interest in relocation quickened when the City of St.

Paul offered the University $190,000 for the campus. Explaining that it wished to use the gymnasium for public recreation, the library as a neighborhood branch of the city system, and other buildings as educational facilities, the city eventually raised its bid to $225,000 and finally to $250,000. Meanwhile, the Carnegie Foundation pledged itself to finance construction of a new library should the trustees decide to relocate. Among several pieces of real estate considered by the Board during the closing months of 1919, the most attractive was a fifty-acre parcel on Marshall Avenue overlooking the Mississippi. Offered by the St. Paul Town and Country Club, it was conveniently situated relative to intercity transportation. Other sites included 100 acres on Lake Johanna owned by J. M. Hackney, acreage on Mississippi River Boulevard between Summit Avenue and Fort Snelling, and plats in Minneapolis, Rochester, Anoka, Albert Lea, and on Lake Minnetonka. After innumerable delays attributed regrettably but understandably to "financial and industrial conditions," the trustees at last decided, on January 17, 1921, not to move the campus.[35]

The President, while keenly disappointed by what he regarded as the Board's unnecessarily cautious disposition, began immediately to crusade for a "greater Hamline." Emphasizing the need to create a new psychology which would highlight the advantages of the Midway site, he rehearsed all the old cliches. "Are we not in the midst of the great laboratory facilities for the study of economic and social problems?" he inquired. Did not Hamline call to mind Longfellow's reference to the scholar who lived "in the dark, gray town?" Was it not wise to follow the lead of the great educational foundations, which increasingly emphasized the need to train students "in the great throbbing centers of population where the opportunities for culture, laboratory facilities, service, and self-help are so much greater than in the quiet cloisters favored by the ancient seats of learning?"[36]

Kerfoot's comments were not altogether on the mark, although his effort to redeem what he continued to regard as a discouraging situation was certainly understandable. The trustees, after all, had never seriously considered removing Hamline to some "cloistered" quarter. What they had debated were questions of space, environment, economics, and timing. Each potential location within St. Paul and Minneapolis would have preserved Hamline's urban opportunities, yet would have provided, in terms of space and natural beauty, an environment wholly conducive to expansion. Still, none could have disputed the fact that the nondescript artery to the west, and the coke plant and railroad yards to the north, seemed to guarantee that future generations of students and professors would have ample opportunity to labor together in Longfellow's "dark, gray town."

The notion that Hamline scholars enjoyed opportunities not afforded their colleagues in remote "hilltop" institutions far from the scene of urban congestion and excitement was hardly a new idea. Indeed, the trustees had moved the University to St. Paul in 1873 partly to secure advantages not available in Red Wing. But over the years, college officials often revealed themselves to be of divided mind regarding the best means of explaining to a conservative and essentially rural constituency the virtues of shipping their uncorrupted sons and daughters off to the wicked city. Thus, college catalogs published during the early years of the century promised students "all the advantage of a residence in a small town at a distance from the noise and disturbance of great metropolitan centers," yet at the same time all the opportunities which such centers provided. By the early 1920s, publicity regarding removal had destroyed for all time the possibility of depicting the campus in terms of its rural, or "suburban," splendor. But in the aftermath of the removal discussion, the University did manage to secure from the city a rezoning ordinance, which it confidently declared would "almost certainly prohibit the closer approach of industrial plants," thus warding off added "menace." This was especially important "from the point of view of the very large proportion of students coming from the rural districts of Minnesota and the Northwest." Hamline would now establish new roots in old soil, "'in close contact with the needs and opportunities of modern urban life, encompassed by, but not altogether of, that life.'"[37] In its perennial effort to dissociate itself from sin and corruption, and to identify its essence with a pastoral life long since departed, the University had therefore continued, well into the twentieth century, to speak implicitly of the manner in which it chose to perceive itself, its presumed mission, and its clientele.

By the spring of 1922, the "greater Hamline," its roots firmly planted in the original patch of prairie soil and its senses within immediate range of a host of environmental pollutants, had begun to materialize. Construction proceeded on a new athletic field and stadium and on a $175,000 women's dormitory, and St. Paul architect F. H. Ellerbe had devised comprehensive plans for long-range physical expansion. As envisioned by Ellerbe, future construction would center upon an east-west mall running from Pascal Avenue to Snelling Avenue along a vacated Hewitt Avenue, and with a magnificent chapel at its head. Grouped about the chapel were to be four more dormitories, while situated on the north side of the mall and facing inward would be a gymnasium, a science building, an administration building, and a dormitory. The new athletic facilities north of Taylor Avenue and another dormitory to the extreme southwest would complete the picture. On March 10, 1922, the *Oracle* published detailed descriptions of the new stadium and of the "Manor House," as the women's facility was grandiosely named. With its picturesque stone tower sheltering the main entrance, and with its half-timbered construction, the new dormitory suggested a scene out of the English Midlands and was surely the most notable structure on an architecturally undistinguished campus.[38]

It was also the last facility erected during Samuel Kerfoot's presidency, for the great program of expansion depicted by Ellerbe never materialized. Even as construction proceeded on the Manor House and the new Norton Field, minor portents of more serious trouble appeared. In December, 1921, the President asked the General Education Board for an extension of time in order to continue collecting unpaid 1916 Advance pledges. Late in 1922, Mr. and Mrs. Russell M. Bennett or Minneapolis came to the rescue by promising to subscribe $50,000 to a forthcoming $1.5 million capital campaign, the money to become available immediately for application to the 1916 deficit. In January and June of 1923, the General Education Board again granted extensions. Hamline's difficulties were not unique, as the histories of other institutions show. But it was obvious, nonetheless, that the University was having much more difficulty meeting its goals than had earlier been the case.[39]

Part of the problem was the fact that it now had to rely much more extensively upon small pledges from Methodist donors. Even before his death in 1916, James J. Hill had ceased contributing to Hamline, explaining that "other colleges in newer districts that are struggling for existence appeal to me with more force." While the Carnegie Foundation had agreed to finance construction of a new library should the University decide to pull up stakes, it had no interest in assisting with enlargement of the 1907 structure. Matthew G. Norton, who with his brother James had earlier given more than $250,000 to the endowment, and who had been the inspiration for the 1916 Advance, had died in 1917. No donor of comparable stature had appeared to replace him.[40]

Thus it was hardly surprising that the results of the $1.5 million 1924 Advance were profoundly discouraging. Although the University came within $147,000 of securing the requisite pledges, collection proved even more difficult than it had eight years earlier. By the summer of 1925, only $89,449 had been received, and by the spring of 1926, only $167,941. After subtracting $78,770 in overhead, $43,000 to defray the debts of a defunct Minneapolis preparatory school, and additional funds to aid the Wesley Foundation at the University of Minnesota, only $40,179 remained from the gross proceeds. In June, 1926, Treasurer William P. Westfall reported that it was no longer possible to determine the precise worth of many subscriptions, for a good number possessed "fictitious values or conditions entailing obligations which the University could not afford to assume." The situation did not improve with the passage of time. In April, 1928, net proceeds stood at only $185,171, and as late as June, 1929, the figure had increased only to $248,617, which included money generously advanced by the Rockefeller board.[41]

Intimately tied to the University's efforts to raise money was the Board's overall attitude toward acquiring and holding real estate. Beginning late in the nineteenth century, Hamline had gradually acquired an extensive portfolio of investments in farm mortgages, most of these in western Minnesota, the Dakotas, and eastern Montana. Encouraged in this endeavor by trustees who saw agricultural mortgages as the cornerstone of long-range endowment efforts, and whose investment philosophy took its cue from a pre-urban past, college officials found themselves continually forced, long after the end of the First World War, to depend upon the productivity of such investments despite overwhelming evidence to the contrary. When the Board decided not to purchase the luxurious but expensive Town and Country Club property in 1921, it did so largely because it had finally begun to sense how precarious it was to wed the University's fortunes so extensively to agricultural real estate. Momentarily disconcerted by the realization that its ancient preference for such investments might no longer be sound, it chose to abandon any thought of risking Hamline's economic condition further by financing the purchase of the Marshall Avenue grounds. Still, the trustees were not wholly persuaded that the depressed agricultural market which followed the 1918 Armistice presented grounds for permanent concern. Thus, they clung stubbornly to their conviction that the University would, within relatively short order, resume reaping the rewards of its agrarian faith.

Had more felt otherwise — in short, had the Board been younger and attuned to postwar economic developments — they might have moved more concertedly to balance the portfolio. Even with their outmoded tendencies, in fact, they occasionally acceded to diversification. Led primarily by J. M. Hackney, who was a member of the Class of 1901, a St. Paul real estate magnate, a state senator, and had been since 1919 the second vice-president of the Board, the trustees gradually altered the portfolio through the acquisition of urban real estate and municipal securities. But as had been the case with J. F. Chaffee before him, Hackney was not above attempting to profit from his position. When he became "financially embarrassed" late in 1922, he quite unintentionally set in motion a chain of events which ultimately focused pointed external criticism upon the University, led to the resignation of Kerfoot's successor, and produced unneeded negative publicity.

The trouble began as a partial outgrowth of the 1916 Advance. In December, 1922, Hackney offered to sell to the University, for $165,000, property which he owned in downtown St. Paul. He then proposed to help defray the 1916 deficit by donating $25,000 of that sum to the University. Uncomfortable with the idea and unsure that the property, located at Fourth and St. Peter Streets, was actually worth $165,000, the Executive Committee countered with an offer of $140,000. Hackney immediately accepted that proposition, received $45,000 in cash, and transferred to Hamline $95,000 worth of mortgages. By January, 1923, the transaction was complete.[42]

Then, in August, 1923, acting on Hackney's motion, the Board appointed a committee to conduct a comprehensive study of University investment policy. It emphasized that its action was not intended to cast suspicion upon earlier investment practices. Rather, it simply wished to examine all relevant data. The report, presented in September, recited past history and indicated that the book value of all farm mortgages held by the University stood at $689,996. But only $284,750 worth were in good standing, it added. Especially dubious, implied the report, was the Board's enthusiasm for Montana and Dakota mortgages. For in that region, where diversified agriculture was conspicuous by its absence, the impact of a depressed market would always be immediate and severe. Calling for the appointment of a competent financial advisor, for an annual audit of the books by a certified public accountant, and for diversification of the portfolio, the committee recommended that the trustees accelerate their purchase of municipal securities and their disposition of agricultural mortgages.[43]

By the end of 1926, the Board had made substantial although hardly profound headway in its work on the recommendations. Most important, it had traded 2,960 acres of foreclosed North Dakota farm land for two apartment buildings located on Grand Avenue in St. Paul. In 1927, it acquired two more nearby apartments through the same process. By June, 1928, Treasurer Westfall was able to report that Hamline owned 8,487 acres of foreclosed land with an endowment value of $159,500. He went on to report that the college portfolio included $231,277 worth of mortgages and $319,579 worth of bonds, along with $662,151 worth of highly improved urban real estate.[44] There was little doubt that the Board had undertaken its investment study partly because it realized that its confidence in the saleability of agricultural real estate was becoming increasingly misplaced. But there was even less doubt that the Hackney transaction had provided the specific stimulus.

Meanwhile, the trustees spent $2,000 refurbishing the property acquired from Hackney. Then, in September, 1924 — after receiving other offers — they leased it to the Greater St. Paul Company, headed by President Kerfoot's son. Open to the obvious criticism, the decision was even more vulnerable on another count. For the charter of the University specified that "all corporate property belonging to the institution, both real and personal, is and shall be free from taxation." Thus, when the Board decided to sign a 99-year lease giving the tax-free use of $140,000 worth of highly improved commercial property to the younger Kerfoot's corporation, it laid itself open for legal inquiries. To be sure, Hamline had twice previously defended itself successfully in the courts against challenges to its tax-exempt status — once in 1891, again in 1922. But the matter remained far from settled in many individuals' minds. The ultimate disposition of the Hackney property only aggravated that concern.[45]

The situation which President Alfred Franklin Hughes confronted when he assumed office in the summer of 1927 following Samuel Kerfoot's long-overdue resignation was therefore potentially highly troublesome. The new president, who had dealt effectively with a host of challenging problems during his previous assignment as president of Evansville College in southern Indiana, chose initially to approach matters gingerly. Especially did he hope that any potential for renewed attacks upon the charter would speedily recede into the background. And at first glance, it appeared that Hughes was precisely the man to restore order. Like each of his five predecessors, the new president was a Methodist clergyman, a fact which rankled the modest band of campus liberals. As president of Evansville, he had revealed a solid business acumen and a flair for generating favorable publicity. Brash and sometimes crude in his administrative dealings, and frequently insensitive in his personal relationships, Hughes plunged into his duties with singleminded intensity. His primary concern was the Church's faltering financial loyalty. In addition, he told the Board early in 1928, only one in twelve Minnesota Methodists of college age was choosing to attend Hamline. Extensive curricular changes, the need to improve faculty salaries, and the advisability of creating an adequate pension and sabbatical plan, together with major physical plant improvements, all called for careful budgetmaking. Responding affirmatively to the President's urgings, the trustees agreed to work toward a $4,000 maximum salary, to include an item for professional travel in the annual budget, to allow 5 per cent per annum for pensions, and to establish a plan for leaves of absence.[46] But the noble goals were destined for speedy oblivion. For the stock market crash of October, 1929, and the prolonged and wrenching economic depression which ensued, promised to test the institution's endurance as never before.

President Hughes, born in Madison County, Ohio in 1882 of deeply-religious Methodist parents, had taken his undergraduate degree from Ohio Wesleyan University in 1907 and had studied at Boston University School of Theology for three years. Serving a succession of charges in Ohio before accepting the presidency of Moores Hill Junior College in 1916 and the Evansville assignment thereafter, he had by 1927 formulated a number of convictions — none of them original — regarding the role of the church-related liberal arts college. He was also an ardent advocate of modern educational trends, many of which endorsed vocationalism as the financial salvation for hard-pressed denominational schools. Although Hughes, as president of Hamline, never succumbed to a wholesale endorsement of such panaceas, he promoted enough of them to lose his job and very nearly ruin the University in the process.[47]

In his inaugural address, the new President wondered openly about the future of institutions like Hamline. "In the five months which I have spent in Minnesota," he told an audience gathered in the Hennepin Avenue Methodist Church on December 13, 1927, "I have heard more said about the precarious position of the church college than in all my previous life." It was a concern, he suggested, which arose out of the fact that Midwestern church colleges had been less well established than their sister institutions in the East when tax-supported educational institutions began to challenge their primacy following the Civil War. Since 1907 alone, enrollment in public universities had grown by 400 per cent. Six new teacher-training colleges and ten junior colleges in Minnesota, along with heightened emphasis upon the desirability of curricular prescription by agencies of the state, made the challenge to institutions like Hamline even greater. It was no wonder that especially in the Midwest, many individuals had begun to "entertain a real question as to the future of the church college."[48]

But there was an "educational service" which Hamline and other private colleges could logically provide, the President went on, and which when sufficiently understood and endorsed might well counter all challenges from the public sector. To begin with, he contended, the past offered little solace and even less justification for keeping the doors open. Reiterating his conviction that small colleges were seldom "strongly enough entrenched to be financially independent of [their] constituency nor indifferent to prevailing educational practice," a statement which provided members of the Conference with much-needed assurance, Hughes then outlined a thoroughly reorganized future curriculum. In it, less rigid entrance requirements would pertain, but admission to upperclass work would become more demanding. This junior and senior college mode of organization would help to solve enrollment problems by opening wide the gates to high school graduates, he implied, yet would simultaneously afford the University ample opportunity to provide a distinctive academic environment for upperclassmen. And, should it ever become necessary to abandon freshman and sophomore work to tax-supported junior colleges, Hamline could easily make the necessary adjustments.[49]

The President's concern over the fate of church-related education in the Midwest was not merely hypothetical. Rather, it reflected widespread interest in the then-current patterns of enrollment within higher education nationwide. Since the end of the First World War, college and university enrollments had shown dramatic increases after growing steadily but slowly prior to that point. From 1890 until 1918, the average annual increment had never exceeded 8,000, and until 1900 had remained below 4,000. But beginning in 1918, collegiate enrollments rose sharply, moving from 239,707 to 695,219 within ten years, an average annual increment of 45,000. In Minnesota, where the comparable figures were 6,104 and 16,647, the picture was similar.[50]

Of greater concern to Hughes and his executive associates was the fact that Minnesota's church-related institutions lagged well behind this trend. While private college enrollments had increased nationally more rapidly than had those of tax-supported institutions, enrollment figures for private institutions in Minnesota were roughly 25 per cent below the national norm. There seemed to be no immediate threat from the College of Arts and Sciences at the University of Minnesota, but the fledgling junior college system appeared to pose significant problems. Begun at Hibbing and Rochester in 1916, the system by 1927 included six campuses with a combined enrollment of 903, and was growing steadily. For Hamline and other private colleges, the implications of that development were uncertain and therefore disquieting.[51]

Nor could Hughes have overlooked the fact that between 1917 and 1927, the colleges within Minnesota with which Hamline enjoyed comparing itself had experienced significantly greater growth. Carleton had enrolled 545 students in 1917 and 845 in 1927. Macalester had grown from 320 to 520. St. Olaf had almost doubled its student body from 549 to 1,009. Hamline, meanwhile, had enrolled 408 students in the autumn of 1927 — ten fewer than in 1917. Comparative statistics on endowment growth were equally unsettling.[52] Thus it was hardly surprising that Hughes, while holding to his initial view that it would be best to wait at least a year before making formal policy recommendations, felt it imperative to broach the subject tentatively.

Despite the fact that much of Hughes' address seemed to argue otherwise, the President knew perfectly well that there was good reason not to alter Hamline's traditional pattern of undergraduate educational service. But he also knew that in terms of endowment, enrollment, physical plant, and capacity to attract major gifts, the overall situation left much to be desired. In this view, he mirrored the attitudes of Samuel Kerfoot, who had felt all of the same pressures but found himself powerless to confront them effectively. But unlike Kerfoot, Hughes displayed no hesitancy in making administrative judgments which he hoped might advance his overall goals. One such judgment occurred within less than a year of his assuming office. Apparently persuaded that the University could not hope to prosper without the wholehearted support of its more conservative constituents, who formed the mainstay of the Conference and filled most of the pews as well, the President made a crucial and ultimately disastrous decision in the spring of 1928. Abandoning forever any remaining possibility of aligning himself with liberal elements both inside the University and beyond it, he decided to fire Professor of Philosophy Gregory Dexter Walcott. The ramifications of that decision were soon apparent.[53]

Never, since his appointment to the faculty in 1907 by President Bridgman, had Walcott consciously sought to alienate or antagonize. To be sure, his B.D. from Union Theological Seminary was suspect in conservative circles, and he had long made it clear that in his view philosophy was a secular discipline. But his background as a pastor and his kind and gentle demeanor seemed to counterbalance any suggestion that Walcott was irreligious. Nor did President Hughes attempt to explain his decision on such grounds. Instead, he merely observed when questioned that he had come to his decision "with great reluctance and keen regret." He had done so, he told the alumni vaguely, only after receiving advice from "prominent" educators and former students and in accord with "the policy as announced fully in my inaugural address."[54]

During the summer of 1928, Hughes and Walcott corresponded frequently about the matter. The Hamline chapter of the American Association of University Professors secured the intervention of the national organization, and, pressed by that agency to explain his actions, Hughes responded lamely that he had made his recommendation because of Walcott's "inability to cooperate as a member of the faculty in carrying out the policies of the institution." The trustees eventually gave Walcott a special hearing, but upheld the President's decision. And the A.A.U.P., falling back upon the convenient if timid rationale that "in distinctly denominational institutions a professor is under certain obligations which would not be recognized in those that are non-denominational," withdrew its services. But if Hughes felt relief following resolution of the Walcott affair, his consolation was short-lived. For in February, 1930, the Board of Education of the Methodist Church published the results of an institutional survey which set in motion a chain of events that again challenged the President's will to survive. The report, which originated in a 1928 General Conference resolution to survey all colleges of the Methodist Church, was by far the most systematic and thorough effort at such analysis ever attempted. In Hamline's case, it was also a disturbing analysis.[55]

The survey opened by declaring bluntly that Hamline was in no way distinguished from "the better denominational colleges generally." Indeed, it was difficult even to regard the University as a liberal arts college. For 38 per cent of the student body, including 66 per cent of the women, were studying to become teachers. Another 17 per cent were leaning toward careers in business, 6 per cent were enrolled in pre-engineering courses, and an ever-diminishing number were choosing careers in religion. In fact, only 24 per cent were currently majoring in subjects clearly identified with the liberal arts. And, while the college was located in the heart of a great metropolitan area, it was not doing well in its efforts to recruit students from that region. Undoubtedly, the report conceded, this owed in part to Hamline's proximity to the University of Minnesota. But it also made the task doubly urgent. For if Hamline were to survive in any meaningful sense, it could not ignore the shadow which the University of Minnesota cast. In short, the survey concluded, Hamline's educational program must be truly distinctive.[56]

The report therefore recommended that the college choose "a few special fields for intensive cultivation." It suggested that since a major function of the church college was to prepare students for religious, social, and civic leadership, the most appropriate areas of emphasis were the humanities and the social sciences. By eliminating costly programs in the natural sciences, and by relegating to public institutions the task of training teachers, Hamline could offer inexpensive survey courses to underclassmen, thereby lavishing most of its instructional budget on specialized upper-division courses of exceptional quality. It was hardly a coincidence that the survey's recommendations closely paralleled the policy statements which had been made since 1924 by the General Education Board.[57]

Proceeding from foundations which the faculty had already established in a recent curricular reorganization, and aligning with that
foundation the survey report which he chose to interpret as a virtual
ultimatum, Hughes now announced a series of radical and definitive
proposals. The trustees should move Hamline to a site near the
University of Minnesota, he recommended. There, in a single, architecturally commanding classroom and administration building,
the college should offer, on the one hand, general college work
which would be self-sustaining. On the other, it should offer senior
college work of exceptional stature in the humanities and social
sciences. Students wishing to specialize in other fields could do so at
the University of Minnesota. In sum, Hamline should model itself
after Victoria College at Toronto University (President Bridgman's
alma mater) where a comparable framework existed. It now became
more clear why Hughes had included the dean of Victoria, Norman
Wentworth DeWitt, in his inaugural program almost three years
earlier, and why the President had recently visited Toronto.[58]

The faculty, predictably, opposed the whole idea, for apart from
philosophical considerations, most of them would lose their jobs if
Hughes managed to capitalize on his plan. A number of trustees,
several of whom lived in St. Paul, joined the faculty in their opposition. So, too, did the St. Paul press, which — after years of inattention to the underlying dilemmas confronting college officials —
suddenly chose to wage a vigorous war against removal. And, while
Minneapolis churchmen tended to favor the idea of uprooting the
University in order to transplant it into their own backyard, they
were powerless to provide Hughes with support. For under the terms
of the charter they were disfranchised. By action of the 1894 Minnesota Annual Conference, Minneapolis had become part of the
newly-organized Northern Minnesota Conference. Yet the delegates
to that gathering had not bothered to amend the charter so as to give
the new entity the legal right jointly to supervise the University's
affairs. So it was that in June, 1930, having defensibly but self-
servingly chosen to interpret the wording of the charter narrowly,
the Executive Committee of the Board voted tentatively not to move
the University. One year later, again guided by the Committee, all

Samuel F. Kerfoot.

Alfred F. Hughes.

James S. King.

Gregory Dexter Walcott in 1916. (From the collections of the Minnesota Historical Society. Photo by Lee Bros, Minneapolis.)

but one of whose members lived in St. Paul, the trustees made the decision final.[59]

Thus, for the second time in a decade, the Midway campus was spared. For good or ill, this meant that whatever the future scope of Hamline's educational program, the liberal arts would remain the core of the curriculum. If teacher training institutions continued to grow in number and in size, the University would need to fashion practical responses to that challenge, and yet do so with integrity. If vocational and professional institutes increased in popularity, Hamline would have to ask itself hard questions about its legitimate scope of interest. If junior colleges posed an increasing threat, it would be imperative to devise suitable academic responses to the entire issue of general education. And if the College of Arts and Sciences at the University of Minnesota began to place pressure upon the state's four-year private institutions, it would undoubtedly be necessary to devise a better overall rationale for the very existence of the church-related liberal arts college.

Unfortunately for President Hughes in particular and for the University in general, the trustees' decision did not end Hamline's difficulties. In fact, the academic critique contained in the 1930 survey, and which provided the President with much of his ammunition regarding removal, was only one aspect of that extensive and revealing report. For the document also contained an elaborate discussion of other financial and administrative conditions which only served to highlight the almost hopeless conditions which Hughes faced. For example, the survey recommended reallocation of functions currently centered in the office of the "badly overloaded" dean of administration, a position which Hughes had created in 1928 in order to outflank one of his most articulate critics: Dean of the University Henry L. Osborn. It criticized the fact that in William P. Westfall, the college had "a salaried Treasurer of the Board who has in effect a coordinate authority with the President, and who is given entirely too much personal responsibility in the management of the endowment." It disapproved of the fact that both of the University's living ex-presidents sat on the Board, that college records were not centralized, that the business office continued to allow student debts to accumulate, that management of endowment funds was unsatisfactory, and that investment policies needed a general overhaul. Although comparable institutions were enjoying better than a 14 per cent return on their endowment, Hamline's return had averaged only 3.2 per cent during 1928–29. Real estate income was especially low — 0.5 per cent on farms, 3.2 per cent on urban property. While commending the recent exchange of agricultural land for the Grand Avenue properties, the survey pointed out that 77 per cent of all college-held farm mortgages were past due. Such a circumstance called for radical action.[60] All of this meant, of course, that Treasurer Westfall, against whom the survey directed most of its financial criticism, was certain to oppose the report, and would therefore resist any attempt by Hughes to implement its suggestions.

Nor could Hughes have anticipated receiving support from the rest of the Board, for the survey criticized it as well. "It is recommended," the visiting team urged, "that the . . . trustees take greater interest in the work of the institution." Attendance at Board meetings had been "poor," and there was "no evidence that members of the Board have been fulfilling their function in keeping the financial interests of the institution in the foreground of the consciousness of the constituency, nor have they themselves been large givers in recent years. . . ." The report was especially pointed in criticizing the manner in which the Board had handled the 1921 Hackney transaction. This understandably put the first vice-president on the defensive and assured his opposition to anything that Hughes might recommend. Nor did the University's cumulative indebtedness, which stood at $137,000 as early as 1929, ease the President's burden.[61]

Nonetheless, Hughes worked valiantly to implement the changes sought by the survey. But his overall position had so completely deteriorated by that point that he had become virtually powerless, a fact reinforced by changes in the by-laws, made in 1931, which further undermined his authority. In March, 1932, the Executive Committee called for a change in administration, and on April 7, after counselling continued patience and refusing to accept full blame for the University's difficulties, Hughes resigned.[62]

True to form, he went down swinging. In a scathing, eighteen-page indictment of the Executive Committee and its actions, Hughes explained his decision. He declared that he was "out of harmony with the management of the trust funds of the institution as evidenced by certain transactions in the past," and cited specifically the Fourth and St. Peter transaction. He condemned another Hackney scheme, this involving the projected colonization of tracts of farmland in Mexico by Russian Doukhobors, the sale of stock to raise funds for that purpose, and the implication that Hamline endorsed the venture. He deplored the fact that Westfall continued to draw both a salary from the University and a commission for managing college real estate in St. Paul, and charged that the Treasurer had failed to provide an annual accounting of his work. He complained that changes in the by-laws had made him "inferior" to the Treasurer in authority, had removed budgetary authority from his office, and had enabled the trustees to circumvent him by communicating directly with both faculty and students. This, he pointed out, jeopardized Hamline's academic accreditation. He berated the transfer of $112,000 from endowment to current expenses, an action, he contended, which violated the University's 1923 agreement with the General Education Board. And he attacked the trustees for consistently failing both to authorize an annual audit and to produce a systematic report on the University's financial affairs.[63]

These were shocking charges. On June 2, 1932, a special committee, appointed by the Executive Committee and acting under the signature of President Randall, presented its response. It dealt crisply with the Hackney affair. "There was nothing illegal in Hamline's buying this real estate from a board member," pontificated the report. "No law prohibited it. In 1922 it was common enough for national banks and state banks to buy notes and bonds from one of their directors or from an institution in which such director was interested, and to loan money to members of the bank's board. In recent years the practice of bank directors doing business with their bank is viewed more critically but is still common." Newspaper reports regarding personal benefits which had supposedly subsequently accrued to the president of the Greater St. Paul Company were mere "gossip," it went on, failing to provide proof for its assertion. Allowing that Hackney's judgment in the Doukhobor scheme was questionable, the report nonetheless granted the first vice-president absolution. It found "nothing excessive in the amounts paid to Mr. Westfall for services and nothing illegal or unfair to Hamline in his acts," and contended that there was "room for wide difference of judgment as to the wisdom of having compensated officers upon the Board. . . ." Although it found "some point to Dr. Hughes' criticisms concerning by-laws, faculty control and the making of the budget," it refused to attribute "wrongdoing, malfeasance or nonfeasance" to anyone. But it did urge restoration of the previous chain of administrative command, under which the chief executive had possessed authority appropriate to his office.[64]

If it seemed for the moment that the Executive Committee had effectively manufactured full exoneration for itself, and that Hughes had made careless and unwise charges in his resignation statement, events soon confirmed the beleaguered President's essential rectitude. The first clue was contained in a defensive response to the special committee's report by Hackney, who revealed otherwise unwarranted sensitivity both to Hughes' and the special committee's appraisal of the Fourth and St. Peter transaction. The second was the fact that by 1933 the entire membership of the Executive Committee had changed. The third was the fact that within less than two years of Hughes' resignation, the Board had adopted virtually all of the changes urged either explicitly or implicitly by the former president, including a rewording of the by-laws. Finally, when the North Central Association withdrew accreditation from the University in the spring of 1933, part of its stated rationale was its concern over the administrative structure of the college as established in the by-laws. More than any other single factor, the loss of accreditation caused the Board to review critically both its internal organization and its legal relationships with the University's administrators.[65] Thus, while none could foresee the manner in which Hamline would fashion responses to its difficulties, or the extent to which it would be capable of resolving its financial difficulties, the events of 1932 had ironically laid the foundation for their solution.

But of greater long-range consequence was the fact that after two decades of frequent institutional self-analysis, many critical issues remained unresolved except in the most superficial sense. Most important was the fact that the intellectual relationship between college and Church had not matured appreciably — that churchmen in general had not taken James King's 1925 admonitions to heart and that college officials had not wrestled productively with some of the more discerning observations made by Church agencies. Most Minnesota Methodists seemed to regard Hamline as an institution which was evangelical in its theology, scrupulously upright in its morality, adequate in its academics, and warm and caring in its attitudes toward students. In large measure, these were accurate perceptions with which disinterested observers would undoubtedly have agreed. And they were honorable enough attributes — qualities which had helped create a good reputation for the University and which would remain intimately tied to its future program of educational service.

At another level, however, Hamline's constituency either failed to appreciate or chose to minimize the important fact that for decades the institution had frequently displayed instances of truly significant academic achievement. When left free to pursue their intellectual interests, many faculty had proven themselves capable of noteworthy accomplishments. When appropriately guided and minimally constrained, so were many students, as the selection of two Rhodes scholars by 1919 and the imminent selection of another in 1932 made clear.[66] Creative scientific and literary endeavors, in short, were most likely to flourish in an academic atmosphere unhindered by religious or moral strictures. Especially during the 1920s had it become clear that the University was failing to provide adequate explanations of its objectives, or of the more general relationship between mind and spirit. Nor was it likely, given the historic relationship between Methodism and higher education, that such explanations would be altogether acceptable to the Church. For Methodists had often stressed that character preceded intellect, and the related conviction that Christian credentials became less trustworthy as academic credentials grew more distinguished remained a surprisingly powerful motif. This could only spell frustration for colleges and universities like Hamline, which depended upon evangelical bodies for support, but could not always dispel charges arising out of the conflict between mind and spirit.

Thus, even under optimum political and economic conditions it would have remained difficult for the college to improve upon the coherence and intellectual defensibility of its curriculum. Given the unprecedented stress generated first by the Depression and then by the Second World War, the attainment of such objectives seemed virtually out of the question. It therefore appeared altogether probable, in 1932, that Hamline University would remain in a state of philosophical flux for some time, during which both internal and external factors would continue to conspire against anything but transient solutions to the material and academic dilemmas which confronted the institution.

CHAPTER 5

THE UNIVERSITY IN
DEPRESSION AND WAR

"IN CHANGES OF administrative leadership, differences of idealism may come up for trial," wrote Acting President Henry L. Osborn shortly after the departure of Alfred F. Hughes in the spring of 1932. "But in most cases in the past, these differences have been of minor rather than major significance. It is the purpose of the trustees of Hamline, and the strong intention of the faculty, to operate a strong liberal arts college course here, and I feel that I can assure all our alumni that every effort will be made to do this." On campus, the mood had become one of almost immediate calm. "The events of the past week . . . have probably left many students uncertain what the immediate future of the college is to be," commented the student editor on April 15. "It is a source of satisfaction that there has been no anxiety or uneasiness manifest on the campus, and that affairs have gone on with perfectly normal regularity. . . . Everything has illustrated the really obvious fact," she added, "that a firmly established institution is not dependent upon one or two men, however important they may be."[1]

The confident assertions of Osborn and the editor did not change the fact that the University was in deep trouble. Clearly the budget, which recorded a $90,000 deficit during 1931–32, and with a cumulative deficit of $222,000 since 1923, was the most pressing concern. As early as January, 1932, the faculty had consented to a 5 per cent salary reduction, although they had urged the Board "not to reduce the teaching budget as much as certain other items, such as radio contracts, athletic contracts, and general promotional expense.'' Hamline's economic position, they believed, was essentially sound, and therefore ''the incurring of a small addition to the deficit during the coming year would be less harmful than a too drastic reduction in salaries or staff.'' Nor did the Board overlook any means to save money. In April, 1932, the Executive Committee agreed that the University should loan hoods for honorary degrees to the recipients rather than present them. Business Manager Harold Craig received authorization ''to sell the Packard car'' for whatever it would bring (he got $400), reported that he had received an offer of $200 for the Hupmobile (the Board decided to exchange it for a Ford Coupe), and convinced the trustees that, subject to faculty approval, he should sell the Ford bus for $1,000.[2]

But it was obvious that the University was not going to wipe the red ink from its ledgers by turning the campus into a used car lot. Treasurer William P. Westfall made the magnitude of the problem only too clear. He reported that out of an endowment of $1,863,150, only $949,839, hardly more than 50 per cent, was productive. Net endowment income during 1931–32 had been only $32,571, compared with $9,175 in 1930–31 and $71,960 in 1929–30. Current expense indebtedness to the endowment fund stood at $129,000, he reported, and the University had borrowed $62,000 from the bank, depositing $87,000 worth of bonds as collateral. Although the college still held an additional $150,000 worth of bonds, they were not easily marketable. Of the University's investments in farm loans and mortgages, $327,000 worth were virtually unproductive. Finally, there was the quarter-million-dollar cumulative deficit.[3]

Asked by trustee Samuel L. Parish whether Hamline could continue to operate with its present income, Raymond A. Lee, chairman of the Auditing Committee, assured him that it could, provided the University had 300 students paying full tuition and retained its present endowment income. But he acknowledged that the institution's financial condition was ''deplorable.'' Conference visitor Frank Doran insisted upon the speedy resolution of Hamline's financial problems. The University would soon lose the confidence of the constituency, he insisted, if the Board continued to dip into the endowment. In an ominously prophetic note, he asked whether

Hamline could hope to maintain its accreditation without enlarging its income. Without answering Doran's principal question, trustee Donald Bridgman explained that the probable current deficit would be $30,000, that all colleges were being forced to fall back on their reserves, and that Hamline would probably need to continue drawing upon its endowment for another year or two.[4]

While the Board pondered economics, the faculty concentrated upon administrative matters. In July, 1932, it began a unique experiment in democratic administration with the creation of a Committee on Administration. Comprised of Professors King, Beyer, Muhleman, Kuhlmann, Rife, and Aubert B. Potorf, it divided responsibilities by allocating activities according to "experience, temperament" and choice. As the senior member, King served as chairman and was also responsible for student financial aid, convocations, and maintenance. Beyer was in charge of curriculum, publications, and publicity. Muhleman oversaw graduate study, music, health services, and contacts with the registrar. Kuhlmann maintained alumni and business secretary contacts and supervised the college admissions program. Rife communicated with the deans of men and women, the fraternities, the library, and was secretary to the committee. And Potorf, who was Professor of Bible, was in charge of athletics, church contacts, faculty-student relations, and the Religious Council. Under Kuhlmann's direction, faculty members participated in an aggressive program of student recruitment during the summer of 1932 and repeated the process the following January. As a result of their efforts, enrollment during 1932–33 rose 13 per cent over the previous year to 503, and grew slowly but steadily from that point onward, reaching 690 by the autumn of 1939.[5]

But even as the administrative affairs of the University seemed to be returning to normal, a new and embarrassing circumstance confronted the University. For in the spring of 1933, the North Central Association removed Hamline from its list of accredited institutions. In its specific criticisms, the Association indicated that the experimental Administration Committee was an unsatisfactory means of governing a university. It faulted the 1931 by-laws, which had taken much authority away from the president, and repeated Hughes' charge that the trustees' ability to communicate directly with the faculty and students over the head of the chief executive officer contravened Association rules. It recommended immediate election of a president, unification of campus financial offices, cessation of the sale of University securities, and election of a new Executive Committee. It also charged that, in allowing Athletic Director J. W. Hutton to participate in the 1932 student recruitment program, and that in permitting the average amount of aid to athletes to be higher than the average for non-athletes, Hamline had also violated Association regulations. But it made no criticism of the University's educational program, which it judged "superior." Within a month, the Board had undertaken to reorganize itself along the suggested lines, the faculty Athletic Committee had begun to make the necessary adjustments in the University's financial aid program, and the Presidential Selection Committee had decided to recommend that the trustees elect Minnesota's presiding bishop, J. Ralph Magee. The Board accepted the recommendation, and on June 27, 1933, Magee specified the conditions under which he was prepared to accept the assignment.[6]

The Board, he indicated, must continue to search for a permanent president, who would, he hoped, take office momentarily. The Executive Committee must appoint from the faculty a dean, to be nominated by the president. Together, the faculty and trustees must consent to drastic fiscal retrenchment, and must protect what was left of the endowment by ceasing to sell securities. The Board must implement all other recommendations regarding University reorganization as specified by the North Central Association, must embark upon an organized effort to secure additional income, and must accept the need to amend the by-laws, especially those concerning the chain of administrative command. For his part, Magee pledged to keep all parties fully informed of his actions. He also made it clear that he had no long-term academic executive aspirations. "I have no desire to run Hamline, but only to save it," he declared. "When I have succeeded in that, I will withdraw happily." The Board unanimously approved his conditions.[7]

Together the Board, the faculty, and Magee made rapid headway in overcoming Hamline's difficulties. Again the faculty accepted drastic salary cuts, and by July, following the most diligent fiscal planning in eight years, the trustees had fashioned a budget for 1933–34 which contained no salary guarantees whatsoever, but came within $11,000 of being in the black. James S. King became dean of the University in July. In September Magee urged speedy implementation of changes in the college by-laws. He saw the problems as twofold. First, he declared, splitting his infinitives with abandon, the 1931 changes had "so circumscribed the powers of the President of the institution and so limited his available resources of exact knowledge of its material condition as to not permit him to actually be President." The Executive Committee, for example, possessed total control over formulation and implementation of the budget. Second, the by-laws made the trustees "a rubber stamp and incapable of any real leadership." "These facts more than anything else," Magee commented ruefully, "have caused our grief."[8]

In December, the Board unanimously approved changes which Magee submitted following consultation with President Lotus Coffman of the University of Minnesota, members of the Methodist Church Board of Higher Education, the faculty, and President Henry M. Wriston of Lawrence College, who was also president of the North Central Association. Meanwhile, it had also voted to stop selling securities, to install all business functions of the University in a single office located on campus, and to change the constituency of the Executive Committee. In February, 1934, it added a single, crucial sentence to the new by-laws which specified that "the President of the University is the chief executive officer of the University."[9] From his pastorate in LaCrosse, Wisconsin, Alfred Hughes must have smiled in silent vindication. On March 24, 1934, a North Central Association inspection team visited the campus, and in April, the Association provisionally reinstated the University. So impressed was the Association with the extent to which Hamline had succeeded by 1936 in rectifying the deficiencies which had caused the loss of accreditation that at the end of the probationary period it waived its right to reinspection, and restored the University to full accreditation.[10]

Meanwhile, on September 6, 1934, the period of Magee's interregnum came to an end with the election of the Rev. Charles Nelson Pace as ninth president of the University. Born in Keosauqua,

Iowa, in 1877, the new chief executive had taken his undergraduate work at Iowa Wesleyan College, receiving his B.A. in 1899. Thereafter, he had studied at Garrett Biblical Seminary. Entering the Methodist ministry, he had served a succession of small Iowa charges before becoming pastor of the First Methodist Episcopal Church in St. Paul in 1912. Four years later he had moved to Duluth, where he was pastor of First Methodist Episcopal Church until 1933. During his seventeen years in Duluth, he created an endowment fund, added $250,000 to the church's capital investment, and built an adjoining education building and community house. At the time of his election to the Hamline presidency, he had completed one year as superintendent of the Minneapolis District of the Northern Minnesota Annual Conference.[11]

Pace offered insight into his conception of society and of the University's social role in his inaugural address. His view of the proper relationship between public and private sectors came straight out of the nineteenth century, and would have pleased political and economic conservatives. Noting that the Depression had gradually undermined men's spirituality, causing many to enter upon "a grim struggle for any material advantage they can snatch," Pace lamented the disappearance "of that sense of honor which once gave distinction to character and that honesty which once furnished a sound basis for credit in the business world." Cautioning against foolhardy reliance upon "the chimerical promise of a Dr. Townsend or the foolish fulminations of a Huey Long," the President at the same time urged his listeners "to avoid the intellectual degradation and the abasement of self respect" which came with excessive reliance upon government-sponsored welfare programs. "A paternalistic government that does everything for its people," he contended, in a thinly-veiled attack upon President Franklin Roosevelt and his New Deal programs, could not in the future reverse its course "without inciting rebellion." Moreover, a society which permitted such control automatically forfeited its right to judge the government. Pace believed that the Christian liberal arts college could function as a liaison between public and private efforts at stewardship by raising "the level of life to greater spiritual concepts." In so doing, it would give men and women the "creative

and constructive" abilities necessary to resolve issues of pressing
public concern such as the matter of welfare, which dominated
much of the thought of that day.[12] Pace may well have been naive in
his hopes. But his injunctions faithfully reiterated a message, pro-
pounded since the 1880s by advocates of social Christianity, which
stressed man's individual responsibility for eliminating injustice,
and which promised an earthly Kingdom as the reward.

From the outset of his administration, it was clear that the President intended to retain the activist, optimistic temper which had
marked his earlier professional endeavors. In February, 1935, just
eight months after assuming office, he requested and received from
the Board authority to announce a million dollar development campaign. He explained that it was "good policy even in depressed
times to make a suggestion of deliberate purpose, and to rout fears
by a declaration of faith." The objective of the campaign was to add
$500,000 to the endowment, build a new men's dormitory and
dining hall, construct a music building and a heating plant, and
expand the library and gymnasium. "Instead of a defensive technique with its fear of what may happen next," the President declared, "it seems the wiser course to rout such fears by definite
advance." By September, the President was able to report that
$118,000 was already in hand. Meanwhile, Treasurer John E.
Bowes worked assiduously to reduce the University's debt. By
June, 1935, he was able to report that it stood at only $32,500, and
by the following February, $22,500. In June, 1936, Bowes in-
formed the Board that the entire deficit had been eliminated. For the
first time in thirteen years, Hamline was free of financial encum-
brance.[13]

Encouraged by this happy turn of events, President Pace now
determined to embark upon the limited building program announced
earlier. First on the agenda were the library, which had lacked
adequate shelving space for more than a decade, and the gymnasium, which had increasingly become a source of embarrassment.
Librarian Anna Lagergren had complained annually since 1924
about the fact that there was no longer room available for new
books. In February, 1936, the Board at last responded to her pleas,
as well as to those of a less intellectual variety, by allocating

$60,000 for additions both to the library and to the gymnasium. With John Bowes' optimistic report of the following June, they adopted a more aggressive strategy, authorizing not only the enlargement of the library but the construction of a magnificent field house. The $100,000 athletic facility was dedicated in January, 1937, and the library addition in May. Other construction programs which antedated the outbreak of the Second World War included the renovation of the old chapel on the second floor of Old Main and its rededication as "Bridgman Hall" on November 6, 1939, and the construction of an $80,000 heating plant and student union, opened in January, 1941. The Board also made preliminary plans to build a new residence hall for men, but the European War soon forced postponement of that project and of a contemplated drive to secure an additional $2 million.[14]

The University took particular satisfaction in securing by 1944 what appeared to be definitive court approval for its tax-exempt status. After successfully defending itself against legal challenges both in 1891 and 1922, it had once more found its unique situation under review following acquisition of the four Grand Avenue apartments in 1926 and 1927. Especially did city and county interest in the property intensify after President Hughes' 1932 charges of Executive Committee malfeasance regarding the Hackney real estate in downtown St. Paul. Although the trustees had regularly argued in response to public criticism that the University was actually saving tax dollars by educating students, the Ramsey County assessor had continued to count Hamline business property as tax-delinquent. Despite that fact, the University managed each year until 1937 to secure a stipulation that its property was considered exempt from local improvement assessments, which in turn enabled it to win twelve court judgments.[15]

But in 1937, the county refused to sign another stipulation, stating instead that it wished to await the State Supreme Court's decision in the Pillsbury Academy case then pending. When the Court ruled that Pillsbury was not, as Hamline had always contended in its own defense, the same corporation that had initially received a tax-exemption, and that the entire matter of the territorial legislature's right to grant such an exemption might well bear re-examination, attention once more turned to Hamline's charter. Heightening interest in the matter was a decision made by the office of the attorney general that a farm in Redwood County acquired by the University during the 1935 Advance was also tax-exempt. Thus, with several important legal precedents bearing upon the case, University officials urged Ramsey County to take Hamline to court in order to try to collect taxes for 1937,1938, and 1939. To assist the University in presenting its case, the Board in 1940 asked that Clarence W. Rife of the Department of History document the legal status of the University from 1854 onward, and that he focus particularly upon the crucial period from 1869 to 1880, during which time the Board had continued to meet despite suspension of classes. In his meticulously researched and forcefully argued manuscript, Rife proved conclusively that there had been no cessation of legal functions and that the University which reopened in 1880 was the same legal entity that had conducted business at Red Wing prior to 1869. He therefore undermined the county's principal arguments, namely, that the University had not enjoyed a continuous existence, was therefore not the same institution that had received the charter from the territorial legislature in 1854, and thus should be denied the unique tax status described in the original articles of incorporation. The case, along with a comparable suit brought against Hamline simultaneously by Hennepin County, came to trial in 1942. In both instances the District Court affirmed the University's tax-exempt status, and in May, 1944, the state Supreme Court sustained the District Court's rulings.[16]

"We may safely assume," wrote Supreme Court Justice Julius J. Olson in his 1944 opinion, "that Hamline has travelled the straight and narrow path of corporate rectitude." The eleven-year hiatus, he argued, had not destroyed the University's legal continuity, nor had it caused Hamline to forfeit its tax-exempt privilege. Rather, the trustees had "consistently, through all the difficult years of its early history, made real and effective efforts to build and maintain a worthwhile college." In furnishing "'a consideration more than adequate' to balance the advantages granted by the statutory exemption," the University had amply justified its tax-exempt status. "We should bear in mind," Olson pointed out, "that, while the work of educational institutions such as Hamline is primarily for the advantage of the individuals educated there, it ultimately redounds to the public good. The function of such institutions is largely public, and their property is devoted 'not to private gain to individuals, but to a beneficent use — the education and enlightenment of the citizen.' '' [17]

Although Olson's 1944 opinion seemed to resolve once and for all the matter of Hamline's tax-exempt status, interest in the general issue as it pertained to non-profit institutions remained a lively one. More than two decades after the Ramsey and Hennepin County decisions, the subject surfaced again. In 1967, State Representative Emery Barrette, a Hamline graduate and a Methodist minister, introduced a bill proposing a constitutional amendment to eliminate the tax exemption on business property held by churches, colleges, hospitals, and comparable institutions. The bill died during the closing days of the session. Subsequently, President Paul H. Giddens and Business Manager H. V. Neece prepared a lengthy report for the House Subcommittee on Tax Exemption. In it, they emphasized that it was Hamline's policy to accept any reasonable offer for property which it held, that the University had in fact sold a considerable portion of its property since 1956, that the college had received most of its property as gifts, and that it used income from business property solely to support the educational program. By 1973, the University had divested itself of virtually all business property and the issue of tax exemption was once again dormant. [18]

Even as Hamline's financial condition continued to improve during the latter part of the 1930s under President Pace's optimistic leadership, events elsewhere in the world made increasingly likely the prospect that faculty, students, administration, and trustees would soon find themselves compelled to shift their sights in new directions. Antiwar sentiment grew steadily from 1935 onward, with Hamline students participating in nationwide antiwar strikes. Early in May, 1935, students sent a letter to President Roosevelt protesting naval maneuvers scheduled later that month in the Pacific, 1,500 miles closer to Japan than on any previous occasion. A campus Anti-War Committee existed by the end of 1935 and faculty members occasionally delivered addresses on aspects of the

European situation. The *Oracle* began subscribing to a syndicated international news service and, with Professor Beyer, sponsored a campaign to aid Chinese students who were being driven from their schools by the armies of Imperial Japan.[19]

In the spring of 1934, anti-fascist editorials, most of them written by columnist Ray Smith, began appearing in the *Oracle*. Smith's brilliantly-written commentaries attacked Mussolini, Nazism, and such fascist tendencies within the United States as the vigilante attacks on strikers and union halls in California, the Minneapolis Citizens' Alliance, and the systematic terrorization of blacks then leading an Alabama cottonpickers' strike. Smith was especially interested in "the anomaly of theoretical German superiority seeking expression through the repression of those precise elements which have been responsible for every superior achievement in which Germany can take just pride." Germany under Hitler, he observed, had rejected the brilliance of Goethe and the creativity of Einstein, had betrayed her working classes, and had elevated the military at the expense of culture. Frequently his message was a radical one. Throughout 1934 and 1935, for example, Smith waged war against militarism on the one hand, "dogmatic, inert pacifism" on the other, arguing that social justice demanded revolutionary action, that pacifism could only doom the working class, that "imperialist war, armament and other profiteering, and national economic rivalries" were "products of the capitalistic system. To abolish war," he contended, "capitalism itself must be abolished." Smith was also vehement in his opposition to the American Legion, which stood squarely against the antiwar movement. The Legion, he wrote in January, 1935, "believes in free speech only when free speech means nothing. Such freedom has never been peculiar to American soil. Students who are assailed as 'un-American' for acting in protest against very imminent menaces learn to examine the epithet 'un-American.'" The American Legion's action, he urged, "should warn students of what is before us in the United States unless we refuse to be cowed into silence. The dominant ideas of every era are those of its ruling classes. So long as it is 'safe' that class permits democratic illusions."[20]

But if Smith and a small handful of other radical students were prepared to make an intelligent, thoughtful examination of the European and Asian political scenes, the great majority of Hamline students displayed disinterest and ignorance. When a group of students expressed their opinions on the future of the Saar early in 1935, only one appeared to be resonably well informed, while another was "grossly and humorously misinformed" regarding its geography and five more admitted that they had never heard of it. When the *Oracle* urged that the United States boycott the 1936 Berlin Olympics because of Nazi racist policies, responses from readers revealed hardly the slightest understanding of political conditions within Germany. Nor did the faculty, with a few exceptions, either espouse leftist sympathies or take public stands on important national and international social, economic, and political questions of the day. Overall, the Hamline campus in the 1930s remained inner-directed and conservative, and displayed few indications of social unrest.[21]

Following the outbreak of war between Germany and Great Britain in September, 1939, the *Oracle* urged students to keep their minds open on the question of neutrality. President Pace, too, suggested the advisability of "preserving a calm and objective attitude." James Carlson, president of the Hamline chapter of the American Student Union, reminded students that they "need not be drawn into a war by fears based upon propaganda which arises from an incomplete picture of the world situation." In the autumn of 1940, Pace asked students to respect President Roosevelt's request that they remain in school. "We must have well-educated and intelligent citizens who have sound judgment in dealing with the difficult problems of today," Roosevelt had observed in a letter sent to college presidents across the country. "Young people should be advised that it is their patriotic duty to continue the normal course of their education, unless and until they are called, so that they will be well-prepared for the greatest usefulness to their country." But with the beginning of conscription in October, 1940, the government immediately registered almost 120 Hamline men for possible military training. One month later the first inductees left for the United States Naval Reserve in San Diego.[22]

As the United States moved steadily toward its inevitable involvement in the conflict, students frequently registered their confusion regarding the nature and meaning of America's role in a world at war. On January 10, 1941, the student editor published a highly critical attack on FDR for his increasing emphasis upon patriotic conformity, but in the same issue, bore down unrelentingly upon totalitarianism. In February, he approvingly reprinted isolationist remarks made by United States Ambassador to Great Britain Joseph P. Kennedy in 1939. But students were not wholly unaware of the conditions which had led to war. "The sadistic storm troopers of today are the children who were starved during the food blockade of Germany after the unjust Treaty of Versailles which attached sole war guilt to Germany," wrote the student editor in March, 1941. "Their whole life has been one of desire for revenge against some one for the misery and injustice that is all they have known." Another member of the staff urged caution in the face of propaganda and advocated a qualified isolationism in which the United States would pursue an internationalist, but not interventionist, policy. "Here in the Middle West we are accused of being short-sighted and contented and we are assailed for not working ourselves into an hysterical frenzy over the need for national defense, convoys, and the like," he wrote. "This criticism should be appreciated by students who feel that clear-headed, objective thinking is of primary importance in this time of crisis."[23]

Although the University made certain curricular adjustments during the war, the majority of which provided increased opportunities for vocational and technical training, the liberal arts remained the heart of its academic program. This was in keeping with an Educational Policies Committee recommendation and with President Pace's firm conviction that the college must retain its liberal curricular emphasis. While receptive to Naval Department inquiries regarding potential campus accommodations for certain of its trainees, and while admitting that the college could not overlook such practical necessities as a reduced budget, a more "functional" curriculum, and greater attention to opportunities for community service, the President insisted that Hamline must remain loyal to its heritage.[24]

Events shortly confirmed the wisdom of his view. "At the beginning of this academic year public opinion considered the liberal arts colleges doomed," he told the trustees in March, 1943. Nay-sayers, he pointed out, had assumed that as men were called into military service in ever-increasing numbers, colleges would no longer be able to meet their payrolls and the liberal arts would gradually be abandoned. "To win the war seemed to imply an absorption in military education so complete that there was no room left for any other kind of education." But "wiser counsel" soon prevailed. "The need of trained minds to carry on the mechanized warfare of the present and to understand the continental and global proportions of this vast enterprise made it increasingly apparent that educational institutions should be used, not liquidated," Pace added. "This recognition of the smaller schools was the result of a revaluation of their worth, the contribution they had already made to citizenship, the fact that they represented two-thirds of the number of college students in the United States, that to ignore their equipment in faculty and facilities would be wasteful, but also . . . that liberal arts education was itself important and fundamental to our American way of life." Liberal arts education had for decades "furnished rational, unemotional thinking based on knowledge of history and political science and economics," and more recently had "shown keen interest in postwar plans for the reconstruction materially and spiritually of a world of peace."[25]

If the President remained confident that world events would not cause Hamline and other colleges to compromise their academic integrity, the student editor was not so sure. Would "useful" technical courses, he wondered, soon displace the classics? For if this occurred, the postwar implications were intellectually staggering. "May we surmise," he asked, "that the idea is that in the postwar technological world there will be no room for such non-technical things as wisdom, beauty or the sense of continuity in the human story?" Deploring a recent National Education Association recommendation that high schools and colleges decrease their emphasis upon history and the classics and increase coursework that was of more immediate use, he reminded his readers that the British had emerged victorious from their two-year battle with the Luftwaffe not because they possessed technological superiority, but because of spiritual reserves rooted in their heritage. Russia, he noted, had relied upon the same reserves during the battle for Stalingrad. "Can we expect," he asked rhetorically, "that this western world during and after the present war can wrench itself loose from its roots in the old Hebraic and Classical civilizations and still continue to function 'usefully?' "[26]

In the autumn of 1943, *Oracle* editor Kenneth Oelschlager sought to place the war's impact upon the University in perspective. For months, he observed, American colleges and universities had rushed "to turn themselves into training camps for war." Military units had swelled enrollments on some campuses, while elsewhere, faculty committees had substituted technical courses in place of the traditional curriculum "in an effort to teach college students how to drive tanks and rivet bolts." But some educators had from the beginning sensed the negative implications of such a course. Among these foresighted individuals were Hamline's own faculty and administration. "By their actions," Oelschlager wrote, "they infer their belief that this war is not only a question of guns and planes, of men and ships." Rather, it was "a question of what kind of world we want to live in, of what shall have value, and of how ready we shall be to face the issues of the post-war world. If liberal education ever had any worth," he argued, "it has more in time of war. With all the world in a state of flux it is the responsibility of the institutions of higher learning to make clear the present significance of this struggle and to educate the men and women who will shape the future at its cessation."[27]

Despite Oelschlager's assertions, Hamline's faculty and administration had not altogether resisted the temptation to broaden opportunities for technical and vocational training. New offerings in home nursing and nutrition, physics, physical education, X-ray and medical technology, and other disciplines provided mute testimony to that fact, as did the University's willingness to retain emphasis upon a three-year diploma course in the School of Nursing, established in 1940. Nor was this unusual, in light of the economic pressures which the war brought to bear upon small institutions with limited financial resources. But such developments also raised serious questions about the future of liberal education at Hamline.

Yet if the University still found it necessary at war's end to focus much of its administrative energy upon the task of building a larger and more productive endowment, it no longer found itself faced with the cruel economic choices which presented themselves at the time of President Pace's election in 1934. If the student body remained excessively attracted to coursework in education, nursing, and business, there remained a reasonably strong appreciation for the value of liberal education. And if the college was not precisely the liberal institution that Pace so forcefully described, it was nonetheless the case that without his steady defense of the arts and sciences, Hamline might well have foundered upon the shoals of exigency and discovered by 1945 that the task of reconstructing a liberal curriculum had become very nearly impossible. That the faculty, administration, students, and trustees did not confront such an assignment was in considerable measure a credit to Pace's foresight, and to his confident willingness forcefully to express that vision.

CHAPTER 6

LIBERAL EDUCATION IN THE POSTWAR ERA

"IF ANYTHING IS CLEAR in this bewildering and chaotic world," observed Syracuse University Chancellor William P. Tolley early in 1944, "it is the unbalance between scientific advance and social control. We have a world of twentieth-century technology and stone age international relations; a world of unlimited production and uncontrolled hatred and greed; a world of magnificent intellectual achievement and of catastrophic moral failure; a world of magic and of wonder endangered by ignorance of human relations and the art of government. Thus," he continued, "the instruments designed for freedom have become tools of the new barbarians, and for all the promise of the new day, it may again be written, 'Where there is no vision the people perish.' "[1]

The concerns expressed by Tolley were not lost on the faculty and administration of Hamline University, who recognized long before the Allied triumph that at war's end new and critical challenges were almost certain to present themselves. While President Pace continued to emphasize his conviction, expressed with such certitude during the war, that there would be no revolutionary changes in the general framework of liberal arts education in the postwar era, he nonetheless urged the faculty to re-examine the educational policies of the University, and to ask themselves hard questions about the implications of the past upon both present and future. For its part, the faculty through the Educational Policies Committee began a systematic study of enrollment trends, physical plant, vocational emphases, the impact of returning veterans, and the status of liberal

122

education. Its report, which appeared in the spring of 1944 as *Hamline Studies*, was the most comprehensive self-study every conducted, and the most thorough attempt at institutional analysis since the Methodist survey of 1930.[2]

Central to the report was the judgment that Hamline should remain true to its historic role as a liberal arts college. The University, argued the Sub-Committee on the Status of Liberal Education, should resist establishing an elaborate curriculum. It should continue to confine teacher training and other vocational programs already underway within the liberal arts frame. And it should realize that curricular diversification was financially unwise. "In view of local competition with the state University," the committee contended, "Hamline can best excel in developing specialties within the field of the humanities, using that term in the broadest sense." The liberal arts spirit, it maintained, "should be fostered and conserved" in all of the University's educational endeavors.[3]

But if Hamline's destiny lay in the continuation of its role "as a fostering mother of the liberal arts," what could it do realistically to prepare itself for service in the complex postwar era? Old approaches were no longer entirely satisfactory, for the world was changing rapidly, and the men and women returning from service in the armed forces would make new and unfamiliar demands upon the institution. "Many will have found new confidence and enlarged intellectual power as a result of their training and experiences," the committee observed. "The vision of some will have been gloriously extended while the outlook of others unfortunately will have been cynically narrowed. Not lightly will these returned students tolerate any traces of inefficiency, mediocrity, or indifference in the conduct of their courses. The curriculum must be liberal and progressive, the spirit of the University must be stimulating and challenging, and the teaching personnel must be superior."[4]

To meet the necessary objectives and standards, the report proposed that the faculty rededicate itself "to the broad underlying philosophy that is the life of the liberal arts." It should eliminate barriers between divisions and departments by introducing integrated senior-level courses. It should more forcefully promote opportunities for independent study. It should institute a "great books'' program similar to that in existence between 1922 and 1933, but which would provide greater opportunities for synthesis. And it should make a better effort to familiarize itself with the literature of other disciplines. "Liberal education consists in teaching *how to think* without teaching *what to think*," the committee observed. "That is the business of fascism." The faculty received the report with enthusiasm, and continued to work on problems which it outlined. But further intensive curricular study and planning did not occur during the remainder of President Pace's administration.[5]

Especially problematic to the University as it sought to plan for the postwar era was uncertainty regarding enrollment, which hinged upon the number of returning veterans who would now choose to pursue their educational fortunes. Although President Pace assured the trustees in the spring of 1944 that Hamline would not confront undue difficulties if it planned wisely, it had been obvious for some time that colleges and universities across the land could in fact anticipate major enrollment pressures. For in October, 1943, President Roosevelt had outlined to Congress a program of educational benefits for veterans, and in June, 1944, his proposal, Public Law 346, better known as the G. I. Bill of Rights, became law. According to its provisions, all veterans were entitled to specified benefits provided they were under the age of 25 when they entered the service or could prove, if 25 or older, that military service had interrupted their education.[6]

Throughout the 1944–45 academic year, the Educational Policies Committee continued to regard as "overenthusiastic" United States Office of Education predictions that the provisions of the G. I. Bill would lead almost immediately to a drastic increase in college enrollments. The Sub-Committee on Higher Education and National Rehabilitation argued that Hamline should plan for a maximum of 1,000 students and perhaps as few as 700 in September, 1945. For the University, it contended, would "get only that proportion of returning servicemen and of the increased college population who are primarily interested in liberal arts work." But the committee was wrong. The student body, numbering 652 during 1944–45, increased 46 per cent the following year to 951. By 1946–47, the first full year of complete demobilization, it had risen to 1,215, and by 1947–48 had reached 1,308, a 100 per cent increase in three years and an enrollment record which would stand for twenty-five years. Not surprisingly, the University's physical facilities soon felt the pinch. In February, 1946, the *Oracle* reported that classrooms were filled to capacity, with exceptionally large enrollments in philosophy, economic history, and modern civilization. Dormitories were also jammed, and students had rented virtually every available living quarter near the campus as well. In the autumn of 1946, the University tried to ease some of the pressure by converting the women's gymnasium into a barracks for 120 men and by opening a cafeteria in the basement of Hamline Methodist Church. It also submitted an application to the federal government for funds to build the much-needed men's dormitory, but the government's failure to respond rapidly forced several postponements in the timetable. It sought also to alleviate the housing shortage for veterans and their families by applying to the Federal Housing Administration for assistance under the terms of the Lanham Act, which provided funds for temporary facilities. Soon, seven quonset huts with sufficient space to house fourteen families arose on vacant land north of the field house.[7]

While the administration concerned itself with the matter of physical facilities, the faculty made an effort to publicize curricular packages which it believed returning servicemen would find attractive. The 1945–46 catalog announced that in addition to offering courses leading to the B.A., the University provided fifteen vocational and pre-professional "preparations." Among these, none of which was new but simply received added emphasis, were business, teaching, medical technology, nursing, social work, and courses which would prepare students for graduate work in theology, law, dentistry, and medicine. "The college does not expect to provide special courses for veterans outside the already varied program outlined," the announcement continued. The faculty authorized admission of veterans at more frequent intervals than civilian students, agreed to admit veterans who had not graduated from high school providing they pass preliminary aptitude tests, and affirmed that veterans and their wives should be eligible for scholarship benefits on the same basis as all other students. In every case, veterans would receive eight hours' blanket credit toward the degree, and could apply two of these to the physical education requirement.[8]

Meanwhile, the University had received a financial windfall which made prospects for physical plant development bright. In March, 1944, Minneapolis attorney Charles M. Drew, who had given regularly to the college since the 1930s, made a $300,000 pledge, contingent upon Hamline's raising an equivalent sum. Spurred by the Drew challenge and by a $300,000 bequest from former Board member W. W. Norton, the trustees agreed to authorize a $900,000 campaign to celebrate the college's ninetieth anniversary. "There is a chance to do now what might have been impossible earlier and what might be difficult later," President Pace told the Board in June, 1944. "It is no exaggeration to say [that] much of Hamline's future is going to be determined by the success with which we carry forward this campaign."[9]

Hardly had the campaign gotten underway when Drew died, leaving the balance of his estate in trust with informal instructions that Hamline was to become the principal beneficiary. The bequest, which assured immediate construction of the long-needed dormitory and promised other facilities as well, amounted to more than 1.5 million dollars — by far the largest single contribution which the University had ever received, and a gift which represented the culmination of a long friendship between benefactor and University. Drew, born in St. Johnsbury, Vermont, in 1868, had moved with his family to Minneapolis at the age of three months. Encouraged by his mother, who wanted him to have "every possible advantage," Drew studied in Switzerland for a year following graduation from high school, then matriculated at Wesleyan University, graduating Phi Beta Kappa in 1892. Forced by the economic depression of the early 1890s to abandon plans to enroll in Columbia University Law School, he returned to Minneapolis, enrolled instead at the University of Minnesota, and supplemented his parents' income by working at a law firm and tutoring students. Receiving his LL.B. degree, he began a law practice and acquired real estate interests. Drew's original contact with Hamline came as a result of his mother's friendship with Mrs. Anna Goheen when he was a child. In the

1930s his association with trustee Donald E. Bridgman again stimulated that interest. His happy memories of Wesleyan University, his devotion to education, and his desire "to create in the Middle West a liberal arts college similar to Wesleyan" led him to make Hamline his chief beneficiary. The original bequest of $1,907,162.98, had almost doubled in market value by 1960. Together with income from the Eliza Drew Fund, established by Drew in the 1920s in memory of his mother, gifts from the Drew estate totaled over $4 million by 1968.[10]

The first principal result of Drew's major benevolence was the men's dormitory, scaled down substantially from the architects' initial plans, but welcomed enthusiastically by the college community. Cornerstone-laying ceremonies for the $350,000 structure, named in Drew's honor, took place on April 4, 1946, and after a series of delays opened to the first forty students in April, 1947. Situated on Hewitt Avenue immediately opposite Goheen Hall and the Science Hall, the building occupied the former site of the White House, now relocated on the southeast corner of Simpson and Hewitt. Simultaneously, the trustees expended $168,000 on a new wing for the Manor House designed to accommodate 64 women.[11]

As was true at other colleges and universities during that era, veterans made important contributions to Hamline's intellectual life. Serious and intent upon completing their education, they pursued their work with diligence and brought an air of maturity to the classroom. In the process, younger graduates found themselves stimulated to better efforts. The veterans' numbers made their impact substantial. During the 1946–47 academic year, 455 of the 1,215 students enrolled — over 37 per cent — were veterans, and during the following year, 390 out of 1,308 were returned servicemen and women. Meanwhile, college enrollments nationwide had grown to 2,338,226, almost a million more than in 1946–47, and of these almost half were veterans.[12]

President Pace believed firmly that beyond the veterans' specific contributions, the University could benefit intellectually from the enrollment pressures of the postwar era. While Hamline's door was not "closed and barred," and while the University would seriously consider each student application, he told the trustees in June, 1946, it was important to realize that a "first come, first served" rule was not altogether practical. Instead, selectivity must become the rule. "It is our desire to build a fine arts college of quality as well as quantity," he indicated, and for that reason the admissions office, under the direction of Arthus S. Williamson, had attempted to select students who showed the greatest promise. But not all agreed that intellectual considerations should take priority. Troubled by the secular impact which throngs of veterans were likely to bestow upon a campus previously dominated by an essentially sectarian mentality, these individuals raised substantive questions about the University's admissions policies. One such dissenter was Academic Dean Miron A. Morrill, who had returned to the University in 1943 after an absence of almost two decades. In the summer of 1946, Morrill urged the college to review its admissions policies in relation "to whatever picture we have of the place of Hamline University in the general cultural picture, in the life of our state and whether Hamline still maintains any vital connection with the Church and has any obligations to the Church." Morrill disliked "the fact that the data we really take into account in deciding admissions to Hamline University are almost entirely intellectual data," and wondered whether there was "any reliable way to get at matters of character." Was it possible, he wondered, to find out whether applicants had "Christian backgrounds" or "any genuine Christian convictions?"[13]

Williamson's lengthy and pointed response to Morrill's inquiry was significant not merely as an expression of his own attitudes toward admissions criteria, but because on a broader plane it spoke to the critical issue of Hamline's fundamental nature and purpose. It was significant, too, because President Pace endorsed it, and suggested that Williamson's words defined accurately the spirit in which the University sought to strive for academic excellence within the context of its Methodist heritage. The Director of Admissions opened his statement by responding flatly that no alteration in the University's admissions policy was necessary. If alteration were necessary, it "should await the formulation of any theory of education which would require major changes," and short of "a violent social upheaval" he foresaw no chance of that occurring. "What other main criteria could an institution of higher learning have?"

Williamson asked, responding to Morrill's attack upon the primacy of intellectual criteria. "The one thing that bothers me in Dean Morrill's memorandum," the Director added angrily, "is the doubt he implies that our present admissions policies are bringing in students of good character, Christian backgrounds, and genuine Christian convictions. Is something wrong with our students? I had not thought so. On the contrary, I think they are wonderful young people."[14]

Finally, there was the matter of Christian character. "I interpret this to mean," Williamson commented, "that students who do not produce satisfactory evidence of Christian backgrounds and genuine Christian convictions might conceivably be denied admission to Hamline University." Williamson doubted "the wisdom and propriety" of such a policy "no matter how the terms 'Christian backgrounds' and 'genuine Christian convictions' were defined," and announced that he would adamantly oppose such a policy "if the terms were given a personal or sectarian interpretation." What was a "conviction," he wondered, and who would have the right to decide which convictions were genuine? If Hamline attempted to interpret those terms in a manner fair to all denominations and persuasions, would it in the end really improve upon its present condition? And if the University did not approach such efforts at definition in a spirit of ecumenicity, might it not "be in danger of taking the first step back to the dark age of religious dogmatism and bigotry?" Moreover, it was impossible morally or legally to circumvent the clause in the charter which guaranteed freedom of religion and worship. "That Hamline University wants students with good character and a belief in Christian ideals as well as good scholastic aptitude goes without saying and calls for no elaboration," Williamson concluded pertinaciously. "I believe that our present admission policy, with the main emphasis upon scholastic record and aptitude is the best available device for getting the largest possible proportion of such students; and I believe that such a policy is in accord with the purpose for which Hamline University was founded."[15]

The immediate issue which divided Williamson and Morrill in 1946 — that is, whether or not the University should be prepared and willing to sacrifice a degree of academic integrity if necessary in order to admit as many Methodist students as possible — was but another symptom of the most basic philosophical question that Hamline and all educational institutions of evangelical origin found themselves perennially obliged to confront. At heart, it was a debate which pitted the Reformation's emphasis upon man's limitations and potential for sin against the Renaissance affirmation of life and the limitless possibilities of human existence. To what extent and in what fashion, participants in the debate wondered, should colleges chartered by denominations which preached man's sinfulness, his need of salvation, and the opportunity for redemption through faith explicitly or implicitly promote those doctrines? At one extreme there were those who argued that such institutions were essentially an arm of the Church, and should regard themselves as proselytizers. Thus, they should recruit and hire as faculty only those individuals who could state unequivocally that they had experienced personal conversion — that they had "found Jesus," as a later generation would put it. They should elect administrators in comparable fashion. They should admit students according to the same standards and subsequently enforce adherence to a great body of presumably moral and spiritual expectations. And they should stress the importance of "personal witness" in every academic endeavor. These were the individuals who, in Hamline's case, had declared open war on George Bridgman, had influenced Samuel Kerfoot to fire Charles Horswell and Alfred Hughes to rid himself of Gregory Dexter Walcott, and had inspired James S. King to lecture to the clergy during the 1925 Conference on "Our College." Never more than a minority within the Conference, and hardly conspicuous within the faculty, the convergence of circumstances had sometimes made them more obvious.

At the other extreme there were those who contended that colleges and universities like Hamline could best express their essential purpose by relying upon the ability of each member of the faculty and administration to speak tacitly to mankind's essential benevolence and humanity, and to do so with integrity. These were individuals like Thomas Percival Beyer, Henry L. Osborn, Bridgman, Horswell, Walcott and King; and they were the individuals whose influence upon the shaping of the institution had been most pronounced. But they had also tended to rankle more conservative minds, who saw their impact as anathema. That Hamline was hardly unique in its need to blend and reconcile those frequently adamant and conflicting forces made the challenge no less substantial.

Two years before his disagreement with Williamson over admissions policy, Morrill himself had grappled with the nature of the relationship between Church and college. "The place of religion in our institution has always interested me — and baffled me," he wrote in an open letter to the faculty. Because Hamline owed its origin to a Church spawned by the evangelical revival of the late eighteenth century, it was hardly surprising that evangelicalism was very much at home on the campus during the University's early history. But that movement, he accurately pointed out, had never had "a clear-cut and philosophically grounded theology." Instead, what theology it possessed "was deeply affected by the romantic enthusiasms of which it was, in some ways, the forerunner." Accordingly, when evangelicalism began giving way to liberalism during the latter decades of the nineteenth century, individuals associated with denominations involved in that change felt increasingly compelled to become advocates of the liberal view, for there was no hard and fast theological underpinning upon which to build. This essentially transient circumstance, he implied, had contributed mightily to the attacks upon church-related colleges by denominational officials. "Sometimes I almost think they harbor suspicions that the majority of church-related colleges are not religious," he observed. "That is all a matter of definition. As colleges, we take the faculty given us by the graduate schools of America. If we are not religious within the old definitions, then we reflect the intellectual trends of our day. If we did not reflect them," he appropriately added, "we should be accused of obscurantism."[16]

Yet Morrill, like James S. King before him, knew that part of the problem lay in the clergy's unwillingness or inability to grapple with the contemporary implications of their chosen faith and their consequent displeasure with what they perceived as heresy within academic ranks. Morrill saw "the deeply moving trends in the religious life of our age" as intellectual trends which were causing

Christianity slowly to revert to its philosophical foundations. "The task of establishing these foundations was taken up by the author of the Gospel of John and continued at least through the time of Luther and Calvin," he wrote. "I hope that, eventually, these trends may be apparent on our campus." The danger, he realized, was that in the process, Christianity would "lose its recent liberal enthusiasm for good causes and again become merely a philosophy." Admitting that compulsion accomplished nothing, Morrill nevertheless hoped "that genuinely Christian personalities in both faculty and student body will prove vivid enough, vital enough, upright morally and able intellectually so that the cause of Christian faith may command respect."[17]

In terms of economics, Morrill's concerns and the broader issue to which they spoke gave renewed impetus to another longstanding source of concern: the penurious behavior of Minnesota Methodists. In the beginning, membership statistics provided adequate explanation. But by 1895, there were almost 28,000 Methodists in the state, a figure which doubled by 1920 and reached 83,000 by 1934 when President Pace took office. Yet annual giving by the Church for current expenses had seldom exceeded $5,000, and in most years had been, in Pace's own words, "pathetically small." Methodists, the President complained to the Board in 1934, seemed to have neither an adequate sense of loyalty to Christian education nor a "feeling of responsibility for the maintenance of Hamline as the creation and expression of our devotion to Christian education." How else, he asked, could one account for their $1,578 contribution to the 1933–34 budget — a sum that was just over 1 per cent of the $118,000 budget and a far cry from the twenty-five cents per member actually pledged? Pace was unrelenting in his effort to remedy the situation, but to little avail. For in the last year of his presidency, Church giving amounted to $6,000 — *less* than one per cent of the budget. This was under six cents per member per year, a fact which made ludicrous the frequently-voiced rationalization that the modest incomes of Hamline's overwhelmingly service-oriented alumni made more generous giving impossible. In an economic sense, therefore, Miron Morrill's inquiry about the University's obligation to the Church was essentially irrelevant.[18]

As early as 1945, the President, by then 68 years old, had broached the subject of his retirement. But not until June, 1947, did the trustees accede to his request, stipulating that the resignation might take effect when they had located a successor. In their search, the members of the Board emphasized the need for high academic standards, effectiveness in fund-raising, skill in public relations, a proper understanding of faculty-student relations, Christian character, and activity in church work. Although the majority of candidates considered and interviewed were clergymen, the trustees ultimately broke with precedent by deciding for the first time in the University's history to elect a layman. Chosen was Hurst Robins Anderson, since 1943 the president of Centenary Junior College for Women, Hackettstown, New Jersey. Anderson had received his B.A. from Ohio Wesleyan in 1926, and after a brief period of study at the University of Michigan Law School, had joined the English faculty of Allegheny College. By 1932, he had become assistant professor of speech at Allegheny, and by 1940, a full professor. Meanwhile, he had acquired his M.S. from Northwestern and had gained a measure of administrative experience, serving as Allegheny's registrar and as dean of its summer session. Offered the presidency by trustee Walter C. Coffey, who visited Centenary and was impressed by the administrative procedures which prevailed there, Anderson at first declined, and turned down the invitation again following a visit to St. Paul. But after further appeals, he consented to undertake the venture.[19]

Although Anderson knew little about Hamline when he agreed to accept the presidency, it was clear from the outset that he intended to waste no time formulating and attempting to implement curricular and economic strategies. In his inaugural address, delivered on October 23, 1948, he summarized his attitude toward curricular planning within a liberal arts setting. First, liberal education "must meet the needs of the individual and of society . . . by introducing the student to the good life, with all of its implications, and by arousing within him a desire to use his talents for the welfare of the social, political, economic, religious, cultural world about him." The University should attempt to steer a middle course between the progressive synthesis, which encouraged individualism and tended to justify "any kind of self-expression," and "the social view," which tended to ignore individual differences in the interest of a slavish conformity. Second, liberal education should provide general as well as specialized education. Again, the challenge was to find and develop appropriate middle ground. Third, colleges like Hamline should "seek to educate the whole individual" by providing an appropriate Christian environment. Finally, liberal education must be present-oriented to a degree. Education became vital, the University's tenth chief executive contended, whenever educators placed "the rich social, humanistic, and scientific heritage of our past at the service of the difficult present and the uncertain future."[20]

Three days after his inauguration, Anderson outlined to the trustees what he perceived to be the University's immediate and long-range requirements. Particularly important, he emphasized, was the need to devote a larger percentage of college income to maintenance of the physical plant and to initiate an aggressive publicity program. Communicating effectively with alumni and with prospective students was also important; hence, an augmented public relations program was essential. And in the long run, the University should make major curricular decisions, especially at the level of general education. As early as September, he urged the Educational Policies Committee to renew the curricular investigations initiated five years earlier, and to begin by studying current literature on higher education. During his first year in office, Anderson attended all but three meetings of the committee, and constantly urged it to take "a distinctive position of leadership" among American colleges and universities. It must, he suggested, formulate a precise statement of educational objectives and philosophy. "We have not sold our unique distinction to our constituency," he told the committee. "We can get such distinction. The faculty want it; our constituents want it."[21]

Anderson's vigorous efforts to champion the liberal arts and to promote curriculum review owed in part to his conviction that vocational coursework, which had begun to appear during the early months of the Second World War, had become too prominent, and in part to his belief that no satisfactory rationale existed for the University's core curriculum requirements. Both he and many faculty shared the belief that vocational proliferation should cease, and that the University should ask itself hard questions about every aspect of its curriculum. The President himself posed many of those questions and presented information on curricular innovations already in force elsewhere. Especially did he recommend consideration of the Colgate plan, where students were required to pass a senior comprehensive examination and to complete both topical and divisional fields of concentration.[22]

By January, 1949, Anderson and the committee had produced a preliminary statement. Beginning with the assumption that Hamline would remain "primarily and fundamentally a college of liberal arts" which supported one professional unit, the School of Nursing, the statement, which referred to the "Hamline Plan," was a *via media* approach that accorded with the suggestions contained in Anderson's inaugural address. Thus, it rejected "regimentation on the one hand and . . . complete individualization on the other." The document went on to argue that the University should provide a degree of specialized education, but should confine its efforts to those areas which were appropriate to a liberal arts institution. Nor should it threaten its financial status by offering too many specialized programs. By adhering to these guidelines, President and committee argued, Hamline could become a truly distinctive educational institution.[23]

In April, 1950, after almost two years of effort, the faculty approved the first substantive curricular changes since 1934. By agreeing — unwisely, as events soon demonstrated — to accept the committee's recommendation that it abolish the foreign language requirement, the faculty managed to fashion a more comprehensive body of core courses without significantly increasing the number of credit hours required. It doubled the humanities requirement, making three hours in Bible study mandatory and creating an important course grandiosely entitled "Philosophical and Religious Foundations of Western Civilization," soon dubbed "P & R 19 and 20" by students and faculty alike. It also doubled the number of required hours in social science, stipulating that all students must enroll either in Introduction to Modern Civilization or in Contemporary Problems. It left the English, natural science, and physical education requirements essentially unchanged. Discussing the changes with the trustees, President Anderson pointed out that there had recently arisen a nationwide "reaction against excessive indulgence in the free election of courses of study," and that the trend was toward greater specificity in general education requirements. Stimulated by the suggestions of the General Education Board and the American Council on Education, and by the efforts of the arts and sciences faculties of such institutions as Chicago, Columbia, and Harvard, he told Board members, colleges and universities across the land had begun an effort to improve their undergraduate programs.[24]

Although the President had succeeded in focusing faculty attention upon its educational objectives, two vital curricular considerations remained unresolved. One was new: the fact that the 1950 reforms were won wholly at the expense of the foreign language requirement. The other, which had a longer history, was the institution's seeming refusal to wrestle with the implications of the preponderance of vocational and technical offerings within the curriculum. Both circumstances reflected unfavorably upon the institution when, at Anderson's urging, the Phi Beta Kappa faculty once again sought to secure a Hamline chapter. The President knew that the United Chapters would almost certainly turn down such an application — the first submitted by the University since 1931 — but that the process would be an educational experience. He also sensed sufficient division within the faculty regarding course prescription that he felt an application might help to unify sentiment around a particular body of core courses. After informal inquiries and outside encouragement, Anderson and the faculty decided to pursue the matter.[25]

The United Chapters' 1951 examination and anticipated refusal turned, predictably, upon the absence of a foreign language requirement and upon the tendency toward vocationalism. In their report, submitted in February, 1952, the examiners pointed out that many undergraduates who could not qualify for membership in Phi Beta Kappa because of the extent of their vocational coursework were receiving the B.A. degree. If students preferred to concentrate upon athletics, teacher-training, business administration, commercial art, "and similar courses unrelated to a genuine bachelor of arts degree in a liberal arts college," the report intimated, they should receive other degrees. Furthermore, economics and business administration "consistently outranked every other major, with an enrollment more than twice as large as that in the next most popular subject." The report went on to point out that of 232 seniors enrolled at Hamline during 1949–50, only 39 were humanities majors, 50 were natural science majors, and 56 were social science majors. By contrast, 87 seniors — over 37 per cent of the graduating class — were majoring in economics and business administration, physical education, and speech and dramatics. In the judgment of the United Chapters, that distribution reflected "a vocational bias" in turn reinforced by "the freedom permitted students with regard to vocational electives." On a positive note, the examiners indicated that while the number of Ph.D.'s was low — about half of what Phi Beta Kappa considered desirable — faculty quality was good. Moreover, the University was "unquestionably strong" financially, and had made substantial progress toward educational excellence. The report concluded with the suggestion that Hamline should reapply within a few years. Thus, the long effort begun in 1912 had again ended in failure, but with the effort had come new interest in the prospect of securing a chapter. Under Anderson's successor, the college continued its quest, and in 1973 — more than sixty years after Samuel Kerfoot first broached the issue — the dream finally became reality.[26]

Long before the faculty and administration received the United Chapters' 1952 report, attention had turned once more to the prospect of global war. On June 25, 1950, civil conflict erupted on the remote Korean peninsula, and within short order the clear presence of Communist Chinese support for the North Korean military machine made it clear that the conflagration was only the latest and bloodiest episode in the Cold War. At Hamline, thoughts again focused, as they had ten years earlier, upon budgetary considerations should the war ultimately involve large numbers of American military personnel. In November, President Anderson predicted that by the autumn of 1951, enrollment would decrease by one-third. This meant reducing the budget by $100,000 and releasing several junior faculty. Despite Selective Service assurances that the government would not draft scholastically-competent men until they had graduated, Anderson as late as March, 1951, continued to insist that enrollment problems were imminent. By June, acting with Board approval, he had informed five members of the faculty that the University was not renewing their contracts.[27]

Anderson had wasted no time in opting for retrenchment and had sought little advice. Thus, when the predicted declines did not materialize, he suffered a severe loss of credibility, and his relations with the faculty, who had never been enamored of his forceful administrative style, deteriorated swiftly. When Anderson received an invitation in the spring of 1952 to become president of the American University in Washington, D.C., he immediately accepted, and the trustees named their own chairman, Walter C. Coffey, acting president.[28]

If the political, social, and economic pressures of the postwar years had often seemed to raise unanswerable questions about the future of liberal arts education at Hamline, it became clear in retrospect that emergence to maturity was in fact at hand. Serious discussion regarding the relationship between vocationalism and the liberal arts was well underway and unlikely to end short of satisfactory resolution. The frankness of the Morrill-Williamson interchange regarding the function of the Christian college had laid the foundation, however obscure at the time, for what would soon be the open resolution of that sensitive issue. Rapidly escalating enrollments had made the University's physical shortcomings inescapably clear and had virtually assured that in the long run, comprehensive modernization would occur. There were no simple solutions to these complex matters, and the economic stakes were high. At last, however, intellectual integrity appeared to have the upper hand.

CHAPTER 7

GRADUATE AND
PROFESSIONAL EDUCATION

WHEN WILLIAM PITT MURRAY urged David Brooks and his associates in 1854 to raise their sights by requesting from the territorial legislature permission to establish a "university" rather than an "academy," he was appealing primarily to denominational and regional pride. The bill which he submitted, framed as it was in the broadest possible language, enabled the trustees to create an educational institution whose scope would rival that of any college or university in the land. While the Board, along with faculty and administration, adhered from the outset to the view that Hamline University should devote itself chiefly to undergraduate liberal arts education, and while the subsequent history of the college demonstrated that successive generations of individuals responsible for the fate of the institution adhered to a comparable view, the fact remained that it was legally possible to branch out in many directions. Accordingly, whenever internal or external circumstances seemed to suggest or dictate the implementation of graduate and professional programs, college officials sometimes willingly acquiesced in their creation. Some functioned successfully and productively for years, others had shorter life spans, and still others appeared only on paper. Among the University's excursions beyond the liberal arts arena were a School of Nursing, two Schools of Law, a College of Medicine, a School of Fine Arts, a College of Theology, a College of Business and Administration, coursework in teacher education, and a host of specialized degrees to accompany those curricular endeavors. When the curriculum review of 1949 and discussions

139

preceding the unsuccessful Phi Beta Kappa application of 1952
revealed both spoken and unspoken differences of opinion with
regard to the institution's basic purpose and the extent to which a
liberal arts college should foster professional programs, they only
highlighted a perennial, albeit healthy, tension within the University.[1]

As early as 1858, the catalog listed one student enrolled in the
Law Department. In accord with late nineteenth-century practice in
the United States, students interested in the law could "enter any
class in the University," and could undertake a specified course of
reading while pursuing the baccalaureate degree. Included in the list
of readings for the two-year course were the standard fare:
Blackstone's *Commentaries,* Greenleaf's *Evidence,* Walker's *Introduction to American Law*, Story's *Equity Jurisprudence*, Kent's
Commentaries, and an additional half dozen sources, along with the
Statutes of Minnesota. The catalog announcement indicated that
students would have "abundant opportunity of attending courts,"
and would receive practical training through participation in mock
court. At least two law classes graduated from the University, but
with the outbreak of the Civil War, the course disappeared permanently from the catalog.[2]

If the Red Wing Law Department found itself destined to early
oblivion, the Normal Department was from the beginning the
mainstay of collegiate work. This was hardly surprising, given
Hamline's location on the frontier where elementary and secondary
schools were virtually nonexistent. The course of study, explained
an early Red Wing catalog, consisted of the Business Preparatory
Course — that is, the curriculum designed for students who did not
intend to pursue a college course — plus "special instruction by
lecture and recitation upon subjects relating to the teachers' vocation, such as the Science of Education, Art of Teaching, School
Systems, Relations and Duties of the Teacher, and School Government." The college also maintained a "Model School" where prospective pedagogues received practical instruction. No records exist
to indicate how many students of the Red Wing period were enrolled
in the Normal Course. But the fact that fourteen of the twenty-two
individuals who received their baccalaureate degrees between 1859

and 1869 went on to become elementary and secondary teachers suggests that the numbers were substantial.[3]

Hamline's early impact as a teaching-training institution owed itself in no small measure to the foresight of President Brooks, who recognized the University's unique opportunity for service to state and region. Minnesota made no provision for a statewide system of elementary and secondary education until 1862, when the legislature enacted a comprehensive scheme providing for public schools supported by taxation under local control, and authorizing the creation of an educational fund to be realized from the sale of specified public lands. Until 1849, when the United States Congress admitted Oregon as a territory, it had been the government's custom to grant one section of land in each township of a new territory or state for the purpose of education, with the land to be sold and the proceeds to be devoted to education. But when Minnesota became a territory — also in 1849 — Congress specified that two sections of land (numbers 16 and 36) in each township were to be reserved for educational purposes. This change was largely the result of efforts by Henry Hastings Sibley, who was a delegate to Congress from Wisconsin Territory at the time the Minnesota Territory was created from it. Sibley had been in the area since 1834 as a fur trader and justice of the peace as well as a politician, and was one of the region's outstanding leaders. He was also the well-educated son of a Detroit judge, and appreciated the impact which liberalization of the customary provision regarding education would have upon the new territory. His forceful appeal to Congress resulted in the pacesetting statue of 1849. In turn, the Minnesota legislature of 1862 authorized an educational overseer to distribute money received from sale of the specified sections.[4]

Thus, the entire method of developing a public school system for the state was in its infancy when Jabez Brooks returned to the helm in 1861, succeeding Benjamin Crary, who had resigned to become state superintendent of public instruction. Brooks took advantage of the situation by promoting teacher training aggressively, and in his effort quite naturally had Crary's support. Both of Hamline's Red Wing executives believed that Minnesota should expand its public school system as rapidly as possible. In doing so, they constantly emphasized, teachers in ever-increasing numbers would be necessary. The Methodists' emphasis upon the development of public schools was not wholly attributable to unselfish civic spirit. For as Conference minutes regularly hinted, they were enthusiastic supporters of a tax-supported system partially because they harbored prejudice against the parochial school endeavors of their Roman Catholic and Lutheran neighbors. But it was nonetheless difficult to fault them for their general interest in the promotion of education on the frontier.[5]

With the reopening of the University in St. Paul, the Normal Department disappeared as a separate organizational entity, but the most common vocational occupation of its alumni remained teaching. Between 1884 and 1900, more than 50 per cent of all graduates moved on to careers in education. As Minnesota began to design courses of high school study during the 1890s, colleges and universities throughout the state found it increasingly necessary to focus upon the matter of the proper training of teachers. Soon Hamline was one of many institutions offering formal coursework in education. Recognizing the need to upgrade such instruction, President Bridgman managed, by the middle of the 1890s, to hire Wabasha's Superintendent of Schools John A. Van Dyke as a part-time instructor in pedagogy. Van Dyke, who donated his services, also instructed for the Minnesota Department of Education. Although students received no credit for attending Van Dyke's classes, which he conducted as supplemental to George Innis' spring term course in the History of Education, he was extremely popular with students. In his lectures, Van Dyke briefly surveyed current educational trends, which were beginning to feel the progressive impact. Van Dyke also discussed the organization, development, and administration of public school systems, with particular reference to the laws of Minnesota. With scientific education in its infancy, and with education beginning to gain acceptance as a profession, Van Dyke, in the words of one of his students, "aroused an interest in education as a scholarly profession which was based on science, brought to the young neophytes an idea of the demands of the field," and stimulated interest in the dignity and worth of teaching. The catalog carried Van Dyke's name on its faculty roster until 1902.[6]

The curricular modernization which took place following the retirement of President Bridgman in 1912 soon brought about important changes in Hamline's teacher training efforts, all of which focused upon professionalization of the discipline. Much of this found its impetus in the rapid development of Minnesota's public high school system, which by 1905 was supporting 174 high schools enrolling 20,000 students. From 1905 onward, the catalog listed a sequence of four courses in education, all taught by George Innis. These were the History of Education, Psychology as Applied to Education, School Management, and Practical Pedagogy. When John D. Hicks joined the faculty in 1916, Innis was no longer responsible for history, and therefore added several courses to those which he had taught previously. By that time, Hamline was also providing practice teaching experience for seniors. And in 1919, the University introduced coursework in educational measurements. So prominent had the place of education become in the curriculum by 1920 that the *Alumni Quarterly* urged college officials to create a teachers' college, complete with a high school. "The practice teaching that [Hamline's] graduates do is a farce and every graduate knows that it is," wrote Charles Richardson. "Let us end comedy and get down to business."[7]

By the late 1920s, the state required 16 semester hours of study within the Education Department in addition to practice teaching requirements already in force, and students had begun to reflect upon the wisdom and implications of such a demand for a liberal arts college like Hamline. Noting that the University required students who majored in education to complete six hours of general psychology in addition to the state requirements, the student editor wondered whether this was not "an overdose of the medicine. Many who have gone through the mill contend that all the material that is ever used in teaching could be covered in one year, or six hours of theory and another year of actual training," he wrote. "But the requirements call for ten more hours of education. What is the result? The courses are largely a repetition of previously covered material. . . . No wonder that after wading through 500 pages of one of these books a senior remarked, 'All I remember is that the book had a red cover.'"[8]

Nor did most faculty regard with equanimity the efforts of Professor of Education Raymond B. Nell to establish a doctrinaire education curriculum. Nell, who had taken his A.M. in education from Columbia in 1927 after joining the faculty in 1923, was the first member of the education faculty to have received an advanced degree within that discipline, and was thus the University's first professional educator. Confident in his convictions and supported enthusiastically after 1927 by President Hughes, who regarded himself as an educational modernist and was easily impressed by current educational developments, Nell built the Education Department into a distinct academic entity. But he also became the object both of student complaints about excessive regimentation and of faculty doubts regarding the propriety of giving professional education so conspicuous a place in a liberal arts setting.[9]

President Hughes was personally concerned about the implications upon Hamline's future of the fact that 78 per cent of the University's 1927 graduating class had trained to become teachers. In his inaugural address, he reminded his listeners that Minnesota was currently supporting six teacher-training institutions, all of which offered the B.A., and was supporting as well a strong Department of Education at the University of Minnesota. Those facts, coupled with a high nationwide unemployment rate among teachers, suggested that institutions like Hamline must diversify their curricula by providing other types of occupational training as well. Nor did the situation improve with the passage of time. In 1938 alone, 1,198 senior education majors found themselves competing for 524 teaching positions within the state. "Something may be gained from wholesale competition arising from a slight surplus of candidates," noted an understated report issued by the Council of Minnesota Colleges in 1940, "but an oversupply such as these figures represent is regrettable."[10] While war brought a temporary end to the problem after 1941, it was a condition which would recur more than three decades later.

With the appointment of Kenneth R. Doane to head the Education Department in 1949, the University moved toward curricular reorganization at both elementary and secondary levels. Doane held his Ph.D. from the University of Wisconsin — the first member of the

Hamline education faculty to possess that credential. He had taught high school in Wisconsin and, for three years, had been a member of the education faculty at Montana State College. There, he had acquired a reputation as one of the leaders in the field of education within that state. He had published several brief articles on curriculum matters in professional journals, and during his eleven years at Hamline continued to write and publish regularly. Convinced that urban high schools were especially in need of talented teachers, and that they faced acute problems in recruiting such individuals, Doane spearheaded a pilot program designed to provide aid to promising teacher education candidates who would receive additional practice teaching experience while attending the college of their choice, and would agree to teach for a limited period of time in the St. Paul Schools following their graduation. The project, which began in September, 1957, enrolled 24 students in five Twin City educational institutions, including 10 at Hamline.[11]

In the autumn of 1949, the faculty approved Doane's recommendation that it establish a field of concentration in elementary education. He made the recommendations in recognition of the fact that after decades of effort, the state of Minnesota was finally moving toward the enactment of legislation which would require all elementary teachers to possess the bachelor's degree — a standard finally reached in 1961. Students who elected the new field of concentration planned their programs on an individual basis, and the department sought in each instance to achieve a balance between courses in humanities, social sciences, natural sciences, and professional education. Doane also submitted a proposal which called for greater emphasis on the liberal arts within the secondary education curriculum; the faculty approved that plan as well. Largely as a result of Doane's efforts, the American Association of Colleges for Teacher Education received Hamline into membership in February, 1957, and shortly thereafter the National Council for Accreditation of Teacher Education gave the University its stamp of approval.[12]

By the mid-1960s, interest in teaching as a profession had declined among Hamline students as it had elsewhere throughout the country, with about 40 per cent expressing interest in the field. Under the leadership of its chairman, Kenneth E. White, the education faculty had shifted its emphasis to stress the complexities of the contemporary world. Hamline had traditionally turned out a fine teaching product, White told the editor of the *Bulletin* in 1967, but it now needed to move beyond "preparing nice middle class teachers to teach nice middle class students. We have to change our focus so that students can deal with different cultures and students of different cultures," he added, "and this should be done on both a national and international basis." White proposed a variety of alternative experiences, including rural and inner-city opportunities. He expressed frustration over the difficulty of keeping pace with technological change, and at the fact that state and outside agencies, in demanding ever-increasing curricular conformity, impeded innovative efforts. "I'd almost prefer mediocrity in teaching," he confessed, "to better teachers teaching all children exactly the same things." Through the introduction of a topical approach to its courses and the implementation of a performance-based certification philosophy, both begun in 1970, the department hoped to minimize the difficulties which had come to frustrate it.[13]

Although the University made its earliest and most sustained professional effort in the area of teacher education, its contribution to medical education, while abbreviated, was also noteworthy. When the college reopened in 1880, both the prospectus and the first catalog contained a reference to "the St. Paul Medical College, Medical Department of Hamline University," and presented a list of fourteen faculty, headed by Alexander J. Stone, M.D., as dean. Hamline's first experiment in medical education, conducted in downtown St. Paul and at three city hospitals, ceased within a year when the legislature, accurately recognizing the shortcomings of the school's two-year curriculum, withdrew its certification.[14]

But in 1895, the University renewed its medical endeavors by affiliating with the Minneapolis College of Physicians and Surgeons, the oldest chartered institution for medical education in the state. Founded in 1883 by Dr. Edwin Phillips, Dr. J. T. Moore, and others, and supported largely by the doctors' own financial contributions, it had foundered for a decade. Then, in 1893, the College made several strong additions to its faculty, thereby enabling it to increase the student body fourfold and to become a solidly-established institution. Upon affiliating with Hamline in 1895 after more than four years of negotiation, it lengthened its course of study to four years. In 1896, it announced that beginning with the class which entered in 1900, "a first grade high school diploma, or its equivalent," would become mandatory for admission — the first medical college in the region to establish such a requirement. By 1897, it had affiliated with several St. Paul clinics and had become a member of the American Association of Medical Colleges.[15]

Between 1895 and 1907, the College graduated almost 250 doctors, who were among the pioneers of medical practice in Minnesota and the Upper Midwest. Clinical facilities were the best in the Twin Cities, and its faculty were on the visiting staffs of every hospital in Minneapolis and St. Paul. Although city hospitals were initially reluctant to open their facilities to students, President Bridgman eventually succeeded in persuading most to do so. By 1900, with funds again advanced by its faculty, the College had erected a new building at the corner of Fifth Street and Seventh Avenue South in Minneapolis. There, it continued to function as a successful and prestigious arm of the University until 1907, when, for financial reasons, the trustees voted to amalgamate it into the University of Minnesota Medical School. Observing that the Medical Department had maintained itself almost entirely through student tuition, that stiffer entrance requirements had resulted in decreasing attendance, and that the cost of maintenance was greatly increased by the expensive apparatus needed to remain abreast of the times, the *Alumni Quarterly* added that the School had left a secure reputation behind it. Former dean Leo M. Crofts recalled in a 1923 letter to Bridgman that Hamline Medical College graduates "always took rank everywhere in practice with the best from any other schools. The leading members of the Twin City profession . . . gave their services to teaching on the faculty," he added, "making the school the strong teaching institution it was."[16]

Like the College of Medicine, the School of Nursing, founded in 1940, enjoyed a brief but important existence. In April, 1940, the faculty sent to the trustees for approval a plan which proposed that Hamline affiliate with Asbury Hospital in Minneapolis in order to offer "five years of work leading to the Bachelor of Science in

Nursing degree." Initially the result of Asbury's desire to enlarge and improve its three-year course, the proposal envisioned close cooperation between hospital and University. Students would spend three semesters at Hamline, during which time they would enroll in general education courses heavily weighted toward the natural sciences. They would then receive two and one-half years of practical training at Asbury and affiliated institutions, and would spend the fifth year in residence at Hamline, there to pursue one of two courses — the first in public health nursing, the other in nursing education. The trustees authorized creation of the Hamline-Asbury School of Nursing in June, and the B.S. in Nursing degree remained a five-year course until 1944, when the faculty shortened it to four.[17]

From the outset, the School of Nursing found itself beset with administrative difficulties. By early 1941, Professor of Sociology Robert R. Martin, who had been instrumental in the School's founding, had become worried about the chain of command, and urged President Pace to implement "a closer organization, a clearer definition of a division of labor and some clear definition of responsibility and authority." Complicating the matter, he explained, was the absence of a "clear line of demarcation" between the program at Asbury and the medical technology program just getting underway at St. Luke's Hospital in Duluth. Martin pointed out that accreditation would eventually turn upon the maintenance of academically-defensible standards by the hospital's administrative staff, and hinted strongly that such standards were conspicuous by their absence. "There is constant pressure to change the curriculum," he complained, referring to Asbury's attempts to reduce liberal arts coursework while increasing technical training. "Someone should have the definite responsibility of studying our program in the light of other schools of equal standing and of making final recommendations to the proper bodies." Martin urged Pace to appoint a full professor as director of the school. The President agreed, naming Martin himself to the post.[18]

Clearly, Pace's decision to assert the primacy of Hamline's authority was the University's only academically defensible position. But hospital authorities were unimpressed. The difficulties therefore did not subside, and Martin remained permanently embroiled in controversy. Constantly the hospital staff made administrative and personnel decisions without first securing Martin's approval; constantly the Dean demanded that hospital and University adhere strictly to the highest academic standards in planning and altering its nursing curriculum. At one point, he became so frustrated that he forewarned Dean W. J. Scarborough of Morningside College, whose trustees were considering organizing a School of Nursing, that full control of the operation by the college was absolutely essential. "You will find a constant danger of the hospital being more interested in the care of patients than in the training of nurses," he told Scarborough, "and encroaching upon the time and energy of the nurse." It came as no surprise when Martin, exhausted and harassed by the demands and ambiguities of his thankless role, submitted his resignation on January 17, 1944, to President Pace, who reluctantly accepted it. Pace thereupon gave Academic Dean Miron Morrill the unenviable assignment of clarifying the entire administrative structure under which the School would continue to operate. Aided by Martin's groundwork and temperamentally better suited to the task, Morrill performed his assignment with dispatch, and the long controversy finally ended.[19]

After a brief interregnum, Dr. Alice B. Brethorst succeeded to the deanship. Brethorst was a graduate of Asbury Hospital School of Nursing and of the Northwest Bible School, and had also taken her B.A., M.A., and Ph.D. in education from the University of Washington. After serving briefly on the staff of King County Hospital in Seattle, she had enlisted as a missionary to West China, where she worked as a school administrator and established the first women's college in the area. Returning permanently to the United States in 1929, she completed her graduate work and in 1933 became director of elementary education at Dakota Wesleyan University. Her extensive administrative experience, combined with her training in nursing, made her an ideal candidate for a troubled post, and she filled it with wisdom and dignity.[20]

One of Brethorst's first mandates was the task of pursuing accreditation, which hinged upon the necessity of reducing the importance of the diploma program relative to the full collegiate curriculum. From its inception, the Asbury program had included a three-year diploma course as well as the degree course with its added emphasis upon the liberal arts. The University had initially intended to phase out the former, but the outbreak of war and the consequent appeal by the United States Public Health Service for accelerated programs of training for nurses resulted in the temporary abandonment of the original plan. Substantial monetary contributions by the government to institutions which maintained three-year courses made thoughts of eliminating Hamline's diploma program especially unattractive.[21] Although the University redoubled its efforts to develop a strong collegiate school when the war ended, the diploma course remained integral to the nursing curriculum. This, in turn, caused problems with the National League of Nursing Education, which urged schools seeking accreditation to apply all their resources to the development of baccalaureate programs. As a first step toward securing accreditation, the faculty in December, 1945, approved a proposed curriculum for diploma graduates who now wished to return to Hamline to become candidates for the B.S. in Nursing degree. It also approved a modified three-year curriculum and a proposed new four-and-one-half year degree curriculum. By the autumn of 1946, Brethorst was able to report that the two programs were operating satisfactorily, and that a successful separation maintained between them.[22]

But by the mid-1950s, it had again become apparent that reorganization was necessary. In part, this recognition derived from the increasing expense of maintaining both the three-year diploma course and the full degree course. But it also arose from the fact that when the League renewed accreditation in 1956, it did so for one year rather than for the customary three, and made a series of recommendations which it demanded that Hamline implement by April, 1959, if it wished to retain accreditation. The League's recommendations came as no surprise. Strengthen the academic integrity of the programs, it informed the University, and spend more money on them. As a first step in meeting the suggestions, the Administration Committee, headed by President Paul H. Giddens, proposed in 1956 that Asbury Hospital drop its diploma course. This step, the committee argued, would eliminate internal competition, reduce expenses, end competition with more frugal diploma courses run by hospitals, and enable Asbury to concentrate upon the more academic program. The trustees approved the recommendation, and it took effect that September. In the same year, the faculty voted that all potential B.S. in Nursing candidates must first secure admission to the College of Liberal Arts, with the understanding that they undergo subsequent screening for admission to the School of Nursing.[23]

As a result of these efforts and an on-site visit in December, 1956, the League in the spring of 1957 approved both the three-year and the four-year programs for one more year. But accreditation beyond that point remained contingent upon the University's willingness and ability to carry out the 1956 recommendations. Even before receiving the League's report, President Giddens confided to the Board that he felt certain it would raise difficult questions demanding immediate consideration. The report confirmed Giddens' fears. In extending accreditation through April 15, 1958, the League recommended 1) that Hamline officials consult immediately with a League representative; 2) that nursing faculty re-examine the insufficiently differentiated diploma and degree program statements of objectives; 3) that Hamline study the degree program with a view toward reorganizing it according to sound collegiate nursing principles, including charging full tuition to students (since 1940, the participating hospitals had assumed the clinical costs, with concomitant demands upon student nurses' time), charging students for room and board (again, the hospitals had subsidized costs extensively), and making scholarships available to nursing students; and 4) that the University employ full-time faculty for all direct instruction. "Freedom for education unhampered by service obligations must be assured," the League decreed. Under existing conditions, it noted, the hospitals not surprisingly looked more to the nurses for service than for education; the nursing faculty did not enjoy customary welfare benefits; and overall, the liberal arts received insufficient emphasis. Was there enough collegiate work demanded of diploma students, the report asked, to justify retaining it? Would it not be better to return it exclusively to Mounds-Midway for operation?[24]

These were crucial, substantive questions, and Giddens,

strongly implying that Hamline must either considerably increase its financial support for the School of Nursing or cease its operation, asked the trustees for their advice. Stressing the fact that Hamline could not justify maintaining an unaccredited program, and that to maintain an accredited one would be expensive, he asked whether the Board felt the program was worth retaining. In response, the trustees voted to discontinue the diploma course when all students currently enrolled had graduated, thus freeing additional funds for the baccalaureate nursing program. Subsequent to that decision, the Mounds-Midway trustees re-established their own school of nursing and once more began to offer a three-year course.[25]

Shortly after discontinuance of the diploma course, President Giddens presented a comprehensive financial report on the School of Nursing to the Board. He indicated that Hamline could reasonably expect to spend an additional $10,000 per year in order to continue operating the School along the lines established by the National League of Nursing Education. Still, he indicated, he was inclined because of the School's excellent reputation and because it afforded ''a particularly good outlet for young women'' to proceed with reorganization, and to continue operating the program until the financial picture became more clear. But he added that if the University found itself compelled ''to dig deeper and deeper into current funds and endowment income,'' it would then be imperative ''to review the matter and determine if we should drop nursing altogether.'' Responding to Giddens' request that it study the matter thoroughly, the Educational Policies Committee recommended in April, 1958, that the nursing program be retained. Reiterating the reasons cited by the President in his earlier report to the Board, the committee added that the nursing majors as a group were ''a superior class of students,'' that the program was ''consistent with the liberal arts program'' of the University (a point reinforced by the fact that Phi Beta Kappa had never criticized it), that nursing students contributed significantly to University enrollment, that the program was attractive to potential donors, and that Hamline would receive unfavorable publicity if it decided to abandon its nursing program precisely when other private Minnesota colleges were in the process of launching them. Moreover, ''Hamline's ties with both Asbury Hospital and the Methodist Church'' made it politically unwise to drop a program which was ''a pillar of strength for Asbury and an area of dedicated public service in the minds of many Methodists.''[26]

But in the end, resolution of the issue turned strictly upon financial considerations. During the summer of 1958, Giddens and Dean of Nursing Daphne Rolfe made plans to confer with the League's Board of Review in New York City. Shortly before departing, however, they received word from the League that unless the trustees were immediately prepared to present a long-range plan for financing the School of Nursing, it would be pointless to appear. Presented with that ultimatum, and judging that to meet the League's specifications the University would find it necessary to spend an additional $50,000 annually, the President felt that he had no alternative but to recommend discontinuance of the entire program. On October 28, 1958, the Board signalled its agreement, and the last class of nursing students graduated in 1962.[27]

In addition to the professional programs which it actually implemented, the University dreamed of others which never got beyond the drawing board. In 1895, for example, the trustees voted to organize a School of Theology in memory of Mrs. Anna Harrison Goheen's husband, and to finance it with money derived from rental of the Goheen property at Twelfth Street and Nicollet Avenue in Minneapolis. By 1896, the Board had organized a three-year curriculum, appointed a faculty, and published a formal announcement. But economic depression made immediate opening of the school impracticable. The University remained outwardly optimistic about undertaking the venture until 1900, when reference to a School of Theology at last disappeared from college publications. In 1921, President Kerfoot proposed that the trustees organize a College of Business and Administration, with evening courses leading to college certificates and degrees. ''The time has gone by when well informed people consider college training unessential to the best type of business life,'' he told a reporter for the *Bulletin* in October, 1921. ''Leadership in business, no less than in the professions, calls for broad sympathies and scientific knowledge. In fact, leadership in business is becoming professional in character.''

Again the catalog reproduced a list of faculty together with an impressive array of courses and a statement of justification. But by the spring of 1922, the infant venture was listing dangerously. Kerfoot sensed the tide, recommended that the University abandon ship, and the trustees agreed.[28]

During and immediately following the Second Wold War, the University established a host of pre-professional and vocational courses. If some — most notably those of a medical nature — were relatively easy to justify on momentary patriotic grounds, and others — graduate courses in music, for example — exploited significant faculty talents, most existed uneasily and artificially within the University's undergraduate liberal arts framework. In June, 1941, the faculty approved a two-year ''Associate in Business Training'' course which led to a Certificate of Business Training. In the same year they approved the medical technology agreement with St. Luke's Hospital in Duluth, established a journalism curriculum, and devised courses in electrical, mechanical, architectural, and aviation engineering. In 1942, they authorized a two-year program in occupational therapy, and by 1943 had introduced a nucleus of courses which led to a B.S. in X-ray Technology. They established a School of Fine Arts in 1943, ratified a home economics curriculum in 1945, and approved a commercial art curriculum in 1947. By 1944, the University was offering, in addition to the two basic undergraduate degrees, the B.S. in Medical Technology, the B.S. in Music Education, the B.S. in Nursing, and the B.S. in X-ray Technology. It was also offering five master's degrees — the M.A., the M.S., the M.A. in Education, the M.S. in Education, and the Master of Music.[29]

Although graduate coursework reached its apogee during the 1940s, the possibility of undertaking such work — however loosely interpreted — was present almost from the outset in St. Paul. The 1883–84 catalog announced that the University conferred the M.A. and M.Phil. degrees, respectively, ''on Bachelors of Arts and Bachelors of Philosophy who have been engaged for three years in Literary, Scientific, or Professional studies, and whose character has been satisfactory to the Faculty.'' In 1893, the faculty discussed the subject of graduate work thoroughly, and in 1894 adopted a loose set of requirements. But not until 1906 did they finally recommend "that the second degree for all graduates of the college of liberal arts be that of A.M." At the same time they tightened degree requirements, a procedure repeated in 1913.[30]

While the 1930 Methodist survey and the 1933 North Central Association report flatly recommended dropping the M.A., the faculty took no action, preferring instead to adopt a *via media* approach proffered by Dean James S. King in 1934. "Hamline University," declared King, "does not encourage students to remain for the Master of Arts degree. Her practice is to direct students seeking a graduate degree to institutions especially equipped for graduate study." But in "exceptional circumstances" the University would consider allowing "graduates of institutions of recognized standing" to work toward the M.A. under carefully-stipulated conditions. King's statement appeared in the catalog annually until 1938, when it inexplicably disappeared.[31]

Despite the frequency of faculty discussions concerning the propriety of providing opportunities for advanced study, it was obvious from even the most cursory perusal of commencement programs that the situation had not gotten out of hand. In many years, the University awarded no advanced degrees at all, and on no occasion did the roster include more than a small number of M.A. recipients. As for graduate study within the School of Fine Arts, established in 1943 under the direction of Ernst Krenek, matters redounded wholly to Hamline's credit. For most of the graduate students working under Krenek and his distinguished faculty were a superior breed. Among them were Russell G. Harris, who went on to become an accomplished composer in his own right, Robert C. Erickson, who wrote a master's thesis on Krenek's contemporary music, and several others of equally praiseworthy achievement.[32]

With Krenek as its head, the Committee on Graduate Studies recommended in 1945 that the University expand its graduate coursework in order to attract additional students and to respond to postwar enrollment pressures. The presence of even a few graduate students in various departments had raised the intellectual and scholastic level of the undergraduates, the committee argued, a condition which deserved further encouragement. Moreover, it asserted, there would always be graduate students who preferred to do their work at smaller institutions. Finally, the talents of many Hamline faculty, underutilized in undergraduate teaching alone, would find new and more scholarly outlets. Although it discussed the matter thoroughly, the faculty refrained from endorsing the concept, and when President Pace presented the matter to the Board for its information, the trustees likewise made no formal response. Thereafter, interest in the promotion of graduate study faded rapidly. By 1948, with an administrative reorganization which saw elimination of the School of Fine Arts as a separate entity, and with the virtual disappearance of interest in fifth-year programs for teachers, the M.A. remained the only graduate degree listed in the catalog.[33]

But the idea that graduate study deserved a place in the curriculum was never far from the surface. In 1950, after hearing from Dean Charles Wimmer a report on the advisability of establishing a formal fifth-year program of "inservice" study for teachers, the faculty reversed its previous expressions of sentiment and resurrected the recently-entombed Master of Education degree. Individuals desiring to work toward the reincarnated credential, they stipulated, could complete it either in four summer sessions or in three summer sessions plus Saturdays during the regular academic year. Predictably, the program's demise was swift. Few teachers displayed interest in the program, fewer still completed the degree, and in 1953 the University discontinued it. By 1960, the University had suspended all graduate work indefinitely, although the North Central Association continued to accredit Hamline as a graduate degree-awarding institution.[34]

From the beginning of his tenure in 1964, Dean Charles U. Walker pressed the faculty to settle the issue of graduate study once and for all. He suggested that faculty members ponder the rationale upon which they continued to justify advertising graduate work as a merely theoretical possibility, and that if they wished to rise above pretense, they formulate some concrete means of offering advanced programs. Walker believed that the University had played its game long enough, that none of its graduate programs had ever possessed more than a modicum of academic respectability, and that the time had come to admit it.[35]

In December, 1964, Professor of History David M. Pletcher, then a member of the Graduate Studies Committee, addressed a pungent memorandum to the Dean in which he urged that the University commit itself exclusively to undergraduate liberal arts education. After suggesting that it was virtually impossible to maintain separate classroom standards for graduate students enrolled in upper-division courses, that if Hamline offered a full graduate program in a given discipline it was "likely to be a kind of orphan and stunted at that," and that it was unwise to award graduate credit for participation in summer institutes, Pletcher proceeded to defend his position. "What is our rationale for whatever recommendations we make?" he asked. "No matter what it calls itself, Hamline is and ought to be a liberal arts college. We have no more than enough faculty to offer a respectable undergraduate program. We have nothing like the library facilities necessary for graduate work. As things stand now, one of our obvious (and perhaps unavoidable) weaknesses is anemia in our advanced courses. If we try to expand into graduate work, even in one department," he continued, "the result will be more anemia — a thin program which cannot compete with offerings at the University of Minnesota and which will do Hamline's reputation no good. The best hope for Hamline's future seems to me to lie in doing a good job of liberal arts undergraduate education. I recommend to the committee," he concluded, "a new motto for all curriculum planners: *Age quod agis.*"[36]

Agreeing in the main with Pletcher, the Graduate Studies Committee recommend that the University not attempt to offer a master's program and not offer graduate credit of any type during the regular academic year. But it continued to hold out the possibility of earning graduate credit by attending institutes and other special programs conducted during the summer. Eight years later, by which time economic pressures had begun to make themselves felt, the faculty seized upon the opening which it had left for itself by creating an experimental, three-year pilot program in continuing education. Begun in the summer of 1973, it provided a series of graduate-level courses for elementary and secondary teachers, designed to be financially self-sufficient and flexible regarding structure, time, location, and duration. As Hamline approached its 125th year, the program continued in operation.[37]

Meanwhile, the University proceeded to launch yet another venture in professional education which once more emphasized the curricular diversity permitted by the charter. In February, 1974, the Midwestern School of Law, founded two years earlier by a small group of Twin City lawyers, approached Hamline about the possibility of renting classroom space. The fledgling institution clearly hoped that by establishing an informal relationship with the University, it would expedite its chances for accreditation by the American Bar Association. For his part, President Richard P. Bailey, then struggling with sizeable budgetary deficits brought about by inflation and by the most ambitious building program in the University's history, and concerned over the prospect of severe enrollment declines, also viewed the idea favorably. Beyond pragmatic considerations, Bailey felt that such an affiliation might well lead to an extremely productive academic relationship. Responding to the President's appeals, and with 400 law students already installed adequately if not opulently in Drew Residence, the faculty in the autumn of 1974 instructed Dean Kenneth Janzen to appoint a committee to study the prospect of affiliation. Thereafter events moved swiftly, and in February, 1975, President Bailey and representatives of the law school appeared before the Accreditation Committee of the A.B.A. On February 25, the committee announced its provisional approval of Midwestern, and formal merger took place the following year. With the Board's 1977 commitment to construct and furnish a law school building, and with the faculty's decision to establish a legal studies major for undergraduates, the position of the new Hamline University School of Law seemed secure. Whether it would in the long run significantly benefit the University both intellectually and materially, as its advocates had from the beginning contended, remained to be seen.[38]

CHAPTER 8

MUSIC AND DRAMATICS

BY THE END of the Second World War, Hamline University had acquired a secure and well-deserved reputation as a leader in the cultural life of the Twin Cities. Under the chairmanship of the internationally-known composer Ernst Krenek, the School of Fine Arts had begun to offer both undergraduate and graduate degrees in music, fields of concentration in art and drama as well as music, and training in museum and gallery work. The theatre enjoyed consistent popularity under the able leadership of Anne Simley, who had guided its development since the early 1930s. The A Cappella Choir, directed since 1942 by Robert Holliday, regularly provided audiences with intelligent renditions of works ranging from Renaissance motets through the *avant-garde*. The Twin Cities Chapter of the International Society for Contemporary Music had its home on the campus, and the University enjoyed a close relationship with the Minneapolis Symphony Orchestra, chiefly through its Musical Director, Dimitri Mitropoulos, who took regular interest in the many forms of musicianship exhibited at Hamline, and Jenny Cullen, Instructor in Violin, whom Henri Verbruggen had hired in the 1920s as the first female member of the Symphony. When a specially-selected choir sang an all-Krenek concert before an audience of professional musicians in Mandel Hall at the University of Chicago in the spring of 1947, it seemed a fitting culmination to years of growth under the inspired leadership of a group of artists who had developed a distinctive cultural environment on the Hamline campus.

But if the University's contributions to the arts, and especially music, had come to be regarded by knowledgeable critics as without

159

intellectual peer in the region, the beginnings of that rich legacy were hardly auspicious. Until at least the beginning of the First World War, the University's literary societies provided the principal medium of entertainment. Efforts, however energetic, to establish permanent musical organizations seemed consistently to meet with a dearth of enthusiasm. The germ of a glee club appeared in 1893, but until 1913, when John A. Jaeger began a sixteen-year tenure as its director, it lacked any sense of permanence. A college band existed only by fits and starts until at least 1915, with each fresh appearance greeted enthusiastically by the campus community. At last, observed the *Oracle* on one such occasion, the band had "become an actuality to the extent of some twenty spasmodically blowing individuals located at the small end of variously shaped and constructed horns." An orchestra, too, sought to string along upon occasion, but its existence was equally unpredictable. Nor was there anything surprising in this irregular pattern. For it would have been unrealistic, on a campus whose student body prior to 1915 never exceeded four hundred, to assume that the necessary talent for musical showmanship would consistently be available.[1]

Yet the environment in which those early musical organizations functioned was highly receptive. For the wholesome and essentially uncultured atmosphere which pervaded the campus during the early years of the century assured that however poorly prepared the musicians may have been, and however effusively sentimental their renditions, their efforts would ordinarily enjoy enthusiastic praise. When criticism arose, it was much more likely to take the form of a lament that Hamline's organizations were smaller than those at neighboring institutions, or that jokes told between selections were stale, crude, and "purloined from the Orpheum and Empress Theatres," than to focus upon quality of musicianship or intelligence of selection. And if the musicians felt compelled to respond to such critiques, they almost invariably did so in equally simplistic fashion. One Glee Club member, answering a charge that the organization was interested solely in turning a profit, wondered whether his adversary's notion of pleasure was "riding in dirty trains and eating in cheap restaurants, or trying to be agreeable with families with which one is assigned" — a complaint which surfaced regularly over the years. It was vital to remember, another club member pointed out, implying that in less benighted regions the members could rise to their true calling, that such an organization could never hope to be more than a vehicle of popular culture. For "a small town country audience" was "far different than an audience composed of students with as high tastes as the writer of the article referred to evidently seems to possess."[2]

The modern era of music at Hamline traces its origin, then, not to the dedicated yet often inane efforts of those early years, but rather to the appointment of William Lloyd Rowles as professor of theory and voice and director of the Music Department in 1926. Rowles, who had received his Master of Music degree from Northwestern, and who became the college's first full-time music instructor, quickly set out to organize the department on a sound basis. Thus he both broadened and intensified the nature and purpose of campus musical groups. He remained at Hamline for only three years, resigning in 1929 to accept a position in the state of Washington. But during his brief tenure, he managed permanently to alter the thrust of the University's efforts in musical performance. The Glee Club, so thoroughly the product of an earlier and more uncritical age, disappeared almost overnight both at Hamline and elsewhere when confronted by new and more imposing vocal forms. And in turn, Alec Simson, who succeeded Rowles, proceeded to develop an a cappella tradition.[3]

Simson had trained at Marylebone Parish School, London, then judged by many to be the foremost center of training for oratorio music in the British Isles. Arriving at Hamline, he immediately began to build upon his predecessor's work by introducing oratorio literature. But he was sufficiently familiar with the work of F. Melius Christiansen, who had since 1903 headed the famed St. Olaf College Choir, that he simultaneously introduced a limited amount of a cappella literature. The new director also considered himself something of a horticulturist: perhaps with a view toward turning Hamline's pasture-like south campus into a miniature Kew, he secured for his brother the position of head gardener. Soon the younger Simson was hard at work planting pansies, geraniums and other brave specimens inured to the rigors of Minnesota's uncompromising climate. Although flamboyant, domineering, and self-aggrandizing, the new musical director was a superb craftsman and teacher, a fact demonstrated consistently by his choirs' performances.[4]

By the early 1930s, therefore, the notion that Europeans had actually composed music had begun to sink in at Hamline, and the tradition of excellence which would thenceforth characterize all choral work at the University had begun. Performing serious sacred works ranging from Palestrina through Lvov and Rachmaninoff to arrangements by Christiansen, the Choir under Simson soon developed into an organization which rivalled its more famous competitor to the south. "In this part of the world we have come to feel that such miracles of choral singing as the Hamline Choir produced . . . come only out of Northfield," wrote Florence Fitzgerald in the St. Paul *Daily News*. "After [the recent] appearance of the Hamline singers and their leader, Saint Paul may now claim its own miracles, as bright and perfect as those worked by Dr. Christiansen within the limits of their modest undertakings."[5]

But what musical talents Simson possessed he lacked in administrative skill and judgment, and by the spring of 1932 — as if the faculty and college officers had nothing else to worry about just then — "the music situation" had become a matter of pressing concern. Student complaints of inadequate advisement and intradepartmental confusion eventually led to the appointment of a special committee to investigate the matter. Its report revealed that Simson had staffed many of his courses exclusively with undergraduates, had subsequently presented the fledgling instructors' work for college credit, had not even pretended to supervise what they were doing, and had carried out the entire scheme without once breathing a word of it to the faculty assembly. But well before the committee had managed to piece the musical puzzle together, Simson had resigned to accept a position at Oglethorpe University.[6]

So it remained for the Englishman's successor, John M. Kuypers, to bring order out of the administrative chaos which the talented but eccentric St. Marylebone's graduate had left in his wake. Kuypers, whose musical career had begun as a boy-soloist in the civic chorus of his native Rotterdam, was a Phi Beta Kappa graduate of Carleton, where he had majored in music and English. Following graduation, he had taught and had played violin in the Minneapolis Symphony. In his youth, the Dutch-born musician had aspired to be a sea-captain, and at the age of thirteen had sailed to the East Indies as a "sailor's flunkie" on the merchant ship *Taberman*. "When we passed from the Suez Canal into the Red Sea," he laughingly reminisced in 1935, "I sat up most of the night looking for the dark line which the sailors told me marked the place where the Israelites had crossed when pursued by the Egyptian army." Although momentarily inspired by the voyage to pursue his romantic dreams, Kuypers soon moved to America with his family, and thoughts of the sea receded. Once appointed to the Hamline post, Kuypers immediately determined to convert the Choir's bill of fare into an exclusively a cappella repertoire. He told a student reporter in October, 1932, that among the composers whose works the ensemble would study and perform during that maiden year under his direction were Bach, Palestrina, William Byrd, Brahms, Tchaikowsky, Gretchaninoff, Praetorius, and Christiansen. For a campus less than a decade removed from the glee club tradition, it was an intoxicating fare.[7]

In the years that followed, the Hamline A Cappella Choir developed into one of the most distinctive college choral organizations in the nation. Writing in the spring of 1935, music critic John K. Sherman of the Minneapolis *Star* described Kuypers' choir as "a finely balanced group, able to invoke a sonorous tone and keep it under control, singing with precision and clarity." Critic Frances Boardman, writing in the St. Paul *Pioneer Press,* thought the ensemble's singing "almost beyond praise in a sensitive primary regard for implicit musical values, and the technical security with which to realize them. . . . It is very seldom," she remarked, "that such singing can be heard anywhere." And when Eugene Ormandy, then Musical Director of the Minneapolis Symphony, received an honorary degree from Hamline in 1934, the conductor told a special convocation assembled in his honor that Kuypers' choir "ranks with any I have heard; it has sonority and a difference in color in each number. I came expecting to hear a great deal," he admitted, "and received ten times that much." Annual tours throughout Minnesota and the Upper Midwest and frequent appearance in the Twin Cities gave the Choir a broad regional exposure. Soon musicians in other parts of the country became aware of its stature.[8]

Kuypers believed that the first responsibility of a college choral ensemble was to provide a solid musical education for itself and its audiences. Typically, therefore, the literature performed spanned the centuries, providing choice samples of the spirited polyphonic style which characterized sacred music of the late Elizabethan period, the rich body of German choral literature, the appealing legacy of nineteenth-century Russian romanticism, and the challenging works of contemporary European and American composers. Kuypers' musical integrity was of the highest order. It was clear that under his leadership, quality would brook no compromise with popularity.[9]

Despite his success, however, Kuypers never felt that the administration was sufficiently supportive. It had failed, he believed, to appreciate the extent to which a dedicated and literate choral ensemble might serve as a sophisticated and effective public relations agent. When, for example, the Choir received an invitation from the National Federation of Music Clubs to appear at its annual convention in Philadelphia in April, 1935, Kuypers sought financial support for the prospective venture. But neither the Board, President Pace nor anyone else found the idea of such important publicity sufficiently compelling to make the necessary economic sacrifice. While St. Olaf continued to provide its Choir and director with experienced, sympathetic management and with broad national exposure through frequent and extended tours, Kuypers contended almost annually with bad management and a depressingly limited exposure. Nor did his conviction that the Choir's first responsibility was to perform an educational service strengthen his hand. Educated critics might sing the Choir's praises, and their laudatory words might creep into University publications designed to stimulate interest in Hamline. But the administration, undoubtedly drawing fiscal comparisons with the favorable publicity generated by the college's incredibly successful basketball teams, saw little point in spending money on the Choir. Constrained by a severely limited budget,

John M. Kuypers.

A Sunday Choir trip, about 1930.

Kuypers perennially led tours which remained confined to the Upper Midwest. In turn, this virtually guaranteed that most audiences, while friendly and accommodating, would lack the sophistication fully to appreciate the Choir's rich sampling of sacred and secular fare. It was therefore a vicious circle. As tours to rural regions occurred with what must have seemed to Kuypers like mechanical regularity, the administration contented itself with the belief — accurate enough, given its assumptions — that the Choir was helping to maintain good relations with what had always been Hamline's natural constituency: the Methodists of Minnesota, the eastern Dakotas, and western Wisconsin. Though long-suffering, Kuypers was no martyr, and when an opportunity arose in 1942 to join the faculty of Cornell University, he seized it.[10]

Kuypers' departure coincided with the resignation of another member of the music faculty, John Verrall. During his eight years at Hamline, Verrall had become a composer of national renown. His many works, among them a symphony, a sinfonietta, and compositions for horns, strings, and woodwinds, had received their premiere performances by the Minneapolis Symphony, the New York Philharmonic, and such chamber groups as the Coolidge String Quartet and the Minneapolis Pro Musica. By 1942, Verrall, who acknowledged that he had come to musical maturity while at Hamline, felt that the time had arrived for a change. He therefore left to become a member of the faculty at Mount Holyoke College.[11]

Appointed to succeed Verrall as professor of music and acting chairman of the department was the noted Vienna-born composer Ernst Krenek. Known worldwide almost from the moment that his 1926 jazz opera, "Jonny spielt auf," received its premiere performance, Krenek had received his early musical training in Berlin, studying under Franz Schreker, "a composer of boldly erotic and technically progressive" works. Drawing heavily upon Schreker, Krenek composed the opera, which featured the emotional entanglements of a black jazz musician with white women. Predictably, the work had scandalized the Continent. But just as predictably it had played to capacity audiences in more than a hundred houses, and within short order had been translated into eighteen languages. By the early 1930s, Krenek had earned the enmity of Germany's

National Socialists, who considered the composer demented and his works immoral. It was thus fortuitous that at the time of the 1938 Nazi *Anschluss,* Krenek was away from Vienna, and fortunate that through the aid of friends he was able to escape Europe.[12]

Arriving in Boston in the autumn of 1938 with sixteen dollars to his name, the conductor settled into a regimen of odd jobs before securing a teaching position at Vassar. There he maintained a heavy classroom schedule while simultaneously lecturing at a number of other institutions and giving frequent performances of his own works as piano soloist with major ensembles. Eventually driven from Vassar by a departmental chairman who was unable to accept as musically legitimate the twelve-tone technique which Krenek had adopted in the early 1930s, and who was irritated by statements contained in a book-length essay which detailed the composer's current aesthetic attitudes, Krenek found his way to St. Paul. Accustomed to the sophisticated and elegant atmosphere of Vassar, Krenek initially felt relegated to "humiliating exile" on the prairie and even endured ethnic slurs. But he took comfort in Hamline's proximity to Dimitri Mitropoulos and the Minneapolis Symphony, and in the opportunity to work with an a cappella choir.[13]

By the time Krenek arrived at Hamline in 1942 to teach theory, composition, and piano, he had composed six string quartets, three symphonies, ten operas, two piano concertos, two concerti grossi, a number of song cycles and choruses, and additional works for piano. His presence on the faculty, declared the St. Paul *Pioneer Press* proudly, would bring cosmopolitanism to an already prestigious department. For the new appointee displayed, in the editor's view, "both personally and as an artist, the qualities so often associated with the academic leaders among his compatriots: powerful but controlled energy, and an adventurous spirit yoked with a patient sort of sanity."[14]

If Krenek's appointment seemed notable to outside observers, the situation on campus could hardly have appeared less promising. The Music Department, then housed in Goheen, suffered the dual indignities of student noise from dormitory quarters above and cooking odors from a faculty apartment below. The "music library" consisted of a handful of nondescript volumes. But unlike the uncomfortable and unhappy situation at Vassar, Krenek was now his own man. "I don't know anything about music," President Pace told the composer soon after his arrival, "but I want us to have a strong music department, and I am confident that you are the man to make it so." Krenek soon discovered that whereas the refined residents of Vassar had greeted his twelve-tone experiments in stony silence, the relatively uncultivated clientele at Hamline was surprisingly enthusiastic. Because most students came from unsophisticated backgrounds, they were, paradoxically, highly receptive to his suggestions. For them, Krenek wrote, "Webern was no more difficult than Beethoven, of whom they had not heard much either. In fact," he added, "more than a few found the contemporary sounds more spontaneously congenial than the old ones."[15]

Pleasantly surprised by this discovery, Krenek plunged into his work with zeal. Encouraged by Mitropoulos and by his professional contacts within the International Society of Contemporary Musicians, the composer during his years in St. Paul wrote a number of memorable compositions. In addition to putting the final touches on "The Lamentations of Jeremiah," a work for unaccompanied chorus (1941–42), he also composed "Cantata for Wartime" for women's voices and orchestra (1943) on texts drawn from Herman Melville; "Five Prayers" on a John Donne text for unaccompanied women's voices (1944); and "The Santa Fe Timetable" for a cappella choir (1944). He wrote two symphonies, a piano concerto, a string quartet, and a wide variety of additional vocal and instrumental works. The Minneapolis Symphony premiered his Piano Concerto in 1946, and the New York Philharmonic premiered Symphony No. 4 in 1947. Frequent chamber concerts presented in Bridgman Hall gave his works a regular hearing.[16]

Moreover, stimulated by Hamline's relative intimacy and by its students' receptivity, Krenek for the first time in his life became an enthusiastic teacher. "My own education," he later mused, reflecting upon his newfound joy, "had been centered around the classical languages and designed to foster philosophical methods of thinking. Thus it gave me great satisfaction when I was able to apply these methods to the pedagogical interpretation of music, which in my opinion has its place in the humanities alongside literature, and should not be regarded as a trade the tricks of which may be picked up by instinct and mechanical drill. On the other hand,'' he noted, ''I feel that the intellectual approach to music, as furnished by musicology, may benefit from the impulses that the creative imagination of composers can offer.'' In this spirit, Krenek collected and edited four graduate essays which the University published in 1945 as *Hamline Studies in Musicology*. In his preface to the first volume, Krenek again conjoined practical with intellectual. He explained that the work sought to illuminate the usefulness of musicology for the creative artist, especially the artist of modern times. ''Of all the individuals engaged in the widely diversified branches of music,'' he wrote, ''it is probably contemporary composers that will be found among those most vitally interested in, and best equipped with understanding of, musicological thought.'' *Hamline Studies* achieved immediate renown, and the five hundred copies printed by the University were almost instantly purchased.[17]

By 1947, according to his own account, Krenek was ''running out of steam'' both as teacher and academic administrator. Rather than become content with ''settling down to a routine of repetitive cycles of motions,'' which he saw in many of his colleagues and felt would be unfair to his students, Krenek took a leave of absence in order to accept a temporary position at Los Angeles City College. There, he hoped, he might confront with greater equanimity than would have been possible at Hamline a new generation of students, and do so in a climate more benign than that of Minnesota. Within six months, the California post had become permanent.[18]

But even in his absence, Krenek's influence survived and prospered. Appointed as his successor was Russell G. Harris, who had studied under the composer from 1943 through 1945. The twelve-tone technique which permeated Krenek's compositions provided the basis for Harris' work, which the Hamline Choir under Robert Holliday's direction included in its programs. In 1958, the Minneapolis Civic Orchestra, conducted by Hamline faculty member Thomas Nee, premiered Harris' ''Centennial Prelude,'' and in 1968, the fledgling St. Paul Chamber Orchestra, then directed by faculty member Leopold Sipe, performed ''Three Movements for Chamber Orchestra.'' Harris also trained a number of exceptionally able students. In the work of such undergraduates as Thorkell Sigurbjornsson, a 1959 graduate whose "Agnus Dei" was part of the Choir's repertoire, and Bruce Iverson, a 1962 graduate who went on to study under Paul Fetler at Minnesota, Krenek's influence passed to the next generation. Nor did the University overlook Krenek in its special celebrations. Thomas Nee arranged a Krenek Festival in 1965, and Olive Jean Bailey organized another in 1975. Krenek returned to the campus on both occasions to lecture and participate actively in the schedule of events. In performance, too, the Krenek era fostered a sustained period of brilliance, as the talents of such students as June Peterson, Shirley Hammergren, Jack Jaeger, Neva Stevens Pilgrim, and James Bonn made clear.[19]

Meanwhile, the A Cappella Choir continued to display the quality of musicianship which had made it a favorite of the critics since the 1930s. Especially did director Holliday seek to move away from the style, favored by most a cappella ensembles, which placed emphasis upon the heavy, melodious sound popularized by the St. Olaf Choir and adopted by hundreds of other ensembles. F. Melius Christiansen's name disappeared from the repertoire, and the Hamline Choir became an even more distinct musical entity. Holliday constantly impressed upon his singers the qualities sought before him by Kuypers: balance, tonal beauty, and precise intonation. Moreover, his graceful and unobtrusive conducting style caused audiences almost to forget that such qualities were the ones receiving emphasis. The Choir's principal role, he maintained, was "to acquaint students with a variety of literature. Our purpose," he told a student interviewer in 1970, "is also to rise to a high enough level of performance that the musical satisfactions are deep. Then the music speaks for itself." Holliday was equally firm in his attitude toward the audience. "I think every concert should have one piece that shakes them up a little bit," he argued," — that emits a strong reaction of anger or amusement. We don't give them music that the traffic has already worn out. They can hear that anywhere."[20]

The Choir received a signal honor for its efforts to publicize and promote contemporary music in 1959, when the Association for the Preservation of the American Musical Heritage invited it to make a recording of contemporary compositions. The disc included among its selections Kenneth Gaburo's "Three Dedications," Elliott Carter's "Heart Not So Heavy As Mine" and "Harmony of Morning," Paul Fetler's "April," and Charles Ives' "67th Psalm." In 1961, the Choir premiered Fetler's "Nothing But Nature," which was based upon texts by Ogden Nash, and in 1964 recorded the work with the St. Paul Chamber Orchestra. During the 1962–63 academic year it premiered a specially-commissioned work, "Alleluia," by Gene Gutche.[21]

Thus, by the early 1960s, the A Cappella Choir under Holliday's leadership had acquired a secure national reputation as one of the foremost interpreters of contemporary American music. As a result, it was one of three college vocal ensembles considered in 1963 for a tour of the Soviet Union sponsored and conducted by the United States Department of State. Although it lost in the end to the Oberlin College Choir, it remained in the forefront for future consideration, and in 1966 received word that it would be privileged to undertake a ten-week, thirteen-nation tour of Latin America. Appearing in more than sixty performances during the 20,000-mile tour, which was financed by a grant under the Fulbright-Hayes Act, the Choir sang a varied program ranging from the Renaissance to the present. Music critics throughout the region acclaimed its work, focusing invariably both upon repertoire and interpretation. "As a choral instrument, it is among the most effective that we have heard," declared Enrico Nogueira Franca of the *Morning Courier* of Rio de Janeiro and one of Latin America's leading musical critics. "The young voices are, in a diversification of registers, pure and beautiful. And they become welded into an ideal unity, for individuals are all blended into one generic voice . . . so that they sing together in the same relationship as might the pipes of an organ, under the touch of a superb organist." The Latin American tour was not only an appropriate means of recognizing the Choir's musical ability, but a fitting climax to Holliday's own unique and distinctive career.[22]

Although often overshadowed by the achievements of the Choir, other campus musical organizations provided significant contributions of their own. In the spring of 1948, Thomas Nee conducted a reorganized Symphony Orchestra in works of Handel, Beethoven, and Copland, and for the next nine years the ensemble flourished

Robert D. Holliday.

James R. Carlson.

under his exceptionally able guidance. For much of his tenure, Nee was also director of the University Band. In 1961, several years after Nee's departure, Paul Pizner arrived to take charge of the Band, and during the years which followed broadened and intensified instrumental work in that category. By 1963, he was leading both a concert and a dance band, the latter of which evolved by 1969 into a formally-organized jazz band. And in the 1960s, both Russell Harris and David Rubens created and directed a variety of choral ensembles.[23]

If music provided the University with one reason for pride in its contribution to the cultural life of the Twin Cities, drama clearly provided another. With an existence no less sporadic than that of early musical groups, theatre at Hamline came into its own only with the arrival of Anne Simley in 1930. Bequeathed a $150 annual budget and nothing in the way of permanent facilities, Simley must have viewed the prospects darkly. But the energetic director set to work, and within less than two years had persuaded the administration — which was afflicted by academic and financial problems so overwhelming that her request must have passed practically unnoticed — to convert the third floor of Science Hall into a Little Theatre. Despite difficulty of access and constant fire hazard, drama flourished amid the carnivorous ghosts of Henry Osborn's beloved Museum of Natural History until 1947, when a gift from Minneapolis benefactor Charles M. Drew and two surplus government quonset huts enabled the college literally to piece together an ugly but what seemed then an altogether adequate home of its own. Simley, in addition to her full teaching load and responsibilities as director, not only tailored most of the costumes used by her thespians, but rented many of them out in order to secure additional income. She also managed to secure for Hamline a chapter of the National Collegiate Players. As early as 1936, the student editor was led to praise Simley in what he termed "long overdue recognition" for her truly herculean labors.[24]

But if Simley was the individual who established theatre at Hamline on a sound basis, it was her successor, James R. Carlson, who raised the level of dramatic sophistication to one of pre-eminence. Carlson was a 1940 graduate of the institution, and had studied thereafter under Eric Bentley, one of the world's foremost authorities on the modern theatre, receiving his M.A. from the University of Minnesota in 1948. During his Hamline years, he became well known throughout the Midwest for his work in the theatre. He was also active in a nationwide movement which sought to develop and promote religious drama, and which received its impetus from the Department of Worship and the Arts of the National Council of Churches. Carlson made his Hamline debut in February, 1947, directing Ibsen's "The Pillars of Society." For the next seventeen years, Carlson consistently evidenced a point of view analogous to that of his associates in the Department of Music. For he believed that the role of college theatre was not merely to entertain, but to educate, and that above all it had the obligation to confront the great issues of the age. "Entirely too much time and energy are devoted to theatre productions to justify them only on the basis of fun, recreation, and 'college spirit,'" he told an interviewer in 1956. Active involvement in "the great issues of this and every age sometimes leads to burned fingers and aggravated critics," he admitted. "But theatrical vigor, like intellectual growth, may lead to heat and even to conflagration." The theatre had no desire "to be the means to an end for any cause no matter how important," but had an obligation to define itself "not in isolation but insofar as it plunges into life and its issues." His commitment to an intellectually-defensible drama program was readily manifest. Among his more noteworthy productions were the world premiere of Eric and Maja Bentley's translation of Bertold Brecht's "The Good Woman of Setzuan," Ibsen's "Hedda Gabler," Garcia Lorca's "Blood Wedding" and "The House of Bernarda Alba," Barrie Stavis' dramatization of the activities of labor leader Joe Hill, "The Man Who Never Died," and Eugene Ionesco's "The Lesson."[25]

From the outset, theatre at Hamline had its critics. Sometimes the protests took the form of righteous indignation. "How can we continue to call this a Christian college," asked a student in 1949 after returning from a performance of Noel Coward's "Ways and Means," "and at the same time glamorize those things that we protest? If the profane language had been removed from the script, I am sure the 'artistry' would have vanished along with it. It is going too far when they use the name of our God with evil intent on the stage of a Christian college," the critic admonished. "How can we help build Christ's Kingdom when our college promotes those things which are contrary to the principles of a Christian college?" But another student was not at all sure that the nature and purpose of a "Christian college" were self-evident. "As John Milton pointed out," he responded, "good and evil grow up together in this world, almost inseparably. He that can apprehend vice with all her baits and pleasures and still abstain and distinguish and prefer that which is better, he is the true Christian." While "a few immature minds" might presume to suggest that Hamline ceased being Christian when it allowed "an intelligent freedom of the arts," the "irrational censorship" suggested by adversaries of the theatre would in effect undermine the University's very reason for existence. The theatre's defender might have added that there was a certain irony in the charge of irreligion, given Carlson's own evolving interest in religious drama.[26]

In the spring of 1962, *Select* magazine, which devoted itself to publicizing and discussing the cultural life of the Twin Cities, printed a letter written by Carlson's former mentor. In it, Eric Bentley commented upon an aspect of theatre at Hamline which provided a succinct analysis and summary of Carlson's career. For many years, the editors of the magazine wrote in an introductory statement, the Hamline director had "ventured out to the difficult, problematical and economically chancy realms of the ferocious far-out drama" — the plays of Brecht, Ionesco, and Edward Albee, for example. Recently, they continued, Carlson's announcement that he would revive Brecht's "Good Woman" had elicited a letter from Bentley, who recalled an event involving Brecht, Carlson, and himself. Bentley noted that in 1948, having just translated the playwright's "Caucasian Chalk Circle" as well as "The Good Woman," he was privileged to have had two of his graduate students then employed at nearby colleges produce them. One of these was Carlson, who staged "The Good Woman" at Hamline. "The two events," wrote Bentley, "though taken in stride at the time by the Twin Cities, are nowadays constantly being mentioned in European books as historic occasions. For in the nineteen-fifties both

plays came to worldwide vogue, if not positively a fad. . . ."
Thanks to Carlson, Bentley added, "those who are eager to see
living theater, absurd, far-out, involved, obscure, complex theater
of conscience — have several opportunities every season to do so at
Hamline University."[27]

Carlson would surely have agreed that his efforts as director were
often "economically chancy" and that many of his productions
were distinctly *avant-garde*. "We are not in the popularity business," he told a student reporter in November, 1963, shortly before
leaving the University to become professor of theatre at Florida
Presbyterian College. "The college theatre can no more nourish
itself on warmed-over Broadway than the college music department
can feed itself on rock-and-roll." Assiduously and articulately cultivated, Carlson's philosophy helped bring distinction to the fine
arts, and to the life of the mind throughout the University.[28]

On a broader scale, and as the critics had often made clear, the
trend toward leadership in the arts which had begun under Alec
Simson and John Kuypers had made Hamline an increasingly important agent of community education. Fostered by the hard work and
integrity of individuals like Simson, Kuypers, Holliday, and
Carlson, the University had consistently sought to provide the
broader community with a sense of the intellectual importance of
music and dramatics. Especially was this apparent during the Krenek era, when Hamline enjoyed a particularly close relationship
with the professional musical community of the Twin Cities, and
when Krenek through his personal achievements brought the college
international renown. But as evidenced by Eric Bentley's comments, by the Choir's 1967 tour of Latin America, by the emergence
— beginning under Paul Smith in the 1960s — of a distinguished
Department of Art, by the ongoing achievements of Hamline's
graduates, and by many other such examples, it was obviously not
confined to the Krenek years alone. Drawing upon the rich cultural
environment of the Twin Cities — an environment which had for
decades displayed an exceptional appreciation for the arts and a
willingness to cultivate them, the University simultaneously contributed to that remarkable milieu.

CHAPTER 9

ACADEMIC EXCELLENCE

"I ACCEPT THE presidency of Hamline at an auspicious moment in its history," declared Paul H. Giddens at his inauguration in October, 1953. "Within a few months, Hamline will be one hundred years old. To have existed as a private college despite wars, droughts, panics, financial distress, and other hardships and reached the venerable age of one hundred is something of a distinction in itself. Far more significant, however, are the contributions Hamline has made as a liberal arts college during these one hundred years to the social, religious, political, professional, and industrial life of the state and the nation. Its long record of accomplishments," he added, "is indeed most inspiring and a cause for pride."[1]

The new President next set the tone for his administration by discussing what he perceived to be the vital factors which inhered in Hamline's founding. These included the broad and liberal principles stated forthrightly in the charter, the fact that Hamline was not to be narrowly sectarian, the fact that it was from the beginning coeducational, the emphasis upon perfecting the scholar, and the selection of scholarly Jabez Brooks as its first chief executive. The University's task was therefore clear. "As Hamline approaches the beginning of its second century our aim will be to train young men and women more effectively than ever before in the finest traditions of the liberal arts," Giddens pledged. "There are many who say that the liberal studies are in the main a luxury. My view is that they are a necessity if our free democratic society is to be maintained and preserved." The President closed by promising to "move forward in a vigorous and progressive manner in building a distinguished college of liberal arts,'' and in the fifteen years that followed, never deviated from that commitment.[2]

Born in Bellflower, Missouri, Giddens had received his B.A. from Simpson College in 1924. After completing requirements for the M.A. at Harvard in 1926, he returned to the Midwest to teach history and government at Iowa State College and to begin his doctoral program in American history at the State University of Iowa. Following completion of his Ph.D. in 1930 he taught at Oregon State College for one year, then began a twenty-two year career on the faculty of Allegheny College, Meadville, Pennsylvania. Although he had focused until that time upon political and constitutional history, he soon became interested in the growth of the oil industry, and in 1935 published his first article on the subject. There followed other articles and, in 1938, a book, *The Birth of the Oil Industry*. During the next two decades, Giddens published four more books, including his monumental *Standard Oil Company (Indiana): Oil Pioneer of the Middle West*, and was a prolific contributor to professional journals and other publications.[3]

The Hamline trustees' decision to offer the presidency to a scholar such as Giddens was largely the result of advice provided by their chairman, University of Minnesota President Emeritus Walter C. Coffey, and by Harry A. Bullis, chairman of the board of General Mills and a prominent Methodist layman. Coffey, who was then serving as acting president of the University in addition to his responsibilities as trustee, had visited Allegheny and had come away impressed with what he had learned about Giddens' scholarly and administrative abilities. Bullis was a business acquaintance of Dr. Robert E. Wilson, chairman of the board of Standard Oil (Indiana), and received from Wilson a warm endorsement of the Allegheny historian. Apart from the personal ingredient, the Board as a whole remained persuaded, as it had been in 1948, that the University needed at its helm an individual who combined scholarly achievements, administrative ability, and, as Coffey made clear when announcing Giddens' appointment, the "impressive contacts both inside and outside educational institutions" which would best fit Hamline's current needs.[4]

In his desire to strengthen Hamline academically, Giddens focused much of his time and energy upon the quality of the faculty. Convinced, as was Hurst Anderson before him, that the University should hire the finest teachers and scholars available, he emphasized from the outset the importance of increasing the percentage of Ph.D.'s while simultaneously stressing the centrality of undergraduate liberal arts education. Like Anderson, he also rejected the convenient and frequently self-serving rationale that excellence in teaching and devotion to scholarship could not go hand in hand. Accordingly, he sought to hire faculty who not only possessed the appropriate terminal degree and were interested in research and publication, but who also presented evidence of promise as teachers.[5]

Aided in his efforts by the faculty, who welcomed the presence of a chief executive whose own scholarly orientation made emphasis upon academics inevitable, and by the trustees, who willingly acquiesced in requests to improve salaries and fringe benefits, Giddens made steady progress. By 1963, he had managed to increase the number of Ph.D.'s from 36 to 48 per cent of the full-time faculty. Although the University of Minnesota still headed the list of graduate schools represented therein, he had also managed to diversify that list considerably. For seventeen additional universities, from Cornell and Columbia in the East to California and Washington in the West, had also awarded the doctorate to Hamline faculty. Increasingly, the faculty itself assumed responsibility for the hiring process, until by 1971 it had become possible for Giddens' successor, Richard P. Bailey, to observe proudly that within Hamline's faculty-oriented decision-making structure, it would be unthinkable for a president to ignore their judgments.[6]

None would have disagreed that by the end of Giddens' presidency significant external factors were also working to the University's advantage. Giddens had often complained about the disadvantages posed by a seller's market and about the detrimental effect presented by the scarcity of good housing near the campus. But the buyer's market which emerged by the late 1960s and early 1970s made it increasingly possible for Hamline and other liberal arts colleges to become highly selective in their search processes. Included in the causes of this shift were the rapid rise in the number of new Ph.D.'s emerging from the nation's graduate schools, the general economic impact of the Vietnamese war, the conservative fiscal policies of the Nixon administration, and the overall decline in the number of high school graduates. The same conditions, of course, guaranteed that faculty mobility would decrease correspondingly, and that institutions of higher learning, while enjoying the benefits of added stability on the one hand, would confront tenure and promotion dilemmas on the other. For it became ever more fashionable, particularly among administrators and trustees, to argue that an institution's interests were best served in the long run if a fair number of faculty remained untenured. This important problem, which was essentially philosophical in nature but tended to generate administrative discussions which took economics as their cue, surfaced at Hamline well before President Bailey left office in 1975, and the repercussions continued as the University approached its 125th anniversary. But the immediate effects were impressive. By 1971, 70 per cent of the full-time faculty held the Ph.D., and seven years later the figure had risen to 77 per cent. Another 14 per cent held terminal master's degrees appropriate to their respective disciplines. And the doctoral hoods of forty graduate schools displayed themselves in academic processions.[7]

The ability of Giddens and the faculty to identify and secure devoted and capable teachers was equally apparent. When the *Oracle* polled upperclassmen in 1965 to determine their favorite professors, all but one of the ten individuals so designated had become members of the faculty since 1953. Of the first ten faculty selected to receive the annual Merrill C. Burgess Award for Excellence in Teaching, an honor begun in 1965, seven had arrived at Hamline during Giddens' administration. Just as indicative of the strengths which these individuals brought to the institution was the fact that the overwhelming majority were active researchers and writers who were committed to publication. Finally, there was the fact that many had committed themselves to a long tenure at the University. By 1976, for example, the average length of service to the college of the nine Burgess recipients who remained was just over eighteen years.[8]

In his attempt to achieve greater academic excellence by

strengthening the faculty, Giddens built upon a foundation which was in many cases already strong. The Division of Natural Sciences presented particularly striking evidence of institutional commitment, for the average tenure of the faculty in that division when the President arrived was almost fifteen years. Biology chairman Walter Kenyon was completing his third decade of service. Associates Bert L. Hawkins and Ruth Strandberg Sullivan, both of whom were Hamline graduates with Minnesota M.A.'s, were likewise veteran members of the faculty. Perry A. Moore, chairman of the Department of Chemistry, had arrived in 1939, and Kent Bracewell, beginning his twenty-third year at the University, headed the Department of Physics and Mathematics. And in psychology, which remained part of the division until 1961, the principal faculty were Donald E. Swanson, appointed in 1936, and Theta H. Wolf, appointed in 1946. A division with a reputation for excellence in teaching since the days of President Bridgman, it enjoyed the advantage of modern laboratory and classroom facilities in its new quarters in the Drew Hall of Science.[9]

History and Political Science, which remained one department until 1956, dominated the Division of Social Sciences. Three of its faculty — Clarence Rife, Arthur Williamson, and Grace Nute — had taught at the University since the 1920s. In addition, the department's ranks included historian Richard R. Marsh and political scientists Scott D. Johnston and Wesley A. St. John, the latter of whom Giddens hired in the summer of 1953. Marsh, who joined the faculty in 1950, was completing his doctorate in Modern European history at Minnesota. St. John was a specialist in state government administration and was completing his doctoral work at Berkeley. Johnston, a member of the faculty since 1947, was a Minnesota Ph.D., where he had written his dissertation on the relationship between the Socialist Party and the 1924 Conference for Progressive Political Action, which had spearheaded Senator Robert M. LaFollette's campaign for the presidency.[10]

Although generally less conspicuous than History and Political Science, the Department of Sociology also had on its faculty in 1953 two individuals whose scholarly contributions were notable. One of these was Robert R. Martin, who had joined the faculty in 1938 and had soon thereafter organized the School of Nursing. Martin held all of his academic degrees from the University of Washington and was a pioneering specialist in the infant field of human ecology and community organization. During his residence in the Pacific Northwest, he had accumulated a body of research data which led, in the late 1930s, to the publication of several articles dealing with the social and economic integration of the Inland Empire, whose urban center was Spokane. Martin introduced social work into the Hamline curriculum, founded the Minnesota Conference on Social Work Education, and was an editor of the *Alpha Kappa Deltan*.[11]

The other notable member of the department was Leland R. Cooper, an anthropologist with lifelong research interests in the Indian cultures of western Wisconsin and east-central Minnesota. Cooper had graduated from the University of Wisconsin in 1936 and had then taken a divinity degree. Early in his career he had worked for the YMCA and had been involved in juvenile rehabilitation programs in Madison and Milwaukee. A member of the Hamline faculty since 1944, he held the M.A. from Minnesota. His interest in anthropology and Native American cultures stimulated by childhood summers spent in Indian communities with his father, who was a photographer, Cooper began his first excavation in 1929, working at sites near Rice Lake and Clam Lake, Wisconsin. Cooper published several monographs and articles in professional journals, and in addition to his on-site endeavors, conducted research at Stanford, the University of London, and Hamline, where one or more projects was inevitably underway in the basement of Science Hall. In 1961, he received a National Science Foundation grant to excavate Ojibwa sites on Madeline Island in Lake Superior and to conduct stratigraphic sampling on Wisconsin's Spooner Lake. In 1963, he directed an archaeological dig of an early nineteenth-century British fur trading post discovered in the Snake River valley west of Pine City, Minnesota. Early in his career, he also invented the osteostat, a device for measuring bone angles. Beloved among his colleagues and students, Cooper was frequently joined in his efforts by his wife Belle, who also became known to hundreds of Hamline students in her roles as Drew head resident, University hostess, choir chaperone, and indefatigable worker in the theatre.[12]

Paul H. Giddens.

In the Division of Humanities, the faculty of note in Modern Languages included Dorothy McGhee and Kurt N. Berg, a Heidelberg Ph.D. who had replaced James S. King as professor of German in 1952. The English faculty included chairman Reginald G. Buehler, who had joined the University in 1944 and was a specialist in American literature; George T. Vane, who was completing his doctorate at Minnesota and had research interests in the area of English literature; and Barbara Mertz, who served as dean of women and taught journalism. And in the Department of Philosophy and Religion, two new Giddens appointees, Bernard C. Graves and Thurman L. Coss, joined theologian Keith Irwin, who had been at Hamline since 1948. Graves was a graduate of Boston University and the Boston University School of Theology, where he had taken his S.T.B. in 1935. Thereafter he had studied at Cambridge for two years, followed by graduate study at Boston University while simultaneously holding pastorates in the New England Methodist Conference. From 1941 to 1945 he served with military intelligence, and in 1947 received his Ph.D. from Harvard, with majors in the history and philosophy of religion.[13]

Coss was a native of Ohio and a 1947 graduate of Notre Dame. He had taken his M.A. and his B.D. from Oberlin, and was completing his doctorate at Drew University, from which institution he received his Ph.D. in 1957 with a thesis on ''The Fear of the Lord in Hebrew Wisdom.'' During the 1952–53 academic year he had studied at the University of Manchester on a Fulbright Scholarship, and had concluded that year with a tour of the Holy Land. While at Hamline, Coss became increasingly interested in the Dead Sea Scrolls, the series of ancient manuscripts found in the 1940s by a Bedouin tribesman near Qumran on the northwestern shore of the Dead Sea. In 1963, following several years of research in the United States and Israel, he published a guide to the documents entitled *Secrets from the Caves.* An extremely popular lecturer and teacher who empathized with his students' inner religious turmoil as a result of his own conservative upbringing and subsequent encounter with modern Biblical scholarship, Coss in 1965 became the first Burgess Award recipient.[14]

When three senior faculty retired in the mid-1950s, Giddens once again demonstrated his commitment to improve Hamline's academic stature by hiring faculty of exceptional talent and professional dedication. Replacing historian Clarence Rife in 1956 was David M. Pletcher, who was a specialist in United States-Mexican diplomatic relations. Pletcher, who held all of his academic degrees from the University of Chicago, had published several articles on North American entrepreneurs in late nineteenth-century Mexico, and in 1957 expanded upon the subject in *Rails, Mines and Progress: Seven American Promoters in Mexico, 1867–1911*, which received the American Historical Association's Beveridge Prize. In 1964, his analysis of United States foreign policy during the 1880s, *The Awkward Years*, won a McKnight Foundation Humanities Award. Keenly interested in his students, Pletcher was highly regarded as a teacher, a fact emphasized by his selection in the 1965 *Oracle* poll. But it seemed inevitable that a scholar of his stature would eventually move on, and after nine years in St. Paul, he resigned to accept a position on the faculty of Indiana University.[15]

Succeeding Robert Martin, who retired in 1957, was F. James Davis, who had received his doctorate in 1949 from the State University of Iowa and was a specialist in the relationship between law and society. During his five years in St. Paul, Davis continued investigations begun earlier regarding the treatment of law in American sociology, conducted research on foreign students' perceptions of American minority groups, studied problems faced by black and white families forced to relocate due to freeway construction in St. Paul, and co-authored *Society and the Law: New Meanings for an Old Profession*. In 1962, Davis accepted a position at Orange State College.[16]

The third replacement for a staff member of long tenure was Benjamin M. Lewis, who succeeded Librarian Anna C. Lagergren. Lewis had written his dissertation at the University of Michigan on the history and bibliography of early American magazines. During his nine years at Hamline, he published several articles on the subject and in 1961, published the historical segment of his thesis as *An Introduction to American Magazines, 1800–1810*. Lewis completely modernized library procedures, successfully urged renovation of the dungeon-like basement into an attractive reading room, wrote a brief history of the library's beginnings and growth, and in his spare moments coached the University tennis team.[17]

Having separated Political Science from History in 1956, President Giddens determined the following year to detach Mathematics from Physics. By 1958, with a full complement of faculty, the new department, under the chairmanship of Walter Fleming, was a stable and smoothly-functioning entity. In 1961, Giddens brought long-needed stability to the Department of Economics, and in 1966 separated the Department of Philosophy and Religion into two academic units, a move long recommended by Thurman Coss. Although faculty numerical growth had peaked by the time Giddens retired in 1968, efforts to strengthen it both in terms of commitment to teaching and to scholarship continued under his successors. In the autumn of 1977, Richard Bailey, who had by then left Hamline himself to become dean of the General College at the University of Minnesota, spoke proudly of the Hamline faculty which was, in his estimation, the University's greatest strength.[18]

A major reason for the college's increased ability to attract and retain excellent personnel was the substantial progress made during Giddens' tenure in terms of faculty salary increases. Since 1932, when it had first consented loyally to salary cuts, the faculty had persistently sought to restore wages, adjusted for inflation and years of service. Yet by the end of the Second World War, compensation remained embarrassingly low, with many full professors earning $2,550 or less. President Pace, while on the one hand sympathetic to requests for increases, tended to think of the faculty as a community of devoted servants rather than as a body of professionals, and was therefore essentially unresponsive to the more assertive demands. Fond of calling attention to the fact that the University had not defaulted on a payroll since 1934, he urged the faculty to consider its service obligations. What were the implications, he asked a delegation seeking pay increases in 1946, of the fact that certain faculty had taken off-campus employment in addition to their regular duties? How did the faculty regard the fact that opportunities to earn extra money were ordinarily available during summer sessions? Why did some individuals complain about eight o'clock classes;

why did others resist a six-day teaching schedule? Faced with such a philosophical posture on the part of the administration, the faculty found its repeated efforts consistently thwarted. And if Pace's successor, Hurst Anderson, placed greater priority on the matter of faculty salary increases, there was little evidence of it during his abbreviated administration.[19]

Unimpressed by the incremental gains made during the previous decade, Paul Giddens determined from the outset of his administration to give salary increases preferential treatment in budgetary planning. With the aid of a Ford Foundation grant, he managed to raise salaries by an average of 12 per cent in 1956 and almost 14 per cent in 1957. In the first ten years of his presidency, the average salary rose 63 per cent while the Consumer Price Index rose only 14.5 per cent. During the same period, the mean salary for full professors increased to $9,843. In 1965, as a result of unexpectedly large enrollment increases, the faculty received two pay raises, with full professors the beneficiaries of increases ranging up to $2,950. By 1966, the University's average salary of $10,495 placed it ahead of such institutions as Lake Forest, Ohio Wesleyan, Beloit, and Wooster, and the dramatic overall improvement had influenced the American Association of University Professors to give the institution superior ratings in nearly every faculty category. When Giddens retired in 1968, the average cash salary was 232 per cent higher than it had been in 1953. The Consumer Price Index, meanwhile, had risen only 30 per cent.[20]

From his earliest months in office, Giddens was also determined to secure the long-coveted Phi Beta Kappa chapter, and the University made regular application to the United Chapters thereafter. With full restoration of the language requirement in 1962, the faculty removed the last principal objection to membership. While opinion eventually became divided over the issue, with some faculty members resisting the effort because they felt that the United Chapters' guidelines should not determine the nature and scope of Hamline's educational program, and that securing a chapter was not worth the price, both Giddens and the Board remained unequivocally committed to the quest. Ironically, when the national organization finally awarded the University a chapter in 1973, five years after Giddens' departure from office, the faculty had abolished the once-crucial foreign language requirement![21]

Throughout his administration, Giddens held firmly to the view that the University should concentrate its time, resources, and energy upon doing a few things and eventually become known for doing them well. Especially was it important, he felt, to give emphasis to Hamline's development as "a first-class, private, residential, four-year liberal arts college," whose curriculum was well-balanced, and in which the humanities, the fine arts, and the social studies received emphasis coordinate with the sciences. Writing in 1960, shortly after having attended a meeting of the Association of American Colleges, where the future of the liberal arts had been the focus, Giddens stated his position succinctly. "If a college develops an excellent academic reputation, this is [its] best advertisement," he observed. "It will command public respect, get financial support, and attract far more students than [it] can possibly admit."[22]

The President was especially distressed that the social sciences and humanities had become unintentional victims of the space race. Worse still was the fact that few individuals seemed to care about the increasing disparity between the natural sciences and the other disciplines. "It is particularly surprising," he lamented in 1961, "that businessmen, of all people, do not show more interest than they do in providing financial support to strengthen the study of economics and government." Just as frightening was the apparent fact that Americans in general were "even less prepared to make intelligent decisions on foreign policies and international issues. If we are to deal successfully with the thorny international problems that plague us and avoid war," he contended, "there must be greater emphasis placed upon the study of the nature of Communism and the history, language, economic systems, politics and government, religion and philosophy, and the culture of Russia, Europe, Africa, the Middle East, the Far East, and Latin America. If we are unable to cope successfully with these domestic and international issues, all of which have their roots in the social studies and humanities," he warned, "spending more money on science will not enable us to survive."[23]

The University had not been oblivious to the kinds of issues which Giddens addressed. As early as 1934, a faculty committee appointed by President Pace investigated the possibility of establishing student internships in Washington, D.C., and the following year, the first Hamline student received such an appointment under the aegis of the National Institution of Public Affairs. Hamline joined the Washington Semester program in 1948, and thereafter sent outstanding students twice each year for a semester of study in the nation's capital, where they took coursework and engaged in special projects related to the political process in connection with the American University. And there followed comparable programs elsewhere, all oriented toward the encouragement of cosmopolitanism and a better understanding of international affairs.[24]

In the autumn of 1968, the faculty approved a statement which noted the University's commitment to international education and urged continued support for special programs. The basic objective, it declared, was to continue emphasizing similarities and differences between Western and non-Western cultures. The foreign student population at Hamline, which had first received concerted emphasis in the early years of President Giddens' administration and was one of his proudest achievements, should not only be continued but expanded if possible. Both on- and off-campus programs which concentrated upon international affairs should receive added financial support, and once again there should be greater non-Western emphasis. And the faculty should seriously consider requiring students to study abroad at some point during their college years. Reiterating many of the same concerns was a prospectus prepared in defense of an East Asian Studies major, approved in 1973. "Whatever one's definition of liberal education," it observed, "institutions that transcend the traditional Western orientation of higher learning enhance the alternatives for liberating learning influences over those that confine their curricula to nearly exclusive emphasis on Graeco-Roman or European-American curricula."[25]

Part of the faculty's interest in a non-Western curriculum stemmed, of course, from its ongoing effort to keep the entire curriculum both viable and meaningful. In that regard it agreed twice between 1962 and 1970 to implement major curricular changes. The first such effort, which was in part the outgrowth of a suggestion made by trustee Donald E. Bridgman that Hamline develop a comprehensive honors program, resulted in the adoption of a "3-3" trimester calendar. The second, which emerged largely from encouragement and leadership provided by Academic Dean Charles U. Walker, led to the adoption of a "4-1-4" calendar, wherein the month of January became a period for "interim" study in special areas of interest.[26]

Interest in providing special opportunities for gifted students, which lay at the heart of Bridgman's proposal, was hardly new. As early as 1909, Harold Quigley, then associate editor of the *Oracle*, had lamented what he perceived to be the lack of emphasis upon scholarship not merely at Hamline, but among the nation's colleges and universities in general. "Scholarship is not being relegated to the background," he wrote, "but those who are trying to make scholars of themselves are not being encouraged by our colleges as they might be. In this respect, Hamline is no nearer the front than others." Calling for recognition of academic ability through the presentation of prizes, scholarships, and other inducements, Quigley highlighted the scholar's often-overlooked status. "You will say, perhaps, that such recognition is unnecessary when college age is reached and that the only real reward is the innate satisfaction that comes from the knowledge that you have done a thing well," he observed. "Then please tell us why this principle should apply to the regular school work any better than to athletics." Less than four months later, President Bridgman appointed a committee consisting of Professors Beyer, Osborn, and Walcott to consider formulating a policy concerning the awarding of honors for scholarship. By 1916, after first experimenting with the idea informally, the faculty implemented a system of departmental honors, including the establishment of specific criteria for honors at graduation.[27]

In 1921, the National Research Council sent a representative to the University who subsequently urged it to consider means of encouraging and assisting "the unusually gifted student." Led by Beyer and Registrar Roger Johnson, the faculty in 1926 adopted a "Plan for Exceptional Students" which exempted seniors with course averages of C or better from class attendance in an effort to stimulate a greater degree of independent effort. Discussions concerning honors courses and individualized instruction surfaced regularly over the years, although never again with an eye toward honoring the C student. But neither at Hamline nor at neighboring institutions did a comprehensive program take root. Thus, in May, 1952, President Anderson found it important to remind the Board that the college was continuing to focus too much of its energy upon the backward student in order "to get him over the hurdles" rather than upon gifted students. Anderson admitted that the idea of creating a thoroughgoing honors program was a difficult one to implement, for it was "much easier to treat all students alike." But there was greater need than ever before, he argued, since society's leaders emerged from the ranks of the gifted. Under President Giddens' guidance, interest in creating an honors program remained high, and in February, 1959, the faculty formally implemented the Individualized Study Program. Under it, superior students could obtain credit for independent study by means of individualized readings, by examination, through advanced placement, and through opportunities for special projects in regular classes.[28]

By the early 1960s, public interest in special educational opportunities for gifted students had increased markedly. "One of the big questions in education today," noted the Minneapolis *Tribune* in February, 1960, "is what to do with the bright student — how to help him make the most of his talent within a school or college primarily geared to the majority having less talent and more need of systematic teaching." Donald Bridgman's 1961 proposal was one response to that need. Arguing that the existing Independent Study Program was too limited and that the college could afford to do much more, Bridgman suggested that when the range of intellectual ability among students was wide, as at Hamline, the need for an honors program was especially great. The college, he urged, should devise and implement such a program immediately.[29]

Concluding that college resources were "extended to their limits," a special committee charged to study the proposal insisted that major changes await a thorough investigation of the alternatives. Although this precluded meeting Bridgman's insistent timetable, another committee drafted and submitted a frank but essentially optimistic report in August, 1962. Charging that "coordination and communication between the faculty, the administration, and the Board of Trustees had suffered deterioration to the detriment of the morale of the whole University community," it urged forthright corrective action. In calling for the establishment of "a distinct, accurate and attractive" public image and for "the retention and acquisition of a first rate faculty" by means of competitive salaries and "the maintenance of opportunities for effective teaching and research compatible with the best professional standards," the members of the committee seemed to imply that responsibility for flagging morale lay at the President's doorstep. But in suggesting that if Hamline were "to survive and prosper as a distinguished liberal arts college" there must be commitment by everyone interested in its future "to an imaginative program, a willingness to take calculated risks, forceful leadership, and above all mutual confidence in one another," it managed to spread the blame considerably. The committee recommended that every major culminate with independent study. It urged that every department devise an imaginative introductory course. And it suggested that existing opportunities for individualized study be promoted aggressively. But it was unnecessary, the report added, to create special honors courses. When the faculty agreed in March, 1963, to implement a fully revised curriculum based upon the three-course, three-term concept, it incorporated into its plans many of the suggestions made by the special committee.[30]

Although the new curriculum had been in effect for only a year when Charles U. Walker became dean of the University in 1964, the new chief academic officer turned attention once more to the question of curriculum renewal. Predictably, initial faculty reaction was cool. But by the autumn of 1965, the Academic Policies Committee had begun such a study, and by the spring of 1966 had established a series of general guidelines. Calling for renewed emphasis upon breadth through general education and depth through preparation in the major, for increased faculty involvement in introductory courses, and for a radically improved student advising system, it then interjected a cautionary note. "The momentum of change will have to be vigorously sustained," it warned, "and provision made for constant review as the various features are introduced and improved.'' When the committee presented its initial curricular proposal in 1967, Walker sought to provide a degree of momentum himself by suggesting that while Hamline's faculty had always tended to fear change rather than regard it as inevitable, he was optimistic about the current prospects. For the 3-3 program had been a bold experiment, and had worked. Increasingly, students were taking advantage of independent study opportunities. And the faculty was beginning to respond to societal pressures. It appeared, Walker added, that they were willing, despite risks, ''to translate into reality'' their ''desire to be distinctive.''[31]

As ultimately adopted in May, 1969, the revised curriculum incorporated few specific changes within the several major fields of emphasis, but presented greatly enhanced opportunities for flexibility and independent study. With an ''open curriculum'' option introduced at the eleventh hour by Professor of English Quay Grigg, the new format offered ''a custom-tailored program'' to any student desiring it. This meant, Grigg noted, that Hamline had ''adapted the elite education of the 'honors college' to an entire college under the concept of the 'open curriculum.''' Requiring proficiency in English, a foreign language, physical education, eight to fourteen courses in the major, and a demonstrated interrelationship among courses taken outside the major, the new curriculum took effect in September, 1970. In succeeding years, the tendency toward flexibility continued. Most notable of the subsequent modifications was the introduction of a competency-based degree plan.[32]

In his final Matriculation Day address, delivered in September, 1967, and entitled ''On Being an Uncommon Man,'' President Giddens provided a fitting commentary on the quest for academic excellence which had marked his administration, and which had resulted in part in the curricular modifications of the 1960s. Taking note of America's anti-intellectual tradition, of the relationship between that tradition and higher education, and of the challenge presented to anti-intellectualism by society's increasing need for highly educated men and women, the President spoke of the nation's debt to the ''uncommon'' individuals who had done so much to shape its destiny. Out of their early democratic idealism, he observed, the

American people had developed "a deep anti-intellectual attitude" that still persisted. Characterized by "a pronounced tendency to distrust educated persons, fear men with ideas, scorn superior intellectual performance, hold men of outstanding ability and talent in low esteem, elevate and glorify mediocre men, and laud mediocrity as a virtue," it had fostered in "the mass of common people" resentment against "any evidence of intellectual superiority as reflecting upon themselves and their own shortcomings." Its unwritten code had given rise to anti-evolution statutes, to the banning of textbooks which discussed Communism, and to loyalty oaths. It had sent to the White House men born in log cabins and heroes returned from war rather than "first-rate men of intellectual ability and distinction." And it had manifested itself at Hamline in the form of letters critical of faculty members with unpopular views, critical of the theatre for staging a play which allegedly indoctrinated its audience with Communist tenets, critical of the administration for allowing the appearance of a commencement speaker who advocated birth control, and critical of the faculty for recommending certain candidates for honorary doctorates.[33]

But despite the persistence of a strong, native anti-intellectualism, two factors had gradually begun to transform society's attitude toward its "uncommon" men. The first was the rapid growth of technology and the recognition that society's complex problems were beyond the ability of the average citizen to understand or to solve. The second was America's gradual move away from its historic policy of isolationism toward a much more healthy internationalism. Like technological growth, this altered emphasis had increasingly forced the nation to utilize the talents of its best minds. And in the process, colleges and universities across the land had responded "by revising and making the undergraduate curriculum more pertinent and relevant to changing conditions," had recognized the need for emphasis upon excellence in teaching, and had increasingly sought to identify and adequately train "promising and gifted students." Only in recent years, Giddens added, had the American people begun to appreciate "the fact that the common man did not ferret out the riddle of the atom or fling a satellite among the stars or discover polio vaccine or shrink the globe with jet propulsion. They are becoming more aware,'' he observed, ''that all of these things were brought about by distinctly superior men.''[34]

When he retired the following summer, Paul Giddens could take pride in the fact that during his administration, Hamline had made great strides toward becoming an institution which valued the talents of the ''uncommon'' young men and women who might well play leading roles in the future of the nation and the world. If it appeared to some that academic excellence had triumphed at the expense of the aging physical plant, Giddens would surely have argued, as George Henry Bridgman had argued three-quarters of a century earlier, that educational distinction proceeded in the first instance from quality of faculty and curriculum. If it occurred to others that the President had been selective in his curricular emphases, he would undoubtedly have repeated his frequently-voiced contention that Hamline could not hope to be all things to all people. And if it seemed that Giddens was attempting to downplay extracurricular activities which had brought the University a form of prestige in the past, he would just as certainly have answered that such activities, while worthwhile, were not central to the institution's purpose. That Giddens held firmly to these educational principles throughout the fifteen years of his administration was the primary cause of the frustrations which he encountered. But it was also the reason that Hamline, by 1968, was academically far superior to the institution over which he took charge in 1953.

CHAPTER 10

INTERCOLLEGIATE ATHLETICS

"IF INTERCOLLEGIATE ATHLETICS are to be saved from extinction," warned President Giddens in an article published by the *Atlantic Monthly* late in 1965, "it is high time that college and university presidents, deans, and faculties exert strong and courageous leadership, assert greater control over athletic coaches, eliminate practices not in accord with sound educational principles, and restore intercollegiate athletics to an amateur basis." Lucrative broadcasting contracts, enormous stadiums used once a week or less, preferential treatment for athletes both before and after matriculation, and a host of well-publicized scandals involving college athletic programs — these and other sordid aspects of sport were a clear embarrassment to the academic community. And while the major intercollegiate conferences shouldered most of the blame, small colleges and universities suffered more painful consequences. For these institutions, Giddens pointed out, were "already hard-pressed for funds sufficient to maintain the quality of their faculty and educational program," and simply could not long afford to remain "in the mad race to recruit and subsidize student athletes."[1]

The concerns which Giddens so candidly voiced had of course long troubled many academicians. From the moment enthusiasm over intercollegiate football first achieved momentum in the 1880s, college and university presidents, along with their academic and administrative associates, had frequently pondered the place of competitive sports within the structure of American higher education. In the early days, critics most frequently directed their barbs at the more whimsical aspects of the situation. ''I will not permit thirty men to travel four hundred miles merely to agitate a bag of wind,'' responded President Andrew D. White of Cornell University when a team from the University of Michigan issued a challenge to battle on a Cleveland gridiron in 1873. But before long, the concerns had become more serious. For football, as it developed late in the nineteenth century, soon became not merely ungentlemanly, but downright dangerous. When eighteen players died and 159 more sustained serious injuries during the 1905 season alone, the need for a thorough housecleaning seemed unavoidable. Chiefly as a result of this carnage, representatives from sixty-two academic institutions met in December of that year to form the Intercollegiate Athletic Association of the United States, which took as its initial assignment the elimination of violence from football and the supervision of all intercollegiate sports. And in October of the same year, President Theodore Roosevelt, who championed physical exercise but deplored its darker side, called a group of coaches and physical directors to the White House for a discussion. He urged them to clean up the game while preserving what he considered to be its healthful aspects. It was important, Roosevelt told his guests, that physical culture receive effective promotion, for no college should turn out weaklings. But care should accompany its implementation.[2]

Only by stretching the imagination mightily could one have justified labelling any species of physical activity that occurred at Hamline during the Red Wing days ''organized athletics,'' and the concept of ''physical culture'' was still some years in the future. But with the reopening of the University in St. Paul, both preparatory students and undergraduates showed an immediate interest in competitive sports. In the spring of 1881 the first baseball team journeyed to South Minneapolis to play a game — which they lost — with the University of Minnesota. Soon students were scheduling contests with Carleton and with St. Paul and Minneapolis high schools as well. In 1882 a group of undergraduates formed a football team and split a two-game season with the State University. But with a paucity of males to man the teams, and with little available competition, it was difficult to sustain enthusiasm. Moreover, both Presidents John and Bridgman had quite enough to worry about —

physical plant needs, operating capital, endowment — without taking on the task of financing a program of competitive sports as well. By the late 1880s, the *Oracle* had begun to complain about the waning of interest among students in organized sports. Between 1884 and 1892, the University fielded a football team only once — in 1891, for a single game with the State University, which it lost 44-0. Then, in January, 1893, the entire situation changed with the appointment of Raymond P. Kaighn as physical director. And for the first time in its history, Hamline began to examine the relationship between athletics and academics.[3]

Kaighn, who was twenty-three years old when he enrolled as a student and agreed to meet tuition expenses by serving simultaneously as physical director, came to St. Paul from the YMCA School in Springfield, Massachusetts. There he had studied and played under Amos Alonzo Stagg, who had subsequently become head of the Department of Physical Culture and Athletics at the University of Chicago. Both at Springfield and at Chicago Stagg had revolutionized collegiate physical education programs by tying them to athletics and by introducing compulsory physical culture for undergraduates. At Hamline Kaighn began immediately to instill in his students the habits of discipline and devotion which he had acquired under Stagg, and the results were soon apparent. In 1894 he organized men's basketball on an intramural basis, and by 1895 had put together a women's team as well. During his first year he organized field and track teams, and in 1898 introduced tennis. He also guided an inexperienced but devoted football squad to victories over both Carleton and Macalester in 1898. In 1899 the baseball team was so accomplished that, although Kaighn was no longer present, it won eleven out of twelve games and therefore the pennant, and in 1900 it played an undefeated season. By this time, the faculty had become sufficiently interested in athletic matters that, in 1899, it appointed Dean Loren H. Batchelder to serve as a one-person Committee on Athletics, with authority to supervise and report on athletic matters.[4]

Kaighn was scrupulously professional in his work. He insisted that the football team have a training table, and sought to enforce the same eating, exercise, and sleep regulations that Stagg had imposed at Springfield. Finding "almost virgin soil" when he stepped onto the campus in 1893, he quickly spurred interest in the formation of an athletic club, secured new equipment, rebuilt the primitive handball court in the basement of Science Hall into a passable gymnasium, started classes in calisthenics, required participants in organized sports to have heart and lung examinations, and impressed upon his charges the necessity of teamwork. But in both purpose and scope, Kaighn believed that college and university sports must remain strictly amateur. "While we took our training and practice seriously," he recalled almost forty years later, "there was not the sense of strain and importance of winning that seems to be the present order of the day." Athletic activity was integral to a college education, not superior to it, and was best done in moderation.[5]

But Kaighn's immediate successors, of whom there were eight within a decade, did not share his Aristotelian views. With the appointment of J. W. Hollister in 1904, conditions soon took an embarrassing turn. Affirming that the University encouraged its students "to work for a better athletic standing among its rivals," Hollister invited them to participate in intercollegiate sports. And he advanced an argument concerning recruitment of athletes which, though fallacious, had already gained widespread acceptance. Hamline must soon build a modern athletic field, he urged, for male high school graduates were increasingly tending to enroll in those institutions which offered "the best advantages along athletic lines." The University could not "hold its own against the competition of others," he warned, holding forth the spectre of institutional humiliation should athletic fortunes flag, "unless it keeps itself strictly up-to-date in this matter, and this she cannot do without an athletic field."[6]

Within short order, the predictably negative results of Hollister's crusade had become apparent. In the spring of 1905, the Minnesota Athletic Conference, which Hamline and five other schools had formed in 1901 to police athletic activity and guarantee the maintenance of amateurism, investigated and sustained charges of professionalism on the baseball team. Commenting on the embarrassment, the student editor deplored the fact that an investigation had been necessary but assured his readers that the student body approved this "vigorous blow" against professionalism. "A Christian college," he contended, "should above all others foster and cherish clean athletics, and clean athletics only." Still, it was irritating to know that while Hamline had paid the price for its indiscretion, its equally-tainted competitors had gone unpunished. It was therefore not surprising that Hamlinites who had "not yet reached a certain moral and spiritual eminence" were "just a little bit sore over the progress of events." The editor perhaps felt vicarious satisfaction when the Minnesota Athletic Conference collapsed one year later — victim of its inability to wrestle conclusively with the issue of professionalism.[7]

Yet a trace of melancholy must have colored any such perverse pleasure, for the events which culminated in dissolution of the conference had clearly destroyed any lingering notion of institutional innocence. When *Collier's Weekly* published an article revealing startling instances of football mismanagement and misconduct, *Oracle* athletic editor Arthur W. Hoover was not surprised. Persons unfamiliar with such matters might be shocked, he admitted, but college students were not so naive. For they knew from experience that "the desire to win at all costs seems to be the bane of college athletics as well as of so many other departments of life." And there was no obvious solution. For "so long as human nature is what it is and intercollegiate, competitive athletics are indulged in" the evils would remain. Rejection of intercollegiate athletics, he wisely observed, would not cure the disease. The humiliation of rebuke apparently had its effect, for by the autumn of 1906, Athletic Director Lewis Drill detected "no taint of professionalism in any of the different branches," and assured Hamlinites that under his administration there would be none. Drill promised that henceforth admissions standards and financial policies would be the same for athletes as for other undergraduates, and thanked his associates for being liberally disposed "toward the encouragement and support of athletics."[8]

In 1909, stimulated largely by Athletic Committee chairman Thomas Beyer and by the completion of the new gymnasium, Hamline again formalized its athletic commitments by helping to organize the Minnesota-Dakota Intercollegiate Athletic Conference.

Simultaneously, Will Baird became director of athletics. Together, the events signalled renewed stability and prosperity for Hamline's athletic fortunes. Baird, like Kaighn before him, believed that college athletics existed primarily to give every student an opportunity for all-around physical development rather than to produce championship teams. Still, there was no dearth of athletic success during his eleven-year tenure. Between 1909 and 1920, the baseball team won three conference championships, the football team two, and the basketball team six. In 1913 the relay team won the Drake Relays, and in 1914 was invited to the Penn Relays, where it placed second in its class. During the autumn of 1913, football was the subject of the lead editorials for five consecutive weeks. By 1917, the *Oracle* was devoting more than half of every four-page issue to athletics.[9]

If the University's intercollegiate athletic fortunes waxed more than they waned during the second decade of the century, it was not because the faculty had relinquished its responsibilities. As early as 1913, it voted that no student could serve as captain or manager of a team if he was deficient in his work, and in March, 1915, passed a resolution which urged that intramural sports also be encouraged. Shortly thereafter, it proposed a controversial one-year residency requirement for intercollegiate eligibility, a two-sport limit on participation, normal progress toward the degree, and a twelve-hour minimum course requirement per semester, all of which President Kerfoot supported. "The aim," reported the *Oracle,* was "to develop as many students as possible in the various sports of college life, instead of centering all the attention on the naturally gifted athletes." Faculty and Conference alike debated the residency requirement vigorously, and after exhaustive discussion approved a compromise in which freshmen would be eligible after one semester. Alumni were conspicuous in their opposition to the proposal, as was the student editor, who charged that, if approved, it would lower athletic standards without giving proportional benefits, and would encourage "the all-around athlete" to seek his fortunes elsewhere. Early in 1917, five former student athletes wrote to the *Oracle* to suggest that since many of the better athletes attended Hamline and other small colleges for only two years, then transferred themselves along with their enhanced reputations to more prestigious institutions, the proposed restriction would seriously inhibit-the University's future intercollegiate efforts.[10]

At this point, Henry Osborn decided that he had had enough. Objecting vociferously to the contention that superior athletes who dropped out of small colleges in order to pursue fame elsewhere damaged the condition of those colleges, Osborn suggested that perhaps Hamline would be better off without them in the first place. The University wanted "men and women who desire Hamline's diploma," the Dean argued. Students and alumni alike could only gain from a college's enhanced academic prestige, and such prestige was in no way "compatible with two years' residence with athletics as a major." In Osborn's view, the new residency requirement provided "ample opportunity for participation in football by the student who plans for a full course" and that student alone deserved the University's attention. Two weeks after the appearance of Osborn's sternly-worded epistle, President Kerfoot assured the faculty that he would enforce the requirement. But war soon put an end both to the residency issue and to the Minnesota-Dakota Conference itself. Accordingly, decisions regarding eligibility and other matters passed to its postwar successors — the Minnesota Intercollegiate Athletic Conference, organized in 1920, and the Mid-West Conference, formed in 1921. From 1930 onward, the M.I.A.C. alone survived.[11]

While the University's gladiatorial condition entered a long period of decline after the 1921 football squad won the M.I.A.C. championship, faculty interest in athletic policy did not wane. In his 1923 annual report, written as acting president, Henry Osborn more by implication than assertion intimated that his colleagues should aid in restoring academics to primacy within the University's life. While it was commendable to applaud the achievements of the 1921 team and to take pride in the recently-dedicated Norton Field, it was even more important to remember that the college lacked adequate dormitory space and that laboratory and classroom facilities were strained to capacity. Although he avoided mentioning the hornet's nest in his report. Osborn spoke angrily in private of alumni criticism directed at Athletic Director Benjamin Beck for the University's sudden fall from intercollegiate athletic glory. In turn, Osborn's intellectual integrity soon won him a mild reproof from President Kerfoot. Further comments on the ticklish subject were unnecessary, Kerfoot admonished the Dean, inferring that Osborn was too casually blaming the alumni for negative publicity which had reached the newspapers.[12]

Meanwhile, the faculty sparred regularly over the role of intercollegiate athletics. Their discussions were not without humor. Endeavoring to define "eligibility," for example, they finally agreed that "passing in at least twelve hours" one week before a game did not necessarily mean that an athlete had to maintain passing grades in all subjects from the beginning of the semester onward. Rather, he need only be passing in the "current week," which, as it turned out, was not the current week at all, but the previous one! Having reached this magisterial decision, the faculty now found itself condemned to maintain a running account of each athlete's eligibility, and inflicted upon University registrar Roger Johnson the task of keeping score. Johnson, to his credit, threw the entire matter back at the faculty, and at a score of special meetings the status of academically marginal stars received attention. But once again the faculty's efforts to maintain intellectually defensible athletic standards were not universally applauded. Because of unnecessary interference, the *Oracle* charged in 1924, Hamline had suffered from defeats, alumni displeasure, a general disinterest, and high attrition among athletes. "It is not the office of a school to pamper a man because of his athletic ability, to make concessions in his studies or to pay his way through college," the editor acknowledged. "But it is the duty of the school to give considerate attention to those who spend hours daily in practice to defend the name of the school in contest."[13] If the editor knew what he meant by "considerate attention," he did not bother to elaborate. And if he grasped the irony which inhered in his reference to Hamline's good name, he failed to indicate that as well.

Finally, an alumnus got into the act. In a letter to the *Alumni Quarterly*, Harold Quigley — Rhodes Scholar, professor of political science at Hamline from 1917 to 1920, and in 1925 a member of the faculty at the University of Minnesota — delivered a scathing indictment of his *alma mater*'s athletic policy. Castigating the University for failing to stand behind Coach Beck, Quigley reminded the alumni that one of the first signs of creeping professionalism, wherever manifest, was the tendency to fire the coach the moment the team failed to win. "Athletics," he wrote, "is becoming a training of automata for which the strings are jerked by coaches while other automata scream from the stands, their strings jerked by 'rooter kings.' Where," he asked, remembering the days of Will Baird when emphasis upon winning was secondary, "is the soil for soul-growth in athletics unless the players are really matching wits while their comrades looking on voice spontaneous applause? Coaches and even rooter-kings have their value," he admitted, "but when the team goes on the field let the coach retire and let the 'king' lead the cheering, not dragoon the spectators." Another student editor of the period admitted that winning football teams made for good copy and good advertising. But most students, contended Andrew Brandt in the autumn of 1929, came to college to study — not to play or even watch football. Why, he wondered, should the University draw the line at athletes when displaying willingness to reward talent with cash?[14]

By 1930, the thoughts of most individuals concerned with the fate of the University had moved, by the force of world and national economic affairs, toward the more urgent matter of institutional survival. Thus, the arrival of Joseph W. Hutton as basketball coach in December of that year and the almost instant success which his teams enjoyed provided much-needed relief from the acrimonious discussions that had marked debate on the 1930 Methodist survey and President Hughes' efforts to move the University. It would have been difficult for Hamlinites to contend that a winning basketball team was central to the institution's purpose. But in an age of economic crisis, it would not have been at all difficult to argue that the stunning success which Hutton brought to the court produced a much-needed psychological boost. And it might well have been possible to claim, in addition, that the favorable publicity generated by the Pipers' early victories under their new coach laid the foundation, however obscure it may have been at the time, for the resurrection of Hamline's own financial fortunes.

Hutton had graduated from Carleton in 1924. He had played

basketball there for four years, was annually named to the all-state team, and following graduation had been a high school coach in South Dakota and Minnesota. Two months after his arrival at Hamline to take up the reins as basketball coach, President Hughes named him athletic director and placed him in charge of football and track as well. In his initial football season, Hutton guided the Hamline eleven to its first conference victory in two years, and in his second year as basketball mentor produced the University's first M.I.A.C. championship since 1920. Between 1930 and his retirement thirty-five years later, his teams won 588 games while losing 186, a record which in 1965 ranked him sixth among the nation's coaches. Under his tutelage, Hamline teams captured or shared nineteen M.I.A.C. championships and between 1932 and 1957 never placed lower than second. In conference play they won 347 games while suffering only 99 defeats. Twelve times his squads advanced to the N.A.I.A. championship play-offs in Kansas City, and three times, in 1942, 1949, and 1951, they captured the championship, a record matched by only one other school prior to 1961. At the time of his retirement in 1965, Hutton's 36–10 record in N.A.I.A. tournament play remained unmatched. Six of his players went on to pro careers, and three ranked among the top ten in all-time N.A.I.A. scoring. Hutton was the first coach selected to the Helms Foundation Hall of Basketball Immortals, an honor which three of his players later shared.[15]

If Hutton had his campus adversaries during the 1930s and 1940s they were a silent lot, for it was not until 1946 that the first flurry of opposition appeared, and it was short-lived. Athough the basketball team that year had compiled a relatively mediocre 12–8 record, it received a bid to participate in the N.A.I.A. tournament. Asked by the Committee on Physical Education and Athletics to consider the invitation, the faculty by a margin of only one vote approved acceptance. Three days after the vote, the student editor wondered about the benefits supposedly realized from such a perennial venture. What had the 1942 first-place trophy secured for the University in the way of *bona fide* benefits, she asked, and precisely what were those benefits? How many students had actually enrolled at Hamline because of its basketball prowess? Many students, she contended in response to her essentially unanswerable questions, "would have chosen this University whether it had a team or not," an unknowing paraphrase of Andrew Brandt's 1929 contention. In her judgment, it was time for faculty and students to display "a bit more discretion" in their choice of "causes." Calling for a poll of the student body in order to determine reasons for matriculating, she concluded with a plea "for a re-evaluation of our sense of proportion as applied to sport."[16]

Predictably, reaction was swift. What had championship basketball brought Hamline "in the way of benefits?" asked a student correspondent. It had "made the student body proud of our team and school; made the city of St. Paul proud of our school; made the state of Minnesota proud of our school; made the country conscious of our school. If these are not to be classed as benefits," the anonymous author concluded, "I must be sitting in the wrong chair." Another reader endorsed the idea of a poll, but suggested that it be extended to include students, alumni, faculty, and trustees. Such a comprehensive survey, she contended, would not only justify past athletic policy, but would place the "thoughtless" and "misinformed" editorial, which should never have been allowed to appear in the first place, in its true light. Unruffled, the editor struck back satirically, labelling advocates of athletics "Toe Stubbers" whose code was "to love mercy, to ignore evils, and to walk cautiously among the stones." Thereupon, public discussion of the issue ceased.[17]

The controversy, while brief, had raised important and complex questions about the relationship between a winning tradition in athletics at a college like Hamline and such an institution's ability to attract students. In subsequent years, many liberal arts colleges, including a number that had excellent academic reputations, sought to determine and analyze from the standpoint of perceptions the reasons that students chose to enroll, and why they decided to remain. The answers were seldom conclusive and sometimes shocking to those who believed that athletics had little to do with matriculation and retention. In the early 1970s, for example, a study conducted by Lewis and Clark College showed that more than three-quarters of all male students perceived intercollegiate athletics as very important in their decision to enroll. Other comparable studies elsewhere corroborated that discovery.[18]

Meanwhile, in the year following the 1946 controversy, Hutton's teams commenced their longest uninterrupted domination of the M.I.A.C., winning every state championship from 1947 through 1953, advancing to Kansas City every year except one, and winning the N.A.I.A. tournament twice. Basketball became an even more important aspect of college publicity; in the last year of his administration a smiling President Pace posed proudly with Hutton's 1948 championship team for a photograph which appeared in the University catalog. In 1950, the Pipers were pictured and identified in the catalog as "Champions by Tradition," and in 1951, when University publicists devoted three pages of photographs in the catalog to athletics, basketball was the only sport featured.[19]

From the beginning of his career, Hutton had contended and proven that with a disciplined style which relied partially upon good offense but particularly upon consistent man-for-man defense, a reasonably talented team would win the majority of its games. While many coaches came increasingly to adopt a more open style, in which a flashy, high-scoring offense became more important than an effective defense, Hutton continued to rely upon the controlled screen-and-set pattern which had become synonymous with Piper basketball. The free-switching style characteristic of the new approach, he explained, made it much more difficult to set up screens, to control and contain individual opponents' offensive specialties, and to establish consistent shooting percentages from the floor.[20]

If questions concerning the academic propriety of post-season games and the seemingly perennial student hegira through frozen Iowa cornfields to Kansas City and the N.A.I.A. tournament sometimes arose, they seldom had a major impact upon college policy. Lacking any alternative form of distinction that presented equally attractive opportunities to publicize the institution, and in the absence of a chief executive who was prepared to put his job on the line regarding the role of intercollegiate athletics, the University in the late 1940s and early 1950s remained content to identify itself in the public mind with its unarguable prowess in basketball, and with the persuasive, soft-spoken coach who was singularly responsible for that phenomenon.

But in the spring of 1953, it suddenly required little imagination to see that priorities were about to change. Nowhere in his earliest references to athletics did Paul Giddens suggest — as critics would soon charge — that Hamline should de-emphasize either athletics in general or basketball in particular. But the new President's educational philosophy rested upon premises which, by definition, disallowed sanctioning the primacy of any one sport, and an administrative change in attitude toward basketball was therefore a foregone conclusion. Athletics, Giddens told an *Oracle* reporter in a telephone interview prior to leaving Allegheny, "should be a part of a general balanced college program," and should be integral to a well-rounded physical education program which emphasized developing talent for a lifetime of satisfying and healthful participation in continuation sports such as golf and tennis. Although he neither explicitly stated nor implicitly suggested that basketball had overshadowed other intercollegiate sports as well as the entire physical education program for almost twenty-five years, it was clear that if his hopes for Hamline were to be realized, basketball could not continue to occupy its position of supremacy. Giddens found his views reinforced by past circumstance. He was troubled by the discovery that aid given to athletes in contravention of North Central Association rules was the immediate cause of Hamline's temporary loss of accreditation in 1933. He learned that innocent but unwise solicitation of prospective athletes during the summer of 1932 had carried almost equal weight in the North Central Association's decision. More than anything else, however, he was persuaded that an athletic policy which emphasized intercollegiate sports alone was too expensive, gave the public a distorted impression of the University's objectives, and would impede progress toward his goal of making Hamline a first-rate liberal arts college.[21]

Within short order, the President's critics seized upon a variety of issues which they saw as related to what they perceived that Giddens was attempting to achieve. When the Pipers failed to win the M.I.A.C. championship both in 1954 and 1955, Twin City sportswriters aired rumors that Hamline had begun to de-emphasize athletics. Hutton himself saw the difficulty hinging on two factors: Giddens' decision to employ women as admissions counselors, and the institution's preference for a strict interpretation of North Central Association rules governing athletic matters. He did not mention that prior to 1953 there had been no admissions counselors at all, yet Hamline's basketball fortunes had somehow flourished anyway. Nor did he indicate that the first individual Giddens had hired was a male admissions counselor. For what was obviously at stake was not the sex of admissions counselors, but the right of coaches themselves to recruit. On the subject of North Central Association rules, Hutton was especially candid. Unless every member of the conference obeyed the rules to the letter of the law, he told a reporter for the St. Paul *Dispatch,* it was pointless to expect that Hamline could maintain a rigid position and yet expect to retain its competitive edge.[22]

Throughout the spring and summer of 1955, Hutton and the alumni H-Club urged Giddens to make a more thorough commitment to intercollegiate athletics. In September, the President finally referred the matter to the faculty Committee on Athletics for study and recommendation. Meeting jointly with the Committees on Admissions and Student Aid, it soon recommended that Hamline hire another male admissions counselor, preferably an alumnus who was "enthusiastic about Hamline's total program as well as its athletic program," and adhere strictly to all regulations governing the administration of financial aid.[23] In their effort to provide Giddens with a set of concrete guidelines, the faculty were obviously attempting to help resolve a difficult and potentially disruptive situation. But in phrasing the recommendations as they did, they implied a general lack of confidence in the University's admissions and financial aid programs.

Acting on the committee's advice, Giddens offered the admissions position to an alumnus recommended by Hutton and the alumni H-Club. Although the candidate declined the position, the H-Club continued to agitate for his appointment, threatening Giddens with unspecified trouble if he did not capitulate and brazenly sending a letter over the President's head to members of the Board.

Joseph W. Hutton and a championship team.

Giddens thereupon outlined his view of the situation in no uncertain terms. The latest move, he told the trustees, was but another "in a long series of efforts . . . on the part of the Director of Athletics and the H-Club committee to determine what college policies on admissions and financial aid to athletes shall be, what personnel shall be employed by the college, what duties shall be assigned, what salaries shall be paid, what the composition of faculty committees shall be, and what other college policies shall be. It presents an issue," he continued, "as to who is responsible for determining these matters — the President of the University or the Director of Athletics and the alumni H-Club committee." Unless the Board resolved the matter immediately, he warned, "harassment of the Administration" and "incitement of the alumni and students" would continue, and the University's academic reputation would suffer "irreparable damage." Other educators and educational organizations were "silent witnesses to the events which have transpired since June," he concluded ominously, raising unmistakably the spectre of 1933, "to see what the answer of this college may be." In uncompromising language the Board presented its response to Giddens' implicit threat of resignation. The President had handled the matter admirably, it declared; ultimate responsibility was his alone; and while efforts of the alumni H-Club were undoubtedly expressions of "interest and loyalty," that body would immediately learn of the Board's decision. The message was clear: Hutton and the H-Club had a right to their opinions, but the Board would stand behind Giddens.[24]

From that moment until his retirement, the President never again questioned his standing with the Board regarding matters of athletic policy. Of course this did not mean that he was permanently free of difficulty. Late in 1957, for example, the M.I.A.C. presidents proposed to ban participation in post-season games. They did so, as Giddens later explained, on the grounds that such contests unnecessarily lengthened the season in any given sport, handicapped participants scholastically, interfered with other intercollegiate sports, pre-empted other long-scheduled college events, caused undue and unhealthy mass migrations away from the campus, and overemphasized "the role and place of intercollegiate sports in any college

educational program.'' For his efforts, the students — no doubt
smarting over the basketball squad's third-place finish in the conference and willing to blame the most convenient target for their frustration — hanged Giddens in effigy. The student editor accused him
of dishonestly hiding his opposition to Hutton and basketball behind
conference-endorsed opposition to all post-season play. Hutton
lamented taking what he regarded as ''a backward step'' just when
nationwide interest in post-season competition seemed to be increasing. But faculty and Board alike again expressed their confidence in
Giddens' leadership, although they suggested that the President had
been remiss in failing to forewarn students of the presidents' proposal.[25]

In 1959 the N.C.A.A. reprimanded and censured the University
for having violated its prohibition against informal athletic workouts
between college representatives and prospective students, a circumstance fraught with irony for the President, who had made a concerted effort to enforce conformity to regulations. In 1962 Giddens
again fell victim to student charges. This time the stated offense was
his decision so to restrict the athletic budget that hockey uniforms
were ''in a dismal, mungy state'' as a result of six years' use and
storage at the end of the previous season ''while still sweaty wet.''
Incensed at the suggestion that college officials had carelessly
ruined the school's hockey sweaters by stuffing them into cardboard
boxes before the armholes had dried, Giddens opened fire. ''Is
engaging a new coach to improve football, allocating $5,000 to buy
equipment for wrestling, and spending $30,000 to $35,000 to provide better dressing-room facilities for teams in football, hockey,
track and baseball a 'down-grade athletics' policy?'' the President
asked in a letter to the *Oracle*. Did the editor know that the sweaters
were damaged not by carelessness, but by rain dripping through a
leak in the fieldhouse roof? Would it not have been better to seek out
the facts before printing his uninformed and erroneous allega-
tions?[26]

Giddens' most noteworthy decision with respect to the development of a broadly-based intercollegiate athletic program was the one
to which he referred in his letter about the hockey sweaters: the
successful effort to hire Dick Mulkern as head football coach in

1962. In doing so, the President ultimately demonstrated to his own satisfaction the truth of his conviction that an institution could have a first-rate intercollegiate athletic program without sacrificing academic integrity. For decades Hamline's football fortunes had languished. The University had not won an M.I.A.C. championship in the sport since 1921, and had won only two out of the previous forty-six games — one of those by forfeit. The coach who had most recently presided over that barren scene had resigned in despair. Giddens, long worried about the disadvantages that institutions like Hamline encountered when competing for the number of athletes necessary to field a respectable football team, wondered why anyone would even want the vacant position. Complicating the problem, he felt, was the athletic department's tendency to spend most of its time looking for prep basketball players. But when Mulkern's name came to the head of the list of candidates, the President gamely decided to give it a try.

If Mulkern were to take on the seemingly hopeless assignment, Giddens explained to the candidate, it must be on the University's terms. This meant strict adherence to M.I.A.C. rules and respect for the educational principles which had become the hallmark of his presidency. It meant acceptance of Giddens' conviction "that college athletics exist primarily for the enjoyment and benefit of students who wish to participate in them." It meant willingness to subscribe to the position that intercollegiate athletics at Hamline must share the stage with all other extracurricular activities. If the White Bear Lake coach were to consent to head Hamline's football program and seek to lead the University out of its long autumn of discontent, he must do so with the understanding that there could be no preferential treatment for athletics, no high-pressure recruiting, no double admissions standards, and no financial irregularity. The University would be supportive, and with classroom assignments and the added opportunity to develop a wrestling program, Mulkern could carve out a new career for himself. But the strictest propriety must prevail.[27]

To the surprise of many, Mulkern accepted the University's offer of an appointment. He did so, as he later explained, because he had always wanted to coach college football and was eager for a new career. Although he knew that he could not produce a winning team overnight, he believed that if he could give his players the immediate experience of winning some non-conference games, both time and improved morale would be on his side. He therefore asked — and received — permission to add another non-conference contest to the 1962 schedule. And he privately set for himself a five-year timetable during which to build the championship team. "I wanted to cooperate one hundred per cent with the President's goals and Hamline's educational policies," he later reflected, "by bringing in a first class student who would be an all-around asset to the college as well as a football player." It was vital to recruit scholastically-motivated players, he explained, not only because such individuals were much more likely to give a coach four predictable years of service, but because academic failure could have damaging effects upon a student. Mulkern knew that in the absence of a winning tradition, it would initially be difficult to recruit talented football players. But he believed that by stressing the chance to play in several sports, the greater likelihood of seeing regular action, and the superior quality of Hamline's educational program, the task would not prove insurmountable.[28]

He wasted no time proving himself correct. In his first season, he guided Hamline to victory in both of its non-conference games. In 1963 the Pipers moved into the conference's first division, and in 1964 they scored upset victories over St. John's and St. Thomas. In 1965 they upset reigning champion Concordia. Although picked for a seventh-place finish at the beginning of the 1966 season, Mulkern's squad defied the odds-makers by winning the championship, and in doing so meeting Mulkern's timetable. No one could have been more pleased than President Giddens, who had proven through Mulkern that a small liberal arts college could build a successful intercollegiate sports program, even a successful football program, without sacrificing its hard-won academic integrity. Mulkern had "lived, worked, and coached within the educational principles set forth in 1962," Giddens commented early in 1967. "He won the championship in the hard but right way."[29]

Many observers undoubtedly regarded as ironic the fact that Hamline had won the championship less than a year after Giddens in his

Atlantic article had roundly condemned ''the shoddy and questionable practices and policies followed by many colleges and universities in an effort to have a winning team, win public acclaim, and make money.'' But the President saw the situation quite differently. For Mulkern and his teams had resurrected football from oblivion and won the cahmpionship, he reminded the trustees, ''by playing within the educational principles for which I have firmly stood and staunchly contended.''[30]

Those principles were abundantly clear. Hamline's ability to secure publicity because of athletic success was much more likely to mislead the public regarding the University's nature than to enlighten it. Its ability to attract and retain good students, and to secure funds for endowment, faculty salaries, and physical plant, supposedly bore no relation to success in intercollegiate athletics. The University's reputation and prestige was likewise essentially unrelated to its athletic prowess. The President might well have added that while intercollegiate athletics gave faculty, administration, alumni, and students something to occupy their attention, whether mentally or physically, vicariously or in the flesh, such activities had nothing to do with the institution's reason for existing in the first place.

CHAPTER 11

UNDERGRADUATE LIFE AND THOUGHT

"COLLEGE STUDENTS ARE the most conservative people on earth," wrote student editor T. Otto Nall early in 1921. "Of course they embrace every new radical movement which comes their way, but they do this because radicalism is the vogue — because everyone else is 'modern.' By himself the undergraduate dares not take one step."[1]

Nall's blunt assessment of the undergraduate scene applied with particular force at Hamline, where conservatism meant not merely conformity but a much more basic orientation toward life in general. As at other midwestern educational institutions populated largely by the children of hard-working, middle-class parents, most Hamline students regarded a college diploma not as an inborn right, but as the reward for a period of reasonably dedicated study. Such a distinction, they and their parents typically reasoned, would provide access to greater economic opportunity and security and perhaps to enhance social position as well. If students at more prestigious institutions often regarded themselves as heirs to an educational tradition in which their parents and grandparents shared, Hamline undergraduates were almost always first generation collegians. That fact, while hardly preventing the presence of a typical undergraduate social climate, tended to work against the growth of a radical climate of opinion and to convey a bland and rather unexciting overall impression to visitors. Nor did the situation change with the passage of time. For as recently as the late 1960s and early 1970s, when colleges and universities across the land degenerated into battle-scarred scenes of confrontation and even death during the trauma of Vietnam, Hamline's student body — despite isolated flurries of protest — remained essentially tranquil.

If socioeconomic origins were one ingredient which conditioned the general nature of the University's undergraduate community, geographic origins were another. For overwhelmingly, Hamline students came from Minnesota and the border regions of adjoining states. In 1921, the year of Nall's commentary, 97 per cent of the student body claimed homes within the five-state region, and fully 90 per cent hailed from Minnesota. Not until the early 1960s, following a concerted effort by President Paul Giddens to diversify the geographic makeup of the student body, did the number of undergraduates from the immediate region drop below 90 per cent. And never — whether for reasons of climate, distance, or, in the case of the Great Plains and Rocky Mountain regions, sparsity of population — did the University manage to attract more than a handful of its enrollees from distant locations. By contrast, roughly 75 per cent of Carleton's students came from outside Minnesota by the 1950s and St. Olaf was simultaneously attracting approximately half of its undergraduates from other states. Furthermore, despite Giddens' efforts, the picture did not change markedly. For out of a total enrollment of 1,196 in the autumn of 1975, 728 students, or 61 per cent, came from the Twin Cities, while 279, or 23 per cent, came from other parts of the state. Of the remainder, all but 71 hailed from adjoining states, Chicago, and northern Illinois.[2]

Hamline students also revealed their conservative leanings when making political choices, for they preferred Republicans over Democrats by a wide margin, and were frequently out of step with choices made by the state electorate. They enthusiastically supported William McKinley in 1896 and 1900, Theodore Roosevelt in 1904 — at best a qualified concession to liberalism — and William Howard Taft in 1908. They endorsed Herbert Hoover not only in 1920, when the Republicans would have done well to nominate him rather than Warren G. Harding for the presidency, but by a four to one margin in 1932, when 23 million voters, including the majority of those in Minnesota and forty-one other states, cast their ballots for Franklin D. Roosevelt. In a straw vote conducted in 1940,

Wendell Willkie defeated Roosevelt by a margin exceeding two to one. Thomas E. Dewey prevailed over Harry Truman by the same ratio in a comparable poll conducted in 1948. Republicanism triumphed again in 1952, with Dwight Eisenhower receiving 377 straw votes, Adlai Stevenson 190, and Pogo two. Ike repeated as winner in the autumn of 1956, although Republican Senator Margaret Chase Smith of Maine surged to victory in a mock political convention held the preceding spring. Richard Nixon overwhelmed John F. Kennedy in 1960, and Barry Goldwater edged out Lyndon Johnson in 1964. Meanwhile, the Texan romped to a sixteen-million-vote plurality in the November election. And in the aftermath of the tumultuous 1968 Democratic National Convention in Chicago, Hubert H. Humphrey barely managed to edge out Richard Nixon, defeating him in a straw poll by only thirteen votes.[3]

In the early years, the administration reinforced the students' naturally cautious disposition by imposing an extensive group of regulations governing their behavior. President David Clarke John both assured parents and forewarned students in 1880 that paternalism would brook no challenge. "Every pupil whose name is placed on the register of this institution becomes thereby pledged to render a cheerful obedience to all its rules and regulations," he admonished. "Every one will be received upon honor, and implicitly trusted until by misconduct he forfeits the confidence imposed in him. Morals and manners constitute an important factor in the cultus of college life, and they will be as carefully taught as science and literature." Morals and manners were predictably Victorian. Not only were "gentlemen and ladies" enjoined against visiting each other's rooms, but against taking "walks or drives together" and against seeking "opportunities for private conversation." As if this were not sufficient preventative, conditions within University Hall were even more doleful. Students were cautioned against "running, rapid walking, whistling, singing, boisterous laughing and talking" in the building, and the strictest segregation prevailed: "gentlemen" were required to use the western staircase to reach the assembly hall, "ladies," the eastern. Tobacco was strictly anathema as was liquor. Finally, if anyone fell prey to such proletarian instincts, there was to be no spitting on the floor.[4]

Presented with these strictures on their adolescent urges, Hamline students, the majority of whom were then enrolled in the Preparatory Department and, to be fair to President John, perhaps needed such rules, often found themselves called upon to answer to misdemeanor charges. One uncharacteristically rowdy student received five misdemeanors from the faculty for "dragging a fellow student out of bed at midnight, resisting the owner of the house when ordered to go to his room, and using profane language to him," and was ultimately expelled for dating without the services of a chaperone after solemnly promising to enlist them. "Gross immorality" was a frequent cause for expulsion, although the faculty primly avoided spelling out the precise nature of so frightful an offense. "Disorderly conduct," too, was a constant source of irritation, as were unauthorized "visits" to "ladies'" rooms. But faculty and administration were not altogether without heart. In May, 1883, for example, they rescinded a series of reproofs and misdemeanors administered earlier to future president Samuel F. Kerfoot, then a preparatory student, and future faculty member Arthur Z. Drew, then a freshman in the Collegiate Department, following "satisfactory explanation." And when President Bridgman assumed the reins in the summer of that year, the faculty must have breathed a sigh of relief when the new chief executive announced that the pamphlet of regulations prepared by President John would no longer be in force. Honorable individuals, he contended optimistically, needed no such code in order to behave properly.[5]

Certain students of the era, apparently blessed with greater control over their primitive instincts than their more hapless associates, regularly castigated their peers for inattention to deportment. "Annoying and hectoring other people is no way to get an education, and much less is it a proper way of amusement," ran a typical injunction, delivered in 1888. "If a good time is necessary, it is far easier and much better to seek it in some social way or legitimate sport, than by marauding in the dark, removing property and discommoding folks." In 1907, an *Oracle* correspondent wondered whether Hamline students were "a civilized community or merely a band of rowdies, vandals and petty thieves. Annoying disturbances during chapel exercises have become the regular thing," he reported. "Pieces of chalk and headgear are thrown about during prayer. Some buy, borrow or steal keys with which to enter society rooms where they have no business whatever. Gymnasium lockers are broken into by force and rifled of their contents." Students themselves, the writer declared self-righteously, must decide "whether this is to stop or go on; whether we shall be known as a decent community, or whether we shall hang our heads in shame and confess that Hamline is overrun by a set of persons who have no consideration for the rights, feelings or property of others, and are utterly devoid of all sense of common decency."[6]

But if failure to control the wilder impulses prompted stern admonition, devotion to scholarship fared no better. Again and again the *Oracle* urged students not to spend all their time studying. "The college curriculum does not prescribe all that is necessary to an education," the paper observed in 1889, endorsing the popular collegiate notion that institutions of higher learning in America should concentrate upon fostering the development of well-rounded personalities. "An important part is the cultivation of the social side of our natures. Social intercourse makes us more sunny in disposition, and gives us opportunity to cultivate the art of conversation." Another editor elevated the art of avoiding study to the level of virtue. "The student who rises up early and sits up late and has his nose buried in a book the whole while may fancy he is storing up knowledge and piling up scholarship much faster than his neighbor who spends his afternoons in athletics," ran a 1902 commentary, "but it is questionable whether he will know much more about his textbooks, and it is certain he will be in a poorer condition to make use of his knowledge than his less studious classmate."[7]

Was anti-intellectualism among students unique to Hamline? One editor who knew that it was not chose to place the issue in a national context. "We are still too busy laying rails and erecting smokestacks to give attention to such insignificant matters as mere scholarship," wrote Frances Conkey in 1908. "As a natural consequence we have no scholars to boast of, none to place beside those of 'effete Europe.' Our smug self-complacency received somewhat of a jolt when Owen Wister declared that America has no scholars that are pre-eminent in their field, and only three that are candidates for high rank at all. And yet we cannot gainsay the truth of his charge, we cannot answer him.'' Editor Henry Allan Moe had no time for the suggestion that lack of scholarship at Hamline could be excused by appealing to the national temper. He suggested in 1915 that the University must discharge its obligation to foster scholarship and the intellectual life rather than choose to take its cue from the public at large. ''The scholar labors incessantly for four years and in complete obscurity,'' he observed. ''And for his work he is dubbed a 'grind' who seeks to take all from and give nothing to his university.'' Hamline's primary purpose for existing, Moe reminded his readers, was ''to disseminate learning. Hence, all who help raise her standards of scholarship are worthy of the highest praise.''[8]

It was not difficult, of course, for those who rejected ''the grind'' to find extracurricular diversion. For in the typically cloistered environment of the late nineteenth-century denominational college, organizations created to foster special interests provided virtually the only social outlets for student exuberance. A campus literary society, featuring weekly ''entertainments'' and debates on professedly heady intellectual topics flourished from the first in St. Paul. There followed in its wake a succession of such bodies, usually organized according to sex and ostensibly devoted to intellectual as well as social uplift. Parading across the years from the early 1880s to the First World War ran a collection of more than fifteen literary associations. Their presumed virtues received regular notice. To a late nineteenth-century student editor, society work was ''the epitome of college life, and all who miss it miss valuable training.'' Another regarded it as ''more and more an important item in the make-up of the ideal student,'' and considered ''humiliating'' the inability of non-members to discuss with intelligence the broad and sophisticated array of subjects to which members devoted themselves. But almost from the beginning storm clouds hovered over the societies, for there were always more students seeking admission than there were spaces to accommodate them, and invariably jealously and meanness reared their ugly heads. Competition for members and group loyalty inevitably brought out the worst in human nature. ''In the present conditions,'' wrote an *Oracle* reporter in 1903, ''a person hardly dares vote for even a Y.W.C.A.

president unless she is a member of her own society. We have heard that one society even went so far as to have its members promise faithfully to be present at a certain religious meeting in order to elect one of their own members president.'' While comparable complaints directed at the social fraternities and societies which gradually made their appearance would echo down the years, the days of the literary societies were already numbered. As early as 1900, other activities had begun to assume positions of priority, and thereafter interest in the societies waxed less frequently than it waned. By the end of the First World War they had become outmoded relics, and within a few years had disappeared forever.[9]

Meanwhile, their competitors proliferated. Men's and women's scholastic honorary fraternities appeared in 1910 and 1912 respectively, and by 1915 there existed an H-Club, a forensic club, a wireless club and — hardly in keeping with the staid image projected by the institution — a chapter of the Intercollegiate Socialist Society. Encouraged by President Kerfoot, students established men's and women's student councils by 1916. The Hamline Players made their debut the same year, and in 1917 a journalistic fraternity and Torch and Cycle — then a senior honor society — joined the ranks. By 1920, thirty-two agencies of enlightenment and reform were energetically hawking their wares, causing distress within faculty ranks regarding their "alarmingly high birthrate." But no regulatory measure eventuated, and as late as 1938, Dean of Students Charles Templer was continuing to lament the "congestion" on the social calendar. It was not until 1951 that the faculty, encouraged to do so by Dean of Women Barbara Mertz, finally adopted procedures for recognizing organized groups.[10]

Nor were students themselves altogether enamored of the plethora of pet creations which dotted the extracurricular landscape. As early as 1888 the *Oracle* prophesied the problem accurately. "At the present day we as a nation are organized to death," the editor observed. "Almost every conceivable form of society, association, combination, union and trust is in existence, having almost every imaginable object or aim in view. This organizing spirit pervades every college, where it sometimes works as much harm as good." Concern over the issue did not subside. "Sloppiness begins to describe one of the biggest curses to American educational institutions, that of over-organization,'' wrote an editor of the 1920s. ''The insidious malady has attacked the communal life of society in general, but it becomes increasingly evident that Hamline is getting her share of the disease.'' He then proceeded to list 67 clubs, fraternal organizations, and ''more or less undefined activities'' which he had managed to identify in less than an hour of random contemplation. Many years later a comparable picture presented itself, for in 1953, 57 organizations appeared on the roster of extracurricular bodies, and in 1965 there were 42.[11]

But whatever distress arose as a result of extracurricular proliferation paled in comparison to the mental energy expended in an effort to wrestle with the conjoined issues of drinking and dancing. Written into the Discipline of the Methodist Church were prohibitions against both, and the administration quite properly felt impelled to enforce that code. In the early years, both the general attitudes which students brought with them from their homes and the University's relative isolation from the real or presumed sins of city life made the issue somewhat meaningless. But well before President Bridgman left office in 1912 the myth of a Midway Eden had long since exploded,. and by the end of the First World War the ''Amusement Problem,'' as Methodists of that era were euphemistically prone to label it, had become a source of genuine concern.

While alcohol was a flatly forbidden fruit and was therefore beyond even theoretical discussion, dancing soon became another matter. As early as 1913, a letter to the *Oracle* suggested that since students were ''getting their recreation away from the institution, and in many cases under conditions that are not desirable,'' the only logical solution was for the University to sponsor supervised dances on campus. ''There is an old adage of good standing among parents that if the home life of the child is made suitable to his wants he will be kept from the outside world and will not travel the wayward path,'' the student correspondent noted, ''and I believe this is the situation which confronts Hamline. It is true that it will be harder for Hamline to cope with this situation than it would be for Carleton or any other college in a smaller city because of its environment, but nevertheless it can be done and has got to be done at once.'' Nor did college officials seem bent upon strict enforcement, for when the University sponsored the first all-college picnic in 1913 aboard a chartered Mississippi River steamboat, dancing took place and was not stopped. But the student body was far from united on the issue. One editor of the period declared that since the Methodist Church forbade dancing, students should adhere to that standard. Another student, reciting third-hand a claim supposedly made by "the matron of a home for fallen women in Los Angeles" that 70 per cent of the residents had lost their reputations because they had danced, declared solemnly that Hamline was hardly "a training place for the public dance and the brothel."[12]

Unsubstantiated as this and other emotion-charged claims may have been, discussion on the subject had become so intense by the 1920s that the Church's attitude toward recreation in general constituted a significant part of the agenda for the 1925 Conference on "Our College." Church and University delegates learned from the faculty Religious Activities Committee that "the social and recreational impulse" was "God-given" and arose "from instinctive tendencies which are our birthright." Fully 80 per cent of Hamline's students danced "whenever opportunity is offered and have danced as a matter of course in the social and recreational activities of their home communities" before coming to Hamline, the committee added. While only a few students were aggressive advocates of a liberalized policy, it was important to remember that the Methodist General Conference had recently urged that laity and clergy alike re-examine their attitudes toward "the subject of amusements in the light of their tendencies." Accordingly, the members of the committee believed, the University should begin formal sponsorship of various types of recreation, one of which might well be supervised social dancing. There were many "wholesome opportunities for fellowship and association among the students and faculty," the committee contended, and all would "conform in every way to the Christian ideals cherished by the University as a character-building institution." Unpersuaded, many clergymen in attendance argued vociferously against the recommendation, and urged that the administration act forthwith to curtail such student enthusiasms. In a particularly notable display of unreality, the Rev. Willard Kern of Rochester suggested that ''a strong spiritual appeal'' might woo students away from their lasciviousness, that the faculty and Twin City alumni had not supported President Kerfoot in what Kern presumed to be the administration's efforts to prevent dancing, and that parents — having however inexplicably allowed their adolescent sons and daughters to dance while in high school — now looked to the University to rectify the error of their ways.[13]

Meanwhile, President Kerfoot had corresponded with the presidents of several other Methodist colleges in an effort to compare Hamline's stance with similar policy elsewhere. Lawrence College, he learned, had permitted dancing for over thirty years, although it had only recently scheduled the first such function on campus. Illinois Wesleyan chaperoned off-campus dances, while Ohio Wesleyan permitted fraternities and other organizations to sponsor them in order that ''the unwholesome conditions'' existing in nearby Columbus would not invade and pollute the campus. Elsewhere, Kerfoot discovered, the situation was similar to that at Hamline: neither Albion, Baker, Morningside, nor Cornell allowed dancing in any form, although the latter institution enjoined faculty members not to spy on students who danced clandestinely.[14]

All of this, thought alumnus Harold Quigley, was so much nonsense. ''Methodists who have moved out of the orbit of their nativity — and some of those who haven't,'' he observed with typical candor, ''have sometimes dared to dance but they seldom have dared to admit it, preferring to send their children to a depraved college where dancing is committed rather than to be consistent and advocate that dancing be recognized at the institution that deserves their support.'' In so doing, he charged, they made hypocrisy the dominant institutional motif.[15]

Finally, in 1928, the University gave formal approval to on-campus dancing. With President Alfred Hughes and Dean Louise Bollard More acting as advocates, and with the faculty reiterating its earlier stand in favor of supervised dancing, Hamline at last managed to modify one aspect of its outmoded stance. Yet even as it did so, fully half of the nation's Methodist colleges and universities continued to oppose dancing under any conditions, and only ten, in addition to Hamline, allowed dancing on campus.[16]

In one sense, the controversy culminated more than a decade of increasing restlessness among students regarding the general social climate which prevailed within the University. Much of that discontent arose from the fact that in the midst of a rapidly-changing society, Hamline remained in many ways a study in Victorianism. Urged by college representatives "to come to Hamline, where you can enjoy all the resources that . . . Minneapolis and St. Paul have to offer," students discovered upon arrival that many of those "resources" were off-limits. When Samuel Kerfoot assumed office in 1912, college policy not only forbade students to dance, but to go to movies or to attend the theater. Yet few undergraduates were unfamiliar with those popular forms of recreation. While dormitory regulations had changed radically from the days of President John, they were far from acceptable to students. "Girls could not leave the dormitory after the evening meal," noted Grace Lee Nute in her vivid description of the campus scene, "and had to have their gas lights out at ten o'clock." Until the summer of 1912, when the trustees agreed to modernize Goheen Hall by installing electricity, hardwood floors, hot and cold running water in student rooms, and a tiled bath with showers on each floor, steam heat had been the antiquated structure's only visible amenity. And not until 1918 were University Hall and Science Hall fully wired for electricity.[17]

Furthermore, while automobiles, telephones, and motion pictures were revolutionizing the American cultural landscape, Hamline students found themselves consigned weekend after weekend to boring amusements of their own creation — most of these conducted with steadily diminishing enthusiasm by the fast-fading literary societies. Particularly revealing of the increasingly restless student mood was a notorious "yellow" edition of the *Oracle*, published May 2, 1913, and swiftly suppressed by the administration. The scurrilous sheet, which spawned successors every spring for a decade, made reference to Professor Lescohier's "constant absence from his classroom," criticized Professor Beyer's "dictation of athletics," and suggested that the glee club was guilty of snobbery. It alluded to the clandestine presence of campus bingo games, commented upon "Walcott highballs," and expressed disappointment that Richard Strauss' daring and dissonant "Salome" had not been part of the recent grand opera season in Minneapolis. And it discussed means for getting the "girls from the Hall on these balmy spring evenings" — chief among which was clearly the recently-installed system of fire escapes.[18]

Although the European War hastened the process of social change on campus as it did everywhere, and although postwar efforts by the Kerfoot administration to improve the physical condition of the campus altered the overall situation to a degree, Hamline undergraduates remained at the mercy of an outmoded social circumstance. To be sure, social fraternities, the oldest of which had existed since 1901, gradually filled the vacuum left by the demise of the literary societies. But this presented problems anew. For well into the 1920s, the social life of the campus tended to revolve almost exclusively around the relatively small number of students who belonged to those bodies. Meanwhile, administration and faculty did their best to conceal the existence of the fraternities: not until 1927 did the college catalog even mention them, although the faculty had begun in 1921 to lay down pledging policies. Nor did extracurricular organizations satisfy undergraduates' social needs, for most were too narrow in objective to contribute meaningfully in that regard. And while informal activity abounded — ice skating on Lake Como, walks to Frog Pond (Newell Park), nightshirt parades, cane rushes, bonfires to celebrate football victories — it failed to alleviate yearnings for a more mature approach to the provision of social activity.[19]

Ironically but typically, it was a member of the faculty who first proposed a means of achieving consensus regarding the role and nature of such activity. Speaking to a mass meeting held in the spring of 1908, Thomas Beyer presented and explained the idea of a student senate, which would, he believed, serve as an effective method of channeling student desires in the right direction. But it took more than four years of study, and ultimately the personal intervention of President Kerfoot, who enthusiastically supported the idea, before Beyer's proposal became reality. Even then, student opinion remained decidedly mixed. Many felt that the new body was but another agent of faculty and administrative control, while others applauded its achievements and urged support for its work. Across the years, comparable arguments surfaced with regularity. But through frequent change of name and format, student government survived and seemed occasionally to prosper.[20]

Closely related to the issue of student governance was the more fundamental matter of undergraduate participation in the governance of the University itself. The earliest recorded student suggestion that undergraduates receive the privilege of electing their own representatives to the Board of Trustees came in 1923, and was promptly met by President Kerfoot's kindly but patronizing suggestion that such an idea was "perhaps a bit ambitious." Acknowledging that the administration was often guilty of failing to incorporate student viewpoints into the decisionmaking process, the President maintained that he and the trustees alone possessed the ability to protect "the property interests and such ideals, rules and practices as will make for the highest student character." A quarter-century later, the traditional view continued to prevail. When students asked Charles Nelson Pace to be included as participants in the budget planning process, the President hastened to assure the Board that he would never accede to such youthful flights of fancy. "Woodrow Wilson said when he was president of Princeton that he believed he knew what constituted a good education better than any sophomore," Pace observed. "Paraphrasing this, I have the feeling that more than a score of trustees who have had business experience know more about how to conduct the affairs of a six million dollar corporation than a bunch of students." All the same, the President understood and respected their motivation. "Everything in the transactions of the business office or in the administration of Hamline University is open to inspection and review," he pledged. "Often criticism that proves unjustified provokes caution and we presume it proceeds from an honest, though uninformed, loyalty to the welfare of the institution."[21]

Not all undergraduates were impressed with their peers' quest for involvement. One such individual wondered whether his associates actually wanted the rights which they claimed to desire. Students

Two student editors, 1935.

Vietnam Moratorium Day, 1969: Attorney-General Walter Mondale visits with faculty and students.

simply did not take committee responsibilities seriously, he contended, noting that at a recent meeting of one body the majority of student members were absent, and that some had sent substitutes "who hardly knew what the meeting was about." But few seemed to have such reservations. Though lacking in aggressive assertiveness, they frequently issued temperate requests for added responsibility, and quietly accepted that responsibility when offered it.[22]

But by the middle of the 1960s, as student activism accelerated everywhere, Hamline's student body gradually became more vocal in its demands. Undergraduates became non-voting members of five standing faculty committees and voting members of another during the 1964–65 academic year, and simultaneously achieved creation of a system of committees which paralleled those of the faculty. Yet many interpreted this move as institutionalized disfranchisement, nothing more than renewed proof of the administration's insincerity, and when the trustees in 1967 rejected two additional undergraduate proposals, their cynicism was reinforced. Urged to include students in the process of selecting President Giddens' successor, the trustees responded by calling the proposal premature. Asked to meet regularly with a committee chosen from the Student Congress "for the purpose of improving communication," the Board asserted that "adequate and proper official channels already exist" through the president of the University. Distressed by what he regarded as the trustees' intransigence, the author of the proposals issued a lament. "I thought we had left the days behind where we had to take ten steps backward in order to take one ahead," commented Dick Mittleman. "Obviously, I was wrong. I feel sorry for the entire Hamline community." The student editor displayed greater detachment. "If the students can effectively demonstrate their willingness to handle responsibility and their ability to make reasonable suggestions," he wrote, urging Congress to create its own trustee liaison committee," the trustees may reconsider their decision and give the students a voice in determining Hamline's future."[23]

The inauguration of Richard P. Bailey as president in 1968 signalled the beginning of a new era in student-administrative relationships. Whereas Paul Giddens had openly criticized what he regarded as "the challenge to the authority and responsibility of the

Hamline Board of Trustees" issued by various student leaders, Bailey sympathized with the concerns and frustrations of the Vietnam generation. Acknowledging that college campuses had often become "whirlpools of meaningless activity and hotbeds of superficiality," the new President enthusiastically applauded the college student for his skepticism. "He comes to our college campus and frightens all of us," Bailey observed in his inaugural address. "In desperation we grab the handiest weapon we have and threaten him with law and order or with dismissal. We make little attempt to understand him and in our fright at what he may accomplish in changing us and our institution, we find it impossible to enjoy him. He easily sees the falsity of our position as caretakers of the status quo and preservers of the rock-ribbed institution," the President continued, "and he delights in backing us into a corner and watching us squirm and over-react to his exuberant probes."[24]

Bailey's student-oriented predisposition, his liberal and accommodating spirit, and the contemporary climate of opinion nationwide made progress toward greater undergraduate involvement in University governance virtually inevitable. Thus, in February, 1969, students received voting rights on faculty — now re-named "University" — committees and simultaneously began sending non-voting observers to faculty meetings. Within a year, the faculty had approved open attendance for students at its meetings, and by 1971, students had achieved equal representation on all but one University committee. And in March, 1969, the President announced that henceforth, student delegates would attend meetings of the Board of Trustees — although for the time being, Bailey would personally choose those delegates.[25]

Meanwhile, discussion concerning University governance and the manner in which students might become fuller participants continued unabated. Spurred by the zealous efforts of Congress President Geoff Wattles, a sophomore who had been active in the antiwar movement, students during the 1969–70 academic year pressed for a more precise delineation of their role. Principal point of reference for the discussion was the "Joint Statement on Rights and Freedoms of Students," a document based on materials prepared by the Association of American Colleges, the American Association of University Professors, and the National Student Association. First considered in the spring of 1968, the document had received unanimous faculty endorsement but encountered immediate trustee opposition. Prospects for acceptance seemed considerably enhanced by 1970, but Wattles, who had only recently survived a student-led effort to force his resignation, and who had helped to organize a forum for the purpose of examining alternate systems of governance, remained only guardedly optimistic. Yet in May, 1971, the faculty approved a "Statement of Student Rights and Responsibilities," and the revised document became an official part of University guidelines. "Freedom to teach and freedom to learn are inseparable facets of academic freedom," the document declared. "The freedom to learn depends upon appropriate opportunities and conditions in the classroom, on the campus, and in the larger community. Students should exercise their freedom with responsibility." Thus did a familiar theme in American history find a particular application at Hamline University.[26]

In another drive to achieve greater influence, students also attempted, between 1970 and 1972, to gain access to the University portfolio. Many trustees viewed this effort with alarm, causing President Bailey, who did not fully appreciate the depth of student and faculty concern over the issue, to assume a position of intransigence. When the Northern States Power Company proposed, in 1971, to increase the size of its board from fifteen to seventeen in order to include in its number a consumer advocate and an environmentalist, a small but articulate group of students urged Hamline to join other educational institutions owning N.S.P. stock in voting the proxy. Bailey, who later admitted his error, instead directed that Hamline sell its N.S.P. stock immediately in order to avoid further confrontation. He thus alienated not only the student activists, who condemned him for refusing to make what they saw as a moral choice, but several trustees as well, who thought he had displayed cowardice. In fact, the Board had gotten the message. For within a month, it agreed to instruct the Trust Department of the First National Bank of Minneapolis, which managed the portfolio, to vote all Hamline-owned stock "in such a manner as to promote the best interests of the ecology and endeavor to ensure that ecology-conscious individuals are elected to boards of directors of corporations in which Hamline University is a stockholder."[27]

If Bailey and the trustees sometimes lost patience with the daily round of activist demands, they must have taken comfort in the realization that such demands demonstrated a degree of sophistication unknown to earlier generations. Hamline students were hardly unique, of course, for the same process of growth had occurred on college and university campuses everywhere. Yet this made the change no less significant, and the innocently self-righteous messages of fifty and seventy-five years earlier no less unreal. "Could we but infuse the Lord's ideas of labor into some of the thousands of deluded, pride- and vanity-stricken mortals crowded into city hovels, overflowing our alms houses and asylums of every sort and get them to exercise their strength in a noble way," ran a WASPish commentary of 1889, "vacant fields would abound in harvests and waste places become gardens, while dingy hovels would turn to bowers laden with trailing vine and clambering bush." Not to be outdone, a student orator of 1891 displayed comparable nativist leanings. "The typical immigrant," he intoned piously, "is of a narrow mental calibre, with a false religious training, or none at all, with low ideas of life and [typically] from the pauper and criminal classes." Immigrants, he added, were responsible for "71 per cent of all crime" and between 60 and 75 per cent of all liquor traffic — a circumstance explained by the absence of "stern Puritan piety." And in 1896, the student editor submitted that the urban poor, in whose shacks and hovels "thriftlessness and disorder" abounded, could easily raise themselves by their bootstraps if only they chose to do so.[28]

Although student critiques of socioeconomic conditions had for the most part lost their blatantly anti-Semitic and anti-Catholic overtones by the second decade of the twentieth century, and although Hamline undergraduates no longer seemed in awe of the Horatio Alger myth, there was little evidence on campus of the reformist mentality which pervaded the politics of the progressive era. To be sure, the *Oracle* frequently publicized the activities of such reformers as Wisconsin's Senator Robert M. LaFollette and Minnesota's Governor John A. Johnson, and the paper's columns made it clear that such reform-oriented issues as the direct election of Senators, the municipal ownership of public utilities, the conservation of natural resources, and the commission form of city government were the subjects of student discussions. A "small but enthusiastic" Woodrow Wilson Club organized in the autumn of 1912 and cheered the New Jersey governor's election to the presidency that November. Yet only twice between Theodore Roosevelt's accession to the presidency following the assassination of William McKinley in 1901 and the outbreak of the First World War in 1914 — the years, that is, which constituted the heart of the progressive era — did the student editor assume a decidedly reform-oriented posture. The first was in the spring of 1911, when the Minnesota legislature adjourned without even beginning to consider a body of reform legislation then before it. The second was in February, 1914, when the paper endorsed candidates for the St. Paul city council, for mayor, for city comptroller, and for municipal judge, and made it clear that the respective office-seekers would bring "competent, honest and upright" service to the city.[29]

Yet liberalism had its articulate advocates. Few in number, they often held editorial posts or were major contributors to literary publications — circumstances which, when combined with their writing skills, gave them a degree of influence that far exceeded their numbers. Between 1924 and 1926, for example, George L. Peterson, who would in later years become a prominent Twin City journalist, regularly contributed literate and thoughtful essays in a liberal vein which touched upon literature, religion, human values, and philosophy, and which revealed a particular sensitivity to the condition of the working class. Peterson condemned railroad management for failing to pay a living wage, deplored child labor, presented critiques of the industrial system and of the capitalist mentality, and even battled the Minneapolis *Star* for what he saw as its desertion of Minnesota's farmers and laborers in order to gain greater advertising revenue.[30]

Columnist Ray Smith, whose anti-fascist editorials served as a preface to the campus peace movement of the 1930s, was another liberal — and often radical — student voice. Smith saw the Minneapolis workers' riot of 1934 as evidence of capitalism's failure as well as the New Deal's inability to come to grips with the shortcomings of that system. "In the heart of the working man," wrote Smith, "is an ever accentuated questioning of the justice of distribution on an unscientific, unequal, competitive basis. 'Where there is a master, there must be a slave,' call him what you will. And we at college speak of building a brotherhood of equals while we prepare to perpetuate class distinctions and keep the producing class dependent upon the caprices of a few selfish magnates." Not only in the *Oracle,* but in poetry and essays published elsewhere, Smith quietly but persistently advocated the politics of the extreme left, yet never alienated his audience by resorting to verbal overkill or by falling back consistently upon Marxist terminology. When a small group of students met in the winter of 1936 to form a campus chapter of the American Student Union — an organization which opposed militarism in all its forms, was in the vanguard of the civil rights movement, and crusaded for academic freedom — Smith was among the charter members.[31]

Smith was also the first individual to sense and to publicize the danger which racial inequality presented. "Upon the godlike Aryan industralist has fallen the enervating task of equipping the heathen Zulu with sufficient technical skill to render him profitably exploitable," Smith wrote sarcastically in the autumn of 1934, "and not enough to hasten his perception of economic bonds of slavery with the Aryan wage-worker, whom he is equipped to underbid in competition for a bare existence." It was eleven years before the subject of race relations again surfaced in the columns of the *Oracle.* "It may well be that a process of slow change will bring about the correct solution to this problem," observed student editor Kenneth Oelschlager in February, 1945, reflecting upon the general matter of racial intolerance, "but let us be sure that it is not an excuse for inaction on our part. If we believe in slow change, we still cannot sit around and wait for the change to initiate itself. Some Negroes are tired of waiting and are demanding action."[32]

To most Hamline students, of course, the emerging civil rights revolution was virtually meaningless. Few blacks had ever attended the University, and those who did found themselves for the most part sidelined with regard to campus social events. Minnesota's relatively small black population was confined largely to two geo-graphically compact and racially homogeneous neighborhoods within the Twin Cities; in consequence, only a small number of white undergraduates had experienced more than superficial contact with blacks. Fewer still had ever known a Native American, an Hispanic American, or an Asian American. So it was not surprising, given most white Americans' insensitivity to the presence of racial injustice, that a student orator of the 1890s blithely posited the superiority of the Caucasian race and credited Divine Providence for directing ''the overthrow of the Indian in the building up of the American nation.'' Nor was there evidence that anyone seriously challenged the assumptions which underlay an unflattering portrait of the Negro presented in a 1904 student oration; or the willingness of the *Oracle* to accept a 1910 advertisement from a St. Paul busi-ness college which contained the statement ''Colored persons not received as students;'' or a patronizing program of Negro folklore, literature, and music presented by a campus organization in 1932. These were slights of ignorance, isolation, superstition, and myth, and they had their counterparts everywhere. But reasons were hardly excuses.[33]

Yet excuses abounded, and it was not until the charisma of Martin Luther King captivated and energized the civil rights movement in the 1950s that Hamline students, along with the vast majority of their white associates across the land, gradually came to recognize and understand the magnitude of the problem which presented itself. Even then the essentially conservative and homogeneous nature of Hamline's student body served to minimize the movement's impact on the campus. Thus, although the University finally turned its attention to such matters as the education of the culturally disadvan-taged, the need to recognize and eliminate institutional racism, and the advisability of increasing the percentage of minority students and faculty, a full and proper context was always lacking. Accord-ingly, most campus observers agreed by 1975 that much remained to be done.[34]

But the realization that some of the most immediate and practical goals of the civil rights movement had failed of ultimate achieve-ment only served to underscore that generations of Hamline students and faculty had sometimes consciously, sometimes subconsciously, understood. For decades they had recognized that human perfection, however noble a pursuit, would always remain tantalizingly elusive, thereby challenging successive ages to define and achieve it. Truth, the more contemplative members of the University community knew, enjoyed presenting itself in many guises, so that whatever the construct, there were bound to be honest differences of opinion. Nowhere were these differences formulated with greater precision than in the pages of the literary magazines and miscellaneous protest papers which appeared over the years.

The first such vehicle of student — and faculty — opinion was the *Maga*, published by a six-member board of editors chosen from the Senior and Junior Classes, which made its debut in the autumn of 1908. Artistic, well-planned, and innocent, it survived until 1920, when it was succeeded by the *Hamline Review*. Writing in the first issue of the new magazine, Thomas Beyer urged that the *Review* become "a clearing house of Minnesota views, literary, political, social and religious," thereby suggesting that the *Maga* had opted for too limited a scope. While the essays and poetry published in the *Review* were for the most part mediocre, they were occasionally brilliant and sometimes radical in orientation. Especially did Beyer use the pages of the *Review* to promote the labor-oriented views which dominated his thinking in the postwar era.[35]

The *Review* ceased publication in 1927, and after a two-year hiatus was followed by the *Piper*, which survived until 1964. During its thirty-four year history, the *Piper*, often edited by some of the brightest and most creative students ever to enroll in the University, published hundreds of poems, short stories, essays and critiques, many of exceptional quality. When alumnus and trustee Donald Bridgman established the Bridgman Poetry Contest in memory of his parents, the *Piper* announced that it would annually publish the winning entries. And when benefactor Charles M. Drew endowed comparable essay contests in English and the social sciences, the magazine began to publish those award-winners as well. Following the demise of the *Piper*, two other magazines sought to maintain the literary legacy begun in 1908. The *Mousetrap* retained the *Piper*'s format and survived for four years. *Hamline's Literary*

Magazine, the last of its breed, suffered a worse fate. The sole issue, containing six poems and an essay on Kierkegaard, appeared in the spring of 1969.[36]

In truth, most of the publications which served as alternate channels for the expression of student views had fleeting lifespans. The *Piper Pitchfork* surfaced three times between 1926 and 1928 and was nothing more than a scandal sheet. *Pin Feathers,* published irregularly from 1930 until 1950, appeared under the aegis of the Quill Club and seemed to revolve primarily around the sponsorship of Thomas Beyer. In the spring of 1948, the *Hamline Ratical Magazine,* "dedicated to those hardy rats who stop to think when the piper pipes instead of blindly following," devoted its six left-leaning issues to thoughtful discussions of such topics as the dictatorship of Chiang Kai-shek, the fascism of Generalissimo Francisco Franco, the dangers which inhered when high-ranking military officers occupied political posts, Douglas MacArthur's displays of ineptitude, and threats to democracy implicit in universal military training. The *A-Uricle* managed one issue in the spring of 1962, publishing an interchange between two philosophy professors and a critique of the University's most recent failure to provide funds for the A Cappella Choir. "The [members] would probably have preferred something a little more spectacular for all their hard work and practice," chided the editor, "than steaks in Mankato and a movie in Pipestone." The *Pile,* "written by some REALLY concerned people," and the *Heap,* apparently written by the same crowd, were two among several one-page, one-issue news sheets of no redeeming value whatsoever which cluttered the campus post office during 1967 and 1968. Of somewhat greater impact was the *Somewhat,* pacifist and radical in tone, which was largely a response to the frightening developments in Southeast Asia, to the implications of the Democratic Convention of 1968, and to the presidential election of that year. Editor Geoff Wattles summarized the motivations of his staff. "The real 'negative attitude' on this campus," he observed, referring to an *Oracle* critique of his paper, "is shown by those students who refuse to involve or commit themselves to any principle or belief."[37]

Although it was usually difficult, if not impossible, to measure the impact which written expressions of student opinion had upon the University community, there was no doubt that those publications served both as vehicles of communication and as integral parts of the educational process itself. In the latter regard, therefore, their function was analogous to that of many other extracurricular involvements. For like those varied special interests, they provided undergraduates with opportunities for growth and development beyond the classroom, yet in close association with their peers and instructors. The collegiate model, so thoroughly a product of American higher education, remained alive and well at Hamline.

CHAPTER 12

THE MODERN UNIVERSITY

"GREEN, GREEN, GREEN everywhere! It looked like a 1920 park," recalled former president Richard P. Bailey in the autumn of 1977, reconstructing his initial reaction to the appearance of the Hamline campus ten years earlier. "There was an iron chain running from concrete post to concrete post, all around the campus. The posts were painted green, and the chain was an ugly, black, weathered king of thing. And then there were these somewhat bedraggled green benches! The whole thing looked remarkably like a scene straight out of the 1920s. It was as unattractive as it could be."[1]

Bailey's reaction was understandable. Still present were Goheen Hall, eighty-five years old and condemned more than two decades earlier; Old Main, just two years younger, structurally sound but sadly deteriorated; Science Hall, completed in 1887 and recommended for demolition in 1949; the sixty-year-old Carnegie Library; and the gymnasium, built fifty-eight years earlier and still in daily academic use. In short, every building erected during the administrations of George Henry Bridgman and David Clarke John with the exception of the first University Hall was still in regular service when the University's twelfth president took office in 1968. Together, the buildings' average age was just over seventy-five years.

Although minimal, there had been some recent progress. Like Bailey, Hurst Anderson had also reacted negatively to his first sight of the campus — and that had been in 1948. Accordingly, when he took office Anderson had quickly set out to determine what faculty, students, alumni, and clergy perceived to be the University's greatest physical plant needs. When a survey revealed that consensus fa-

240

vored a new science building, a fine arts facility, a new student union, a dormitory to replace Goheen, and better library facilities, the Executive Committee of the Board agreed to request preparation of a master plan for future expansion. Drafted for the honor was the distinguished Chicago architectural firm of Holabird, Root, and Burgee. In June, 1949, after studying the scene for six months, the architects submitted their report. They urged a four-phase program of construction which would result in the replacement or refurbishing of every building on campus except for the gymnasium and the field house. They recommended demolition of Goheen, Science Hall, and Old Main, all of which, they reiterated, were in an advanced stage of deterioration. They envisioned a new science building, a residence hall for women, an administration building, unified facilities for the humanities and social sciences, a fine arts and auditorium complex, and two fraternity houses. Drew Residence, the union, the library, and the heating plant would receive extensive facelifts and expansion. With the entire academic area except for the fine arts building interconnected, and with indoor access from the academic quarter to the women's residence complex as well, the future campus as portrayed by the architects would be totally adapted to Minnesota's challenging climate. In the interest of unity and beauty, the University would ask the city of St. Paul to vacate Hewitt and Asbury Avenues — a recommendation identical to that made by F. H. Ellerbe in 1922. In place of the familiar, eclectic sampling of Renaissance, Romanesque, and Victorian Gothic styles would rise an architecturally-unified superstructure. The estimated cost, reported Holabird, Root, and Burgee, would be just under $6 million.[2]

Within less than a month, the trustees took the first step toward implementation of the plan by contracting to build a fine arts facility. But it was already clear that they had reservations about the overall plan, for instead of authorizing construction of a new $744,000 structure with an 800-seat auditorium, as the architects had urged, the Board voted instead to attach a modest studio and classroom building of inferior design and quality to the quonset huts dragged into position a year earlier. Still, the $200,000 facility, dedicated November 8, 1950, and named in honor of Charles M.

Drew, was a welcome addition. For it unified the several departments of the Division of Fine Arts under one roof for the first time in
the University's history.[3]

When the trustees agreed in November, 1949, to authorize
Holabird, Root, and Burgee to devise comprehensive plans for a new
science building, it appeared momentarily that they might move to
implement the remainder of the master plan. Located immediately
behind Old Main, where it would form the center of a new academic
complex and be fully visible from the mall following demolition of
its venerable neighbor, the $800,000 structure contained
classrooms, offices, a small auditorium, and laboratories dedicated
to Henry Osborn, Loren Batchelder, and alumnus Robert Page, who
had been instrumental in the development of radar. Built largely
through the generosity of the Eliza A. Drew Memorial Fund, which
provided $500,000 for construction and an additional $85,000 for
equipment, the new structure, dedicated in October, 1952, bore the
name of Hamline's great benefactor, Charles M. Drew. Plans also
materialized for the Bridgman Memorial Court, located at the
southwest corner of the campus, which commemorated in sculpture
by John Rood the University's one-hundred-year history. Thus, by
the end of Anderson's brief administration the University presented
a somewhat more attractive public image. But the architecturally-
unified campus envisioned by Holabird, Root, and Burgee had
faded from mind. Not until 1968 would college officials again devote themselves to comprehensive architectural planning.[4]

If Hurst Anderson had sometimes overemphasized the importance
of physical plant modernization and expansion, Paul Giddens' incli-
nations lay in the opposite direction. Still, none could fault him for
inattention to the superstructure. In 1958, the college dedicated
Sorin Hall, an $800,000 residence for women named in honor of
Hamline's first two graduates and located just west of the Manor
House. In 1963, the campus celebrated completion of the A. G.
Bush Student Center, a $1,300,000 structure connected to the field
house by an Olympic-size swimming pool. Bush, then executive
vice-president and chairman of the Executive Committee of the
Minnesota Mining and Manufacturing Company, was a Hamline
trustee who contributed $800,000 to the cost of the structure. His

generous gift was the first of many that significantly aided completion of several new facilities. In 1958, the Board also authorized a $500,000 addition to Drew Residence and modernization of the library basement.[5]

One month after assuming office, Giddens succeeded in persuading the Board to enlist the services of Marts and Lundy, a New York-based consulting firm which agreed to conduct a fund-raising survey. Concluding that Hamline's upcoming centennial celebration encouraged the launching of a capital campaign, the consultants suggested that $4 to $5 million was both realistic and mandatory. They recommended that the University raise $1 million for scholarship endowment, $2 million for endowed faculty chairs, and $3.5 million in general endowment funds. In addition, they urged that the college spend $100,000 immediately on crucial physical plant repairs and $200,000 on the acquisition of property. Overall, Marts and Lundy estimated, it would be possible for the University completely to renovate and modernize its physical facilities for $4,442,000, and for it to raise its endowment to a respectable level by identifying another $6.5 million.[6]

There were problems, the consultants hastened to add. For one thing, the recent history of Minnesota Methodist Conference contributions to the college was discouraging. For another, parents and alumni were not for the most part individuals ''of substantial means.'' Especially did the University's tendency to send its graduates into low-paying service professions work to its disadvantage. There was no annual alumni fund, and hence no pattern of regular giving. Many alumni lived in rural areas, where experience had shown a lower per capita rate of giving. On the other hand, loyalty to the college was abundant. Thus, there was good reason to believe that over a period of ten years, Hamline's constituency would respond generously. Buoyed by the consultants' estimates, but typically conservative in their response, the trustees shortly thereafter authorized a million-dollar Centennial Campaign. Their caution, although perhaps self-fulfilling, proved prophetic. For only with an eleventh-hour windfall in the form of a $175,000 Ford Foundation faculty salary grant was the University able to announce, in September, 1957, that the campaign had succeeded in its objective. If Hamline's constituents were in fact capable of contributing between four and eleven million dollars, as Marts and Lundy had hoped, the fund raising effort of 1953–57 offered no such proof.[7]

The University also sought to strengthen its financial base during the 1950s and 1960s through participation in the Minnesota Private College Fund, organized in 1950. During its first year of operation, the Fund received twenty-one corporate contributions totaling $53,050. Six years later, contributions had increased to $319,796, with 341 firms participating and with Hamline's share of the pledges $18,925. In 1963 the University received $33,607 and in 1967, $52,231. Aided by the Fund, by the Centennial Campaign, by contributions from Church and alumni, and by other gifts, the book value of the University's endowment rose from $4 million in 1949 to more than $6 million ten years later. In 1967 it stood at just under $9 million with a market value of $12.5 million, and by 1977 was declared to be $15,063,632.[8]

Meanwhile, President Giddens was devising responses to other Marts and Lundy recommendations as well as to his own impressions of Hamline's needs. To improve the University's modest public relations program, he established a News Bureau, announced the inauguration of an annual Parents' Day and a Trustee-Alumni Visitation Day, launched an aggressive program of local and regional publicity, and enthusiastically supported the faculty's decision to participate in Twin Cities educational television programs. In an effort to cultivate greater alumni interest, he reorganized and expanded the Alumni Association, enlarged fourfold the number of regional and local alumni clubs, provided additional staff support, was instrumental in the implementation of an annual Alumni Fund, appointed Professor of Education Kenneth Doane to conduct a survey of Hamline alumni and their achievements, and supervised the revamping of the *Alumni Bulletin*. To assist student recruitment efforts, he employed a staff of admissions counselors to visit high schools and talk with prospective students, compiled extensive mailing lists, established an annual visitation day for high school students, and implemented the Competitive Scholarship Examination to attract superior students to the campus. In 1960, Hamline was one

The Holabird, Root, and Burgee plan for the University (1949).

The University in 1967.

of twelve liberal arts institutions to form the Midwest College Council, which sought to interest students from eastern states in midwestern colleges. And among the special programs created by the faculty was an experiment funded by the Hill Family Foundation and begun in 1960 which enabled talented high school students to enroll in regular University science and mathematics courses.[9]

By the early 1960s, it had become apparent that another capital campaign was imperative. In May, 1961 — without formally authorizing such a venture — the trustees agreed that $4–5 million would satisfy Hamline's most pressing needs. President Giddens explained that long-range needs, including the improvement of faculty salaries, would require another $3.3 million. On a related front, the administration began negotiating informally with the city of St. Paul in the summer of 1961 regarding the possible acquisition of recently-vacated Midway Stadium. But city officials failed to respond positively and college officials increasingly questioned both the aesthetic and practical advisability of developing a campus bisected by railroad tracks. The trustees, in turn, postponed their decision regarding the launching of a capital campaign.[10]

Finally, in 1965, several events transpired which renewed interest in such a campaign. In January, the Board appointed a special committee to study development needs. In March, the University Senate of the Methodist Church presented the results of an institutional survey which called attention to the severely damaging impact of recent and dramatic improvements to the physical plants at Macalester, Carleton, and the University of Minnesota. "Hamline now gives the impression of being on the defensive in the presence of sharp contrasts," observed the report, which went on to urge the planning and construction of a modern, architecturally-unified campus — a theme which had become, over the course of more than forty years, almost embarrassingly redundant. The team was especially emphatic in its plea for a new library. In the same month, the faculty voted to create a Long Range Planning Committee, whose functions would be both philosophical and developmental, and which would be part of a comprehensive University development effort. Meanwhile, the Executive Committee contracted with the John Price Jones Company of New York City for yet another financial survey, and in June the Buildings and Grounds Committee voted to recommend that the Board employ the St. Paul architectural firm of Hammel, Green, and Abrahamson to prepare a campus site plan.[11]

During the trustees' discussion of the latter recommendation, member Warren S. Moore spoke ardently about considering the possibility of moving the University to a new campus — the first recorded reference in the minutes to such an idea. In October, during another discussion regarding relocation, Chairman Walter Ringer urged that the Board reach a speedy decision. The trustees responded by appointing a committee to study, report, and recommend on the advisability of moving "after giving consideration to the cultural, academic and economic aspects" of such a choice. They simultaneously agreed to create another committee whose charge was to locate desirable sites.[12]

In December, the Long Range Planning Committee presented a series of recommendations regarding potential relocation. On the positive side, it began by focusing upon projected cost. "To begin *and* end with immediate finances is to foreclose any serious consideration of the possible merits of alternatives that may be more expensive in the short run but might well be less expensive and more attractive in the long range view," it declared. For patchwork solutions, while momentarily less costly, were frequently both "functionally less efficient and aesthetically less attractive" in the long run. Moreover, if the University did decide to achieve the long-sought, architecturally-commanding campus of twice the present size on the Midway site, it would take years to acquire enough land. There were several good tracts of land nearby, and the momentary inconvenience of moving would be more than outweighed by the advantages.[13]

On the negative side, the committee underscored the fact that it would cost approximately $22 million to develop the Midway site and about $33 million to move. "The difference seems significant," it concluded. "While funds may be raised more easily if Hamline should move to a new site, there seems to be no assurance that this factor could account for 10 million more dollars." Since Hamline obviously needed to make rapid and vigorous strides, cost was crucial. The report went on to advise that if relocation would not significantly improve the academic program, there was little justification for considering it. In the future, it argued confidently, academically-oriented students would look for a strong academic program rather than a spacious campus with new buildings. Accordingly, the University could improve its competitive position in the long run only by improving its academic program and its public image. Finally, the report contended, an expanded and attractive campus would have a distinctly positive impact upon the aging neighborhood which adjoined the campus.[14]

It was clear from the committee's report that while the members recognized compelling reasons for pulling up stakes, sentiment both implicitly and explicitly favored remaining. When the trustees' Committee on Expansion recommended unanimously on January 7, 1966, that Hamline not relocate, that it resume purchase of adjacent property, that it expand its facilities, and that it initiate a vigorous development program, many of its arguments reiterated those of the faculty group. Four ingredients comprised the committee's recommendation to the full Board. First, electing to move would mean an immediate expenditure of more than $20 million. There was no indication that a large initial gift was in sight, and so it was unrealistic to think in such grandiose terms. Second, the $20 million would almost certainly come out of the University's academic hide. Third, benefactors A. G. Bush and Mrs. Charles M. Drew opposed relocation. Finally, the present campus possessed the capacity "of being expanded and being made much more attractive." Adjoining real estate costs were high, but not prohibitive. And there was the likelihood of a positive psychological stimulus upon the neighborhood. Following general discussion, the trustees adopted the committee's recommendations, thereby deciding for the second time in forty-five years not to relocate on a more aesthetically pleasing site.[15] But unlike the unfortunate 1921 decision, made when removal would clearly have enhanced the University's attractiveness and rid it of future dilemmas, the 1966 decision was both defensible and sound. Admittedly, it was a decision fully in keeping with the conservative and somewhat unimaginative stewardship which the Board had exercised across the years. Still, taking into account the University's past experience with fundraising, it was a decision that would have been hard to fault.

Four months after the trustees registered their opinion concerning removal, the John Price Jones Company submitted its judgment regarding a capital campaign. At the heart of the University's dilemma, observed the consultants, lay the critical matter of public image. Nothing could better excite the enthusiasm and imagination of prospective donors, they argued, than to agree that a new library was of central importance to the institution's future. For a commitment to build a superb new structure to replace the lovely but hopelessly inadequate Carnegie Library would "be a striking outward symbol of Hamline's dedication to the best in higher education, to the centrality of the library in the learning process, and to Hamline's ability and will, not only to keep abreast, but to lead."[16]

The consultants viewed with apprehension the fact that President Giddens' anticipated retirement in 1968 coincided with the opening phase of the development program. "It is in fact the very prospect Dr. Giddens himself faced upon beginning his presidency," they reminded the Board, "and may well be the explanation for the essentially unsuccessful result of the Centennial Campaign, which was saved on paper only by the fortuitous timing of the unrelated Ford grant of 1956–1957." To alleviate the problem, they urged the trustees to consider hiring Giddens' successor well in advance of the date that he would actually take office, thereby availing him of the opportunity to become familiar with the University and the forthcoming campaign. They also commented upon the potential role of the Church, whose problems with the University could hardly be ignored, but which were "chronic rather than acute" and not unique to Hamline. While it was pointless to deny "the fact that in important Methodist quarters" there was "indifference" to the college, the attitude of the Church as a whole was distinctly favorable.[17]

The report then moved to the heart of the matter. Before formally announcing the $8–11 million campaign goal, it was vital for the University to identify "perhaps fifteen or more" gifts of no less than $100,000 each. Even more important, it would be necessary to identify one major gift of perhaps $2 million, for such a gift would hold the key to the entire campaign. "Otherwise," the consultants stressed, "we think the goal would have to be sharply curtailed, perhaps to $5,000,000 or less, to avoid a damaging failure."[18]

In light of the $22 million projected earlier by the faculty Long Range Planning Committee, the John Price Jones report must have appeared discouraging. But all was not lost, for University officials had good reason to believe that they had already located the major gift mentioned by the consultants. For shortly before his death on January 16, 1966, trustee and benefactor A. G. Bush had left written instructions that Hamline receive from his estate $1 million each year for ten years. It seemed that such a gift would launch the campaign handsomely. The President and the trustees could not have known, in the spring of 1966, that an impending legal battle over the disposition of Bush's $145,000,000 estate would soon place the University's anticipated gift in jeopardy. Spurred by confidence that the $10 million pledge would soon become a reality, the faculty and administration began to develop comprehensive plans for campus modernization and expansion. By early 1967, they had agreed that the most pressing needs were a library, a learning center complex, a dormitory cluster, a central dining facility, and a women's physical education building. And they had determined, in line with the John Price Jones report, that the library should be not merely the intellectual center of the campus but its architectural and visual heart as well.[19]

At the time of his election to the Hamline presidency, Richard P. Bailey was president of Northland College, Ashland, Wisconsin, where he had successfully guided a major campus expansion program. Bailey was a native of Stockton, Illinois and a graduate of North Central College. He had received his M.A. and Ph.D. from the University of Wisconsin, and except for a brief stint on the faculty of Oshkosh State College, where he had taught English and journalism, had spent his entire professional career in academic administration. Between 1953 and 1958 he had conducted research for the Wisconsin State College system, and from 1958 until his move to Ashland in 1962 had been president of Yakima Valley Junior College in the state of Washington.[20]

Unfamiliar with Minnesota and initially persuaded that his future in academic administration lay not in another private institution but within a state university system, Bailey at first hesitated when approached by a representative of Hamline's Presidential Search Committee in the summer of 1967. Nor did his initial impression of the campus itself appreciably alter his frame of mind. But other factors did. Although it had become clear by that point that the newly-created Bush Foundation was showing signs of reluctance to discharge Bush's $10 million, 10-year pledge, trustees with whom Bailey visited assured him that Hamline had every reason to expect the money eventually. The faculty, in Bailey's view "solid, academically strong, and looking for leadership," were anxious for a president who would assume an aggressive posture. Nor was the University's $12 million endowment to be regarded lightly. All in all, it was an inviting picture, and the prospects for success in those halcyon days before the tragedy and sorrow of Memphis, Los Angeles, Chicago, and Kent State seemed encouraging. Despite all the green paint and down-at-the-heels appearance, Hamline looked to Bailey like an exciting institution where stimulating growth could occur. And the prospective chief executive knew that his background in journalism could aid him enormously in publicizing the cause. Accordingly, he consented to accept the Board's invitation to become Hamline's twelfth president, and on August 10, 1967, the trustees elected him.[21]

On December 12, 1968, five months after Bailey assumed office, the University announced a ten-year, $26,550,000 development program. Approximately half of that sum would become part of the permanent endowment and half would be directed toward the physical plant. During the campaign's initial three-year phase, the University would seek $13,475,000 to meet the most pressing needs, including $6 million for the endowment. There were eight specific objectives: $1.5 million for land acquisition (the University had already spent $650,000 since 1953 for 52 parcels), $3.6 million for seven dormitories, $2,772,000 for a library, $2.8 million for two learning centers whose architecture would stress independent study, $1.5 million for a University commons, $650,000 for a women's physical education addition to the field house, $600,000 for an addition to the heating plant, and additional money for modernization and renovation. Of the $13 million allocated to endowment, faculty salaries would claim $6 million and student scholarships $4 million. Two days before issuing a formal announcement, the trustees launched the development effort by accepting bids totaling $2,025,000 for the first three housing units. Then, almost sixty years after Thomas Beyer had guided the plow in groundbreaking ceremonies for the gymnasium, three hundred students and faculty broke ground for the new facilities in identical fashion on January 7, 1969. Students occupied the first unit, named in honor of trustee Paul Schilling, in September of that year. By January, 1970, the second unit, honoring trustee Edward B. Osborn, and the third yet-unnamed dormitory were also in operation. Financed largely by a $1,665,000 loan from the United States Office of Education, the new facilities occupied the southeast corner of the campus, immediately adjacent to the Manor House.[22]

Next on the agenda was the library. After an extensive planning period involving all sectors of the campus community, the Board approved bids which totalled $2,605,880 on May 4, 1970. On May 8, the tone of the gathering subdued by the tragic killing of four students at Kent State University four days earlier, the University held groundbreaking ceremonies. With a capacity of 240,000 volumes and designed to accommodate a fourth floor when necessary, the 83,210-square-foot structure, named in memory of A. G. Bush, was a splendid facility which emphasized curricular flexibility, independent study, and the University's commitment to internationalism. Constructed with the aid of an $890,000 grant from the United States Office of Education, a $517,000 gift from Mrs Edyth Bush, and a $600,000 gift from the A. G. Bush Foundation, the building was dedicated on October 9, 1971. The emphasis upon internationalism received notice in 1975, when Professor S. M. Burke of the University of Minnesota presented his collection of South Asian materials to the University. The $150,000 collection was, in the words of International Studies Center Director W. A. St. John, "the most comprehensive and systematic arrangement of material on South Asia anywhere in the world."[23]

Meanwhile, plans for the learning center, now reduced to a single structure, proceded apace. Campus architects Hammel, Green, and Abrahamson began to design the unit in May, 1969, and in August of that year the University submitted to the Department of Health, Education, and Welfare an application for a $1 million grant and a $587,000 loan. It also established an alumni challenge fund which eventually raised $500,000. The government's disappointing $235,000 grant was partially offset by an award of $1,208,000 from the Bush Foundation, a gift of $50,000 from the Kresge Foundation and $80,000 in other contributions. But the cumulative deficit on the complex finally reached $1 million. Groundbreaking took place on May 22, 1971, and dedication of the structure, which was linked architecturally to the Carnegie Library, occurred on October 19, 1972. The new facility housed the Divisions of Social Science and Humanities and the Department of Education, and contained classrooms, study areas, laboratories, and a large central lounge.[24]

In view of inflation and skyrocketing costs for education, severe cutbacks in government spending on higher education, reductions in tax benefits to donors, the general slowdown in the economy, and a gradual concomitant decrease in enrollment — all of which had an impact upon the University from the end of the 1960s onward — Hamline was fortunate to have completed the most vital segments of its building program. But at the same time, the steady rise in the operating budget during Bailey's presidency, which reflected both general economic trends and the increased cost of maintaining an enlarged plant, placed ever-greater financial pressures upon the institution. Between 1948 and 1968, the budget rose from $810,000 to $3,545,904, for an average annual increase of just under $137,000. By contrast, in the five succeeding years, during which time all of the major development projects were begun and completed, it increased another $2 million, and by the autumn of 1976 had risen to $7.5 million — more than twice the 1968 figure and an average increase annually since that time of just under $500,000. The fact that Hamline was not alone in experiencing such a financial crunch made its circumstance no less difficult.[25]

Signs of difficulty appeared during Bailey's first year in office. After operating on a balanced budget every year since 1946, the college ran a minimal $12,300 deficit in 1968–69 and a more worrisome $140,000 during 1969–70. By 1971, total indebtedness had risen to more than $207,000. The operating budget ran $266,000 in the red during 1973–74 and $273,000 during 1974–75. Thereafter, the Board determined to hold the line on deficit spending, and in September, 1976, Bailey's successor, Jerry E. Hudson, was able to announce that while the cumulative operating deficit stood at $748,000, the 1975–76 academic year showed indebtedness of only $4,217, compared with $44,694 actually budgeted. While tuition income had actually been less than anticipated, he told the faculty, the return on the endowment along with gifts and income from auxiliary enterprises had been better than expected, and had more than made up the difference.[26]

Although the years from 1968 onward were characterized by consistent budgetary imbalance, Bailey and the trustees had hardly been oblivious to the implications of deficit spending. As early as February, 1971, the President had informed the faculty that in an effort to eliminate red ink, there would be no salary increases for faculty or staff the following year. Business Manager Harold Neece tried to soften the blow by indicating that the measure was less drastic than those imposed by officials at many other institutions. But faculty concern over future ramifications of the Board's decision was substantial enough to cause adoption of a resolution requesting that in subsequent years, no decisions "on a freeze of faculty positions" or on priorities to be assigned vacancies be made without first consulting with the faculty Institutional Relations and Budget Committee. Then, in the autumn of 1974, with enrollment down approximately 5 per cent, President Bailey announced a more thoroughgoing effort to balance the books. He called for a three-year retrenchment program, including the termination of several staff positions, a reduction in faculty and administrative staff travel, and accompanying increases in room, board, and tuition. In the spring of 1975, he went still further, proposing to eliminate the equivalent of fifteen faculty positions, which represented 17 per cent of the full-time faculty. In response, the faculty immediately voted to support a student-initiated moratorium on classes. With Bailey about to leave office — he had submitted his resignation to the trustees in January — the faculty also moved to recommend that the Board suspend any final decision regarding retrenchment until the new president had had adequate opportunity to survey the picture.

Ultimately the Board reduced the overall number of faculty to be released to nine. But it also voted to postpone salary increases for another year, and in an additional critical decision announced "that tenure decisions relative to faculty members shall be deferred, extending the probationary status of faculty members affected an additional year."[27]

The Board's mandate concerning tenure struck a particularly sensitive faculty nerve. Since 1950, when the trustees endorsed the first tenure policy in Hamline's history, the institution had followed procedures which accorded roughly with the American Association of University Professors' 1940 *Statement of Principles on Academic Freedom and Tenure*. This was a statement which by 1975 had received the formal endorsement of 97 professional organizations. Relying extensively upon that document for guidance, the 1950 Hamline policy specified that the University would state all terms and conditions of a faculty member's appointment in writing, that tenure was automatic for professors and associate professors after three years of service unless duly notified, and that when advantageous to the University full professors might receive tenure after one year of service. It further stated that a faculty member would not normally achieve tenure without serving at least one year at a rank above that of assistant professor, although by special action of the Board, instructors and assistant professors who had taught at the University for a minimum of five years might also achieve tenure. Except for reasons of financial exigency, the University was obliged to show adequate cause when terminating the services of a tenured member of the faculty.[28]

The 1950 policy was certainly a far cry from the authoritarian 1931 by-laws provision which announced that "any member of the faculty may be removed at any time." But it differed from the 1940 AAUP *Statement* in specifying that under ordinary circumstances, only associate professors and full professors could receive tenure. For the AAUP guidelines stipulated that in no case should the probationary period exceed seven years, and that tenure was a right which every college and university faculty member with full-time status might reasonably expect to obtain. This important variance received critical notice by the 1965 Methodist survey team. "There is more

than a little concern about the current tenure system at Hamline,''
the visitors observed, ''particularly since it involves many instructors and assistant professors.'' The resignation of theatre director
James Carlson in 1964 after seventeen years without tenure, they
pointed out, raised serious questions in many individuals' minds.
Shortly after Richard Bailey took office, the college finally brought
its tenure rules more nearly into accord with the 1940 *Statement* by
including assistant professors within the stipulated seven-year probationary period.[29]

Given the University's relatively recent willingness to strengthen
its tenure policy, the faculty's vehement response to the 1975 retrenchment announcement and to the Board's extension of the probationary period was understandable. Within faculty ranks, collective bargaining immediately appeared as a potential alternative — a
prospect met with alarm by the Board and with uncharacteristic
anger by President Bailey. But after a brief period of intense interest
in such a move, the faculty voted against it. And, in an effort to
rectify what they soon agreed was an action ''contrary to a technical
interpretation of the existing tenure policy,'' the trustees in 1976
granted tenure retroactively to four members of the faculty affected
by the 1975 resolution. But they also resolved ''that because of the
need to retain flexibility in faculty size and distribution among
academic fields in times of uncertainty in enrollment,'' modifications in the existing tenure policy were essential. ''The value of
tenure as a means of preserving academic freedom and recognizing
the contributions which individual faculty make to the University,''
they declared, ''should continue to be recognized in a system of
tenure which also protects institutional flexibility.'' Accordingly,
they soon decided to adopt a quota system designed to insure that no
more than two-thirds of the full-time faculty eligible for tenure at
any given time should actually be tenured. The faculty ''received''
the new policy in April, 1976, and the Board formally implemented
it the following month.[30] Thus, in an era of continuing economic
uncertainty, declining student enrollments, and highly constricted
opportunity for movement from one job to another, the Hamline
faculty could only ponder the implications of the new policy upon
their individual circumstances. Again, the fact that faculties across

the land were experiencing similar dilemmas made the Hamline situation no less problematic.

Yet another ingredient which signalled the University's attempts to balance its operating budget was the sale of virtually all city real estate during the early 1970s. By 1970, the Board had placed all college-owned houses which lay outside the newly-defined campus expansion area on the market, and within short order had sold them. Several major pieces of property likewise changed ownership. In May, 1970, after months of negotiation, it sold for $747,000 the Grand Avenue apartments orginally acquired in 1926 and 1927. In March, 1971, it closed the sale of the property at Fourth and St. Peter Streets in downtown St. Paul which it had owned since 1923. And on June 13, 1973, it agreed to transfer to the Minnesota Orchestral Association, for $500,000, the leased fee rights to the Sheridan Hotel property on Marquette Avenue between Eleventh and Twelfth Streets in Minneapolis. The property, sold to the University by J. F. Chaffee in 1898, became part of the site upon which the Association erected the magnificent Orchestra Hall, which opened to widespread acclaim in the autumn of 1974.[31]

Joining the transformation of the physical plant and the struggle to maintain a balanced budget as evidences of the University's passage into the modern era was the effort, begun in the late 1940s, to make the Board of Trustees a more significant and useful body. In the course of this effort, Hamline found itself drawn once more into a prolonged controversy with the Minnesota Annual Conference over the proper role of a church-related college.

Since 1871, trustee membership had numbered twenty-one, including four individuals chosen by the Conference. In addition, the Conference annually elected seven conference visitors who held *ex officio* powers. While the Board had been, in President Bridgman's day, a powerful and prestigious body with important civic and business connections, changes both within the University and society at large had gradually diminished its native ability and its capacity to stimulate external interest in the University. President Pace had spoken indirectly to the issue as early as 1935 when suggesting discretely to the trustees that they intensify their efforts to raise money for the hard-pressed institution, and he had reiterated his concerns over the years. But Hurst Anderson was the first to approach the problem head-on. "We need to think of the financial needs of the institution," he declared in March, 1949, shortly after the death of Board member Charles Orr. "We need men who have financial resources or who command financial resources. We need men who have sound business judgment and who are prepared for educational leadership. A college," he submitted, "ultimately reflects the character of its leadership." Part of that character obviously inhered in the Board. But like other executives who found themselves upon occasion forced to deal with impediments not by eliminating but by circumventing them, Anderson eventually decided that the easiest means of dealing with the situation at Hamline was to create a new adjunct body. Designated the "Hamline University Associates," and modeled after a comparable entity at Northwestern University, the group was to consist of individuals drawn from business, industry, civic life, and the professions who agreed to accept responsibility for promoting the University's interests. Assured that the new agency would have no legal responsibility, the trustees acceded to Anderson's wishes. Among the charter members, whose names appeared for the first time in the 1951 catalog, were such individuals as WCCO radio commentator and Minneapolis *Star* columnist Cedric Adams, General Mills president Harry A. Bullis, Mrs. Charles M. Drew, alumnus and Guggenheim Memorial Foundation secretary general Henry Allen Moe, fellow alumnus and St. Paul *Pioneer Press-Dispatch* associate editor Alfred D. Stedman, and Northwest Airlines vice-president E. Irving Whyatt.[32]

Paul Giddens, like his predecessor, believed that appointing trustees was an extremely important responsibility. He also felt, as had Anderson, that Hamline's board was too small to perform its job effectively, as proven by the fact that it was sometimes difficult to muster a quorum. Occasionally, during his first ten years in office, he managed to make what he considered to be an appropriately influential appointment. In 1954, for example, he nominated University Associate Dorothy Bridgman Rood, who became the first woman ever to serve on the Board, and in 1956 Associate Harry A. Bullis joined the ranks. Theodore C. Blegen, dean of the Graduate

School at the University of Minnesota and a former Hamline faculty member, became a trustee in 1956. The following year, Walter M. Ringer, Sr., chairman of the board of the Foley Manufacturing Company of Minneapolis, and A. G. Bush joined the Board, and in 1959, Giddens secured the appointment of another Associate, Rollin O. Bishop, who was president of the American National Bank of St. Paul. But Giddens remained frustrated at his inability under the limitations of the charter to make more than an occasional appointment. And the requirement that a minimum of four trustees be Methodist clergymen made it even more difficult to find places on the Board for individuals whose business and civic connections could be financially useful.[33]

Ultimately, the President decided that the only promising course of action was to request that the Conference authorize an increase in the size of the Board by amending the charter, and in 1963 he presented such a plan to the trustees. Broadening the base of membership was the trend among private colleges, he explained, noting that Hamline's board was small in comparison with that of Carleton, which had 32, Macalester, which had 37, and Lawrence and Cornell, each of which had 36. He then asked the trustees to approve and send to the June, 1963, session of the Conference a charter amendment which called for expansion to 32 members by 1966. The terms concerning Conference membership and conference visitors would remain unaltered. The Board adopted Giddens' recommendations, and agreed that Chairman Frank Hodgson would present the plan to the Conference.[34]

By the time the session convened, however, opposition to the proposal had crystallized. Wrongly interpreted both by certain Conference members and by the Twin City press as an attempt by Giddens to reduce and perhaps eliminate the historic relationship between University and Church, the plan encountered its most concerted resistance in the annual report of the district superintendents. The seven administrators opened their criticism by declaring that the Conference's obligation to the University was more than legal and financial, but that in monetary terms alone its annual appropriation to the college approximated the return on a $2.5 million endowment. They went on to argue that "certain tax advantages" which accrued to the University because of its church relationship must be protected, and that Hamline had a particular obligation to "recruit and train students going into church-related vocations." They next moved to what they saw as the heart of the matter. "We shall oppose efforts to take Hamline away from the church," they wrote, "and we shall encourage moves to increase Hamline's service to the church." Without debate, the Conference assigned the proposal to a study committee consisting of the bishop, two trustees, two members of the Conference and two members of the Methodist Board of Education, with instructions to return a report the following year. It also made its displeasure with Giddens clear by refusing to re-elect him to the Board.[35]

Infuriated by the action of the Conference, the President considered submitting his resignation. When several trustees, among them Blegen and Bullis, indicated that they too would resign if he did so, Giddens changed his mind, feeling that in the interest of securing a satisfactory charter compromise and warding off potentially negative publicity, it would be better to remain. But he spared no words in responding to the report of the district superintendents. For they had chosen, he later wrote, to place the worst possible construction on a perfectly straightforward effort to enhance the power and authority of the Board, and thus the best interests of both University and Church. Especially unfortunate, he observed, was the fact that they had "questioned the integrity and motives of the trustees, who had never discussed, advocated, or proposed changing or lessening the relationship between Hamline and the Methodist Church. They were simply interested," he explained, "in enlarging and strengthening the membership of the Board in order to help the college accomplish its objectives." And he sought to remove the edge from the more paranoid complaints by publishing in the *Bulletin* an article which placed in perspective the relationship between Church and college. Entitled "Hamline University — A Methodist Source of Religious Leadership," the article listed the University's most significant contributions to the church, including the fact that 89 per cent of all alumni were members of some church, that 453 were currently on church school staffs, that eleven had become presidents of Methodist colleges and universities, that nearly one-third of all ministers admitted to full membership in the Minnesota Annual Conference since 1897 were Hamline alumni — including Bishop T. Otto Nall, that more than 100 graduates were ministers elsewhere, and that approximately 40 undergraduates were presently preparing for careers in the church.[36]

When the Conference convened in June, 1964, the special committee appointed the previous year presented a compromise plan. Under its terms, membership would increase to 32 as originally suggested, but bishop and president would become *ex officio* members and the conference visitors would become trustees. After brief discussion the Conference approved the plan. And when it agreed in 1974 to enlarge the Board to 40 members, it further enhanced the University's potential for growth by means of trustee participation. Among the early additions to the enlarged body were such prominent individuals as Minnesota Supreme Court associate justice James C. Otis; future United States Supreme Court associate justice Harry A. Blackmun; President Edwin W. Rawlings of General Mills, who was an alumnus and former Hamline Associate; Dean Robert B. Howard of the University of Minnesota School of Medicine; and Paul Schilling, chairman of the board of Waldorf Paper Products Company.[37]

Giddens' battle to secure charter revision was not simply the culmination of an unease which had characterized almost from the outset his administration's relationship with the Methodist Church in Minnesota. Rather, it was merely an additional symptom of the same conflict between mind and spirit, the same inability to reconcile Renaissance and Reformation motif, the same reluctance to endorse high academic standards in the name of service to Church, which had plagued every chief executive from George Henry Bridgman onward. Never far from view, it was a conflict which surfaced with particular frequency and clarity during Giddens' administration. So it was that in 1962 the conference visitors submitted an uncharacteristically blunt report. "Hamline has many outreaches and constituencies," the ministers observed, "but it must not lose sight of its primary constituency. We feel that it must be scholastically possible for all qualified Methodist young people to attend Hamline," they wrote tautologically. It must, they felt, be economically possible as well. While there existed many laudable secondary goals — "achieving a place in the very highest scholastic ranks of American colleges," for example, "or such as finding students who can afford to attend such a college" — those commendable objectives must never obscure the primary goals.[38]

If the 1962 report caused college officials only minor irritation, the document submitted in 1963 — to the Conference session, that is, which received Giddens' charter revision proposal — must have chafed annoyingly. In it, the clergymen chastised the Board for failing to accept an earlier suggestion that the University Senate of the Church conduct a study of the college. They expressed concern over the deletion of the philosophy requirement from the prescribed core curriculum when the faculty implemented the 3-3 system. They urged that the administration inaugurate "an annual pre-registration faculty retreat at which time major attention would be given to the implications of Hamline's role as a church related college." They suggested that the University chaplain involve himself more actively in the work of the Methodist Student Movement and as a liaison with the Church. They proposed that $10,000 of the annual Conference allocation to the University become part of a scholarship fund for pre-seminary and Christian education students. And they recommended the establishment of annual lectures on the Bible.[39]

Still smarting from his June rebuke, Giddens responded immediately, extensively, and with only thinly-veiled contempt. In a September communique addressed to the trustees, he met the first objection by pointing out that the Board had voted neither for nor against a Senate survey, but rather for continued study of all possible options. He explained curtly that no curriculum was perfect, but was rather a series of compromises, and that when the Board had discussed the philosophy requirement, not one of the ministerial members present had raised so much as a single objection. He challenged the implication that Hamline had never held a fall retreat by reminding the visitors that it had regularly done so, most recently to meet with a Danforth Foundation representative in order to discuss the relationship between Church and college! He argued that "representing Hamline in the Methodist churches" was neither the chief responsibility of the chaplain nor of any one faculty member, but was instead an obligation willingly assumed by the entire staff and administration of the college. He questioned the equity and propriety of creating a special fund for pre-seminarians, indicating that it ran counter to college policy, which specified that economic need must determine the amount of aid granted. And he reminded his audience that instruction in Bible and theology was an ongoing part of the college curriculum.[40]

The President was especially perturbed by the administrative implications of the visitors' report, which appeared without prior notice and which the Conference proceeded unquestioningly to adopt. "The conference visitors have a responsibility to report to the Conference," Giddens acknowledged, "but when recommendations or suggestions are made as to what the college should do, an extremely difficult situation is created. The recommendations are made without prior consultation, discussion, action, or knowledge of the Board of Trustees. In effect," he quite accurately maintained, "the conference visitors are going direct to the Conference over the head of the Board of Trustees and asking for legislation on these matters. In this instance, at least one member of the faculty was consulted regarding the recommendations even though the President of the University was not." Giddens wondered openly whether this meant that the visitors' recommendations and the Conference's subsequent acquiescence superseded the Board's legal authority. And he asked the trustees to consider and clarify immediately the serious administrative dilemma which the report had posed. "All of this could be avoided," he maintained, "if the conference visitors as members of the Board of Trustees presented whatever recommendations they wished to the meetings of the Board [for its] consideration, abided by whatever decision was made, and did not make an issue of them in a report to the Conference."[41] There was little doubt that the 1963 report and Giddens' irritation over what he considered to be its temerity and presumptuousness influenced the special study committee to alter the visitors' legal relationship to the institution by making them regular trustees. In so doing, the committee reinforced the administrative chain of command, a move which not only pleased Giddens but was the University's only defensible choice.

The warfare which broke out by the early 1960s unfortunately tended to obscure the fact that Church giving had increased dramatically since 1953. In that year, the Conference had contributed $27,000 to a budget of just under $1 million. Between 1953 and 1959, the budget rose by slightly more than 50 per cent to $1,527,317. Meanwhile, Conference giving increased by 271 per cent to $100,310. Thus the Church, which had contributed 2.7 per cent of the 1953 figure, had increased its giving to 6.5 per cent of the 1959 figure, a circumstance which owed in no small measure to Giddens' personal efforts, and to the respect and support which he received from many of the clergy. To be sure, the Church's contribution, both in relative and absolute terms, declined after that point, as inflation and rapidly escalating operating costs brought new economic pressures to bear. And President Bailey found himself increasingly at odds with Bishop Paul Washburn, who succeeded T. Otto Nall in 1968. But the low point in Church-University relations had obviously passed.[42]

Reflecting upon the budgetary pressures which had confronted President Giddens, and upon the increasingly problematic economic conditions which plagued educators by the early 1970s, Bailey remained optimistic. "It is during lean years that strength develops," he observed in 1972. "The educational institution which finds its way through the '70s with wisdom and grace can emerge in the '80s healthy, strong, and better fitted to serve the needs of students because of the experience." Bailey saw curricular re-evaluation, cooperative educational programs, faculty involvement in budgetary planning, and intensification of creative thought as beneficial both to Hamline and to higher education in general. "When everything is possible, standards of selection are useless," he reminded his associates; "but when only the necessary is possible some hard decisions must be made with a resulting emphasis on goals and standards." Hamline, the President believed, had risen proudly to the occasion. When, he inquired rhetorically, had the college "developed and built more facilities, enrolled more students, supported a larger operating budget, attracted more faculty doctorates, been involved in more foundation-funded innovative programs, gained greater alumni support, boasted of a more illustrious board of trustees, served a larger number of minority students, had greater student participation, watched a thousand people pass daily through its library doors, [and] presented a brighter public image'' than in the present moment, when ''the lean years'' challenged educational institutions everywhere.[43]

As Hamline University approached its 125th anniversary the challenge articulated by Bailey remained uncomfortably real. But the optimism which he voiced, while increasingly tempered by external economic dictates, also remained alive. It was clear that the confident spirit which had motivated Hamline's founders and which had served to aid the University in times of crisis was not lost, and that the college would in all probability confront the future with equanimity.

NOTES

ABBREVIATIONS

The following abbreviations are used in the notes:

AB   Alumni Bulletin
AM   Alumni Monthly
AQ   Alumni Quarterly
FM   Faculty Minutes, MS, Office of the Registrar, Old Main
HUA   Hamline University Archives, Bush Memorial Library
HUB   Hamline University Bulletin
HUC   Catalog of Hamline University
MAPC   Minutes of the Academic Policies Committee, MS, Office of the Registrar, Old Main
MBT   Minutes of the Board of Trustees, MS, Office of the Business Manager, Old Main
MEPC   Minutes of the Educational Policies Committee, MS, Office of the Registrar, Old Main
MFC   Minutes of the Faculty Council, MS, Office of the Registrar, Old Main
MHSA   Minnesota Historical Society Archives, Manuscripts Research Center
MHSN   Minnesota Historical Society Newspaper Department, Historical Building
MMC   Minutes of the Minnesota Annual Conference of the Methodist Church

CHAPTER 1

1. William Warren Sweet, *Religion on the American Frontier, 1783–1840,* IV (Chicago, 1946), 42–44, 52, 64; Sylvanus M. Duvall, *The Methodist Episcopal Church and Education up to 1869* (New York, 1928), 37–39. Two general accounts which discuss the frontier after 1815 are George Dangerfield, *The Awakening of American Nationalism, 1815–28* (New York, 1965), and Francis Philbrick, *The Rise of the West, 1754–1830* (New York, 1965).

2. Duvall, 12; Sidney E. Ahlstrom, *A Religious History of the American People* (New Haven, 1972), 431–432, 436–438; Grace Lee Nute, manuscript history of Hamline University, 1–3, HUA. The original copy of the Nute manuscript is part of the Nute papers, on file in the Northeast Minnesota Historical Center of the University of Minnesota-Duluth Library.

3. Umphrey Lee and William Warren Sweet, *A Short History of Methodism* (New York, 1956), 92; Duvall, 8, 10, 12; Donald G. Tewkesbury, *The Founding of American Colleges and Universities Before the Civil War, with Particular Reference to the Religious Influences Bearing upon the College Movement* (New York, 1932), 103; William Warren Sweet, *Methodism in American History* (New York, 1933), 177.

4. Lee and Sweet, 94; Tewkesbury, 103–111; Sweet, *Methodism*, 177; Winthrop S. Hudson, *Religion in America* (New York, 1965), 155.

5. Sweet, *Methodism,* 207. See also T. Otto Nall, *Forever Beginning* (Nashville, 1973), 12–18; Nute Ms., 14–15; Hellen Asher, "A Frontier College of the Middle West: Hamline University, 1854–69," *Minnesota History*, IX (December, 1928), 363; HUC, 1946–47, p. 110.

6. Tewkesbury, 51; Chauncey Hobart, *History of Methodism in Minnesota* (Red Wing, 1887), 284–285; Laws of Minnesota, Ch. 43, 1854; [J. R. Creighton], *Hamline University Annual* (Minneapolis, 1875). Nute, 4ff, provides a detailed account of the efforts begun under Hobart to establish an academy.

7. Laws of Minnesota, Ch. 43, 1854; *HUB,* XLVIII (October, 1953); Nute Ms., 3, 16–17.

8. Alumni Association of Hamline University, *History of the Hamline University of Minnesota When Located at Red Wing, Minnesota from 1854 to 1869* (St. Paul, 1907), 10, hereafter cited as *Red Wing History;* Leonidas L. Hamline to David Brooks, April 10, 1855, Ms. in HUA; Nute Ms., 5, 18; Walter C. Palmer, *Life and Letters of Leonidas L. Hamline, D. D.* (New York, 1877), 436.

9. Nute Ms., 18; *Red Wing History,* 13; Hobart, 286; Nall, 124.

10. *Red Wing History,* 13; MMC, 1857, p. 16, 1860, p. 24; Duvall, 86–89; *Hamline University Annual;* J. F. Chaffee, "Hamline University," Ms. in possession of MHSA.

11. Paul H. Giddens, "Hamline University Students Fight and Die to Save Union," *HUB*, LI (October, 1961), 10–11; Nute Ms., 49–73; MMC, 1866, p. 44.

12. *Red Wing History,* 22–23.

13. MMC, 1868, pp. 42–43.

14. MMC, 1869, pp. 23–25.

15. MBT, July 6, 1869; *Red Wing History,* 24.

16. Ezra Lathrop, "Historical Remarks on Hamline University," Ms. in possession of MHSA; *Red Wing History,* 25; Asher, 77–78.

17. MMC, 1870, p. 17; Clarence W. Rife, notes and manuscript in HUA; Chaffee, "Hamline University;" Special Laws of Minnesota for 1871, Ch. CXII.

18. MMC, 1871, p. 16; Rife Ms.

19. MBT, November 14, 15, 1871; Rife Ms.; Chaffee, "Hamline University."

20. Nute Ms., 98–100; Rife Ms.; Chaffee, "Hamline University;" MMC, 1872, pp. 5, 16, 36; MBT, September 26, 27, October 28, 29, December 10, 11, 1872. Hewitt made the offer jointly with former governor and current trustee William R. Marshall, William Fry, and Horace Thompson. All were St. Paul residents.

21. *Hamline University Annual;* Rife Ms.; MBT, July 8, 1873.

22. MMC, 1874, p. 43; Chaffee, "Hamline University."

23. Rife Ms.; MMC, 1874, pp. 47–49.

24. Theodore C. Blegen, *Minnesota: A History of the State* (Minneapolis, 1963), 294–295; Rife Ms.; MMC, 1877.

25. Rife Ms.; MMC, 1874, pp. 47–50.

26. Nute Ms., 105; Rife Ms.; *Hamline University Annual;* Special Laws of Minnesota for 1876, Ch. CCXXV; MBT, June 27, July 27, 1876.

27. Rife Ms.; *Hamline University Annual;* MBT, March 25, 1873, June 22, 1875; MMC, 1875, p. 31; Chaffee, "Hamline University."

28. Rife Ms.; MBT, June 27, July 27, 1876; MMC, 1876, pp. 5, 10, 28.

29. General Laws of Minnesota for 1877, Ch. 38; Chaffee, "Hamline University;" MMC, 1876, pp. 23, 28; Nute Ms., 110.

30. St. Paul *Daily Globe,* June 26, 1878; MMC, 1878, pp. 27, 31–32; J. Wesley Hill, *Twin City Methodism* (Minneapolis, 1895), 194; Rife Ms.

31. MMC, 1879, pp. 20–21, 28–29; Rife Ms.; MBT, April 6, July 19, 1880; St. Paul *Daily Globe,* July 21, 1880; Minneapolis *Tribune,* July 21, 1880.

CHAPTER 2

1. Leonard J. Dobner to Henry L. Osborn, November 23, 1935; Frank H. Cone to Henry L. Osborn, January 30, 1937; miscellaneous letters from alumni to Osborn during the mid-1930s; Dobner in *AB,* XXX (January, 1934) and in *Oracle,* November 30, 1893; MMC, 1874, p. 48.

2. *Prospectus of Hamline University* (Mankato, 1880, 3, 13.

3. Dobner to Osborn, November 23, 1935; *AB,* XXX (January, 1934); FM, November 30, December 1, 2, 1881; *The Minnesota Methodist and Hamline Review,* I (March, 1883), 3–4; Minneapolis *Tribune,* February 8, 1883; St. Paul *Daily Globe,* February 8, 1883; Chauncey Hobart, *History of Methodism in Minnesota* (Red Wing, 1887), 292.

4. *The Minnesota Methodist and Hamline Review*, I (June, 1882); HUC, 1880–81, p. 15, 1881–82, p. 17; St. Paul *Pioneer Press,* July 27, 1882; St. Paul *Daily Globe,* July 27, 1882; Hobart, 291–293; J. F. Chaffee, "Hamline University," Ms. in possession of MHSA; E. F. Mearkle to J. F. Chaffee, April 2, 1886.

5. *The Minnesota Methodist and Hamline Review,* I (March, 1883), 4; MMC, 1883, pp. 68, 76–77, 1884, p. 33; Hobart, 293–295.

6. Hobart, 295; MMC, 1883, pp. 63, 67; Cyrus D. Foss, "Mrs. Adeline E. John," in MMC, 1885, pp. 57–58; Dobner to Osborn, November 23, 1935; Margaret S. Kerfoot to Osborn, January 14, 1936, E. P. Robertson to Osborn, January 23, 1937, Frank H. Cone to Osborn, January 30, 1937, George S. Innis to Osborn, January 18, 1936, John file, HUA; *AB,* XXX (January, 1934); Dorothy Bridgman Atkinson, "Hamline Grows Strong," in Charles Nelson Pace, ed., *Hamline University* (Minneapolis, 1939), 27.

7. George H. Bridgman, "My Life Story in Brief," Ms. (copy), undated [1919–21], in Grace Lee Nute papers, Northeast Minnesota Historical Center of the University of Minnesota-Duluth Library; Atkinson, "Hamline Grows Strong," 32–33; W. E. Thompson, "An Appreciation of President Bridgman and His Work," *AQ,* VIII (April, 1912), 2–3.

8. Bridgman, "My Life Story;" Atkinson, "Hamline Grows Strong," 25–26.

9. MMC, 1884, p. 33, 1886, p. 72, 1887, p. 84, 1888, p. 81, 1889, p. 51.

10. MMC, 1886, p. 51; HUC, 1886–87, pp. 32, 36–37, 1887–88, pp. 36–37.

11. MBT, August 16, December 16, 1893, June 6, October 19, 1894, June 5, December 4, 1895, February 26, June 3, 1896, May 24, June 9, 1897.

12. MBT, April 18, 1886, April 24, 1888, January 5, 1891, January 20, 1895; HUC, 1888–89, p. 5.

13. J. Wesley Hill, *Twin City Methodism* (Minneapolis, 1895), 305; MBT, December 16, 1895, February 26, April 7, 1896.

14. MBT, February 26, 1896.

15. MBT, February 26, June 3, 1896, December 14, 1897, February 7, March 18, June 8, December 28, 1898.

16. MBT, May 25, June 8, 1898; *Oracle,* January, February, May, June, 1898.

17. MBT, June 7, 1899, June 6, 1900, June 5, 1901, June 4, 1902, June 2, 1903; *Oracle,* January 15, February 1, 1903. By the mid-1930s, all of the endowed chairs had disappeared, undoubtedly casualties of the Depression.

18. MBT, June 4, 1902, January 26, March 6, June 5, October 13, October 16, October 22, 1906; January 10, November 4, 1907; April 6, 1908; *Oracle,* October 1, 1905, October 1, 1906, May 20, October 4, October 18, 1907; *AQ,* II (July, 1905), 19, III (April, 1907), 5, 10, IV (October, 1907), 1.

19. *The General Education Board: An Account of Its Activities, 1902–1914* (New York, 1915), 3; *AQ,* III (October, 1906), 6, V (April, 1909), 2; *Oracle,* February 11, 1909; MBT, February 16, 1909.

20. St. Paul *Dispatch,* February 4, 1909; *General Education Board,* xiv.

21. MBT, January 26, June 5, 1906, March 5, November 4, 1907, November 27, 1908, February 16, April 6, June 8, 1909; *Oracle,* October 8, 1908, April 8, 15, 22, December 9, 1909; *AQ,* V (October, 1908–January, 1909), 15, V (April, 1909), 6, VI (January 1910), 5–6; Arthur S. Williamson, ed., *Alumni Directory Hamline University 1854–1966* (St. Paul, 1966), 22. The trustees had renamed Ladies' Hall "Goheen Hall" on March 3, 1908.

22. Bridgman file, HUA; St. Paul *Pioneer Press,* June 11, 1911; Frank Doran in *North Western Christian Advocate,* June 14, 1911, reprinted in *AQ,* VIII (July, 1911), 2–3; *Oracle,* November, 1888, October 20, 1894, October, 1895, October 15, 1903, March 1, 1906, February 13, 1908.

23. MBT, April 27, May 1, 1908; *AQ,* VII (October, 1910), 2–3; *Oracle,* October 13, 1910.

24. HUC, 1908–09, p. 82, 1909–10, p. 84, 1910–11, p. 84; *Oracle,* October 13, 20, 27, 1910.

25. *Oracle,* October 27, November 3, 1910.

26. Minneapolis *Journal,* October 6, 23, 25, 1910; St. Paul *Dispatch,* October 19, 1910; MBT, November 7, 1910, June 6, 1911.

27. MMC, 1908, p. 49, 1909, pp. 10, 16, 36–37.

28. General Laws of Minnesota for 1877, Ch. 38; MBT, June 5, 1906, June 4, 1907; *Oracle,* May 1, October 1, November 15, 1905, October 8, 1908.

29. MMC, 1910, pp. 11, 35, 39, 64, 1911, pp. 36–37, 43, 1912, *passim*; MBT, June 1, 6, 1911; *Oracle,* June 15, 1911.

30. HUC, 1883–84, pp. 3–4, 1910–11, pp. 5–6. Laws of Minnesota, Ch. 43, 1854; Special Laws of Minnesota for 1871, Ch. CXII; Special Laws of Minnesota for 1876, Ch. CCXXV; General Laws of Minnesota for 1877, Ch. 38.

31. HUC, 1910–11, pp. 5–6. The quotation is from Grace Lee Nute, manuscript history of Hamline University, 197, HUA.

32. Nute Ms., 197.

33. Thomas P. Beyer in *AQ,* VII (October, 1910), 11.

34. MBT, June 1, 6, 1911; St. Paul *Dispatch,* June 7, 1911.

CHAPTER 3

1. Laws of Minnesota, Ch. 43, 1854; *HUB,* XLIII (October, 1953); Louis C. Hatch, *The History of Bowdoin College* (Portland, 1927), 19, quoted in Frederick Rudolph, *The American College and University, A History* (New York, 1962), 58–59.

2. MMC, 1860, p. 24; *HUB,* XLIII (October, 1953); Alumni Association of Hamline University, *History of the Hamline University of Minnesota When Located at Red Wing, Minnesota from 1854 to 1869* (St. Paul, 1907), 40–42, hereafter cited as *Red Wing History*; T. Otto Nall, *Forever Beginning* (Nashville, 1973), 23–24.

3. *First Annual Catalogue of the Preparatory Department of the Hamline University* (Red Wing, 1855). A copy of this catalogue is in the library of the Minnesota Historical Society, Historical Building.

4. *Red Wing History,* 45; Ezra Lathrop, "Historical Remarks on Hamline University," Ms. in possession of MHSA.

5. HUC, 1857–58, 1862–63, 1865–66.

6. *Red Wing History,* 36–65.

7. *Prospectus of Hamline University* (Mankato, 1880), 4–7; Arthur S. Williamson, ed., *Alumni Directory Hamline University 1854–1966* (St. Paul, 1966), 16–18; FM, May 21, 1914. See catalogs of the University, 1910–1915, for lists of degrees granted.

8. HUC, 1880–81, p. 11.

9. FM, October 31, November 7, 14, 21, 28, December 5, 1883, April 20, 1887 March 16, 1888, February 4, 1891; HUC, 1890–91, pp. 14–22; *Oracle*, March, October, 1891; Merle Curti and Vernon Carstensen, *The University of Wisconsin. A History* (Madison, 1949), I, 622. Rudolph, Chapter 14, provides an excellent discussion of the emergence and evolution of the elective principle. See also Charles W. Eliot, "The New Education, Its Organization," *Atlantic Monthly,* XXIII (February, 1869), 203–220, XXIII (March, 1896), 358–367.

10. Henry L. Osborn notes, checked by George H. Bridgman in 1929, Bridgman file, HUA; HUC, 1883–84, p. 5; J. Wesley Hill, *Twin City Methodism* (Minneapolis, 1895), 289–290; Bridgman, "My Life Story in Brief," Ms. (copy), undated [1919–21], in Grace Lee Nute papers, Northeast Minnesota Historical Center of the University of Minnesota-Duluth Library; Dorothy Bridgman Atkinson, "Hamline Grows Strong," in Charles Nelson Pace, ed., *Hamline University* (Minneapolis, 1939), 34.

11. Bridgman, "My Life Story."

12. Bridgman, "My Life Story;" Atkinson, "Hamline Grows Strong," 34;

Hill, 289; Henry L. Osborn, "Our Dean," *AQ*, XV (July, 1918), 19–21; Henry L. Osborn, "Loren Harrison Batchelder: An Appreciation," *AQ*, XIX (Fall, 1922), 4–5; Henry L. Osborn, *Loren Harrison Batchelder: An Appreciation* (St. Paul, 1923), 13–14, 18–19. Faculty minutes reveal Batchelder's scrupulous devotion to the development of academic standards; see, e.g., FM, February 19, March 26, 1902, April 4, 11, May 9, 1912, October 29, 1914.

13. MMC, 1877, pp. 6, 9, 1878, p. 9, 1879, p. 6, 1880, p. 11; Hill, 289; HUC, 1889–90 and 1915–16; *Oracle*, November, 1891; George S. Innis to Osborn, February 3, 1936, in Osborn papers, HUA. I am indebted to Hope Weber of Columbus, Ohio, for verifying Innis' high school record. Following his retirement, Innis moved to Tacoma, Washington, where he remained active in church and civic organizations until his death.

14. *AQ*, XVII (April, 1921), 3–4; *Oracle*, November 30, 1893, October, 1897.

15. Hill, 289–290, 292–293; HUC, 1883–84, p. 33.

16. Hill, 290; letters of Mrs. Osborn in Osborn papers, HUA; Grace Lee Nute, manuscript history of Hamline University, 142, HUA.

17. Henry L. Osborn, "Structure of Clinostomum," *Science*, XIII (1901), 378; "Notes on the Trematodes of Lake Chautauqua, N.Y., " *Science*, XV (1902), 573; "On Phyllodistomum Americanum (N. Sp.)," *Biological Bulletin*, IV (April, 1903), 252–258; "Bunodera Cornuta Sp. Nov.: A New Parasite from the Crayfish and Certain Fishes of Lake Chautauqua, N.Y., " *Biological Bulletin*, V (July, 1903), 63–73; "Cryptogonimus (n.g. chili n. sp.): A Fluke with Two Ventral Suckers," *Zool. Anzeiger*, XXVI (1903), 695–696; "On the Habits and Structure of Cotylaspis Insignis," *Zool. Jhrb. Anat. Bd.*, XXI (1904); "On the Structure of Cryptogonimus," *Journal of Experimental Zoology*, IX (November, 1910), 517–536; "On the Distribution and Mode of Occurrence in the United States and Canada of Clinostomum Marginatum," *Biological Bulletin*, XX (May, 1911), 350–367; *Invertebrate Dissections* (St. Paul, 1895); *Studies in Elementary Biology* (Washington, 1896); *Studies in the Elements of the Anatomy of the Lower Vertebrates* ([St. Paul], 1897); *Guide for the Laboratory Study of the Smelt* ([St. Paul], 1909); "The Mission of the Public Park with Reference to the Preservation of Our Native Animals and Plants," address delivered at St. Croix Falls, Wisconsin, March 25, 1896; *Hamline University in the World War* (St. Paul, 1920); *Alumni Record of Hamline University* (St. Paul, 1924).

18. Bridgman, "My Life Story;" Atkinson, "Hamline Grows Strong," 43; Hill, 292; MBT, June 5, 1889.

19. HUC, 1895–96, 1896–97, 1897–98; FM, April 13, 1898; MBT, March 18, April 25, 1898; *Oracle,* December 20, 1893, February, 1896, May 25, 1901.

20. MBT, June 7, 1899, June 5, 1906; HUC, 1899–1900, 1906–07.

21. FM, *passim*. Quotations on Beyer are from Nute, 199–200. Examples of Beyer's *Dial* contributions are "The Plays of Strindberg," LIV (January 16, 1913), 52–54, and "The Playboy of American Critics," LV (August 1, 1913), 80–82.

22. Thomas P. Beyer, "The Unpragmatic Truth," *Forum*, XLVIII (August, 1912), 129–144.

23. Thomas P. Beyer, "Educing and Traducing," *Forum*, XLIX (June, 1913), 641–657.

24. Thomas P. Beyer, "A Discord in the Sweet Orchestra of Optimism,"

Forum, L (October, 1913), 417–427. See also "The Art of Everlasting Life," *Forum*, LI (April, 1914), 481–497, and a rejoinder by Mowry Saben, "The Problem of Immortality," *loc. cit.*, 684–694.

25. MBT, August 14, 1901; HUC, 1903–04, 1915–16.

26. Morris LeRoy Arnold, *The Soliloquies of Shakespeare. A Study in Technique* (New York, 1911); LeRoy Arnold, *Hurry, Hurry, Hurry* (New York, 1915); *Oracle,* September 24, 1943; Charles Nelson Pace to the Board of Trustees, October 26, 1943. Arnold's lectures and his pilgrimmages to New York City received regular notice in the *Oracle*.

27. Thomas P. Beyer, "George Wilber Hartwell," *HUB,* VII (November, 1917), 7, 9; *AQ,* XV (July 1918), 3.

28. MBT, January 26, March 6, December 3, 1906, June 4, 1907; Erville Bartlett Woods, "Progress as a Sociological Concept," *American Journal of Sociology*, XII (May, 1907), 779–821.

29. Part II of the *Twelfth Biennial Report of the Bureau of Labor Industries and Commerce of the State of Minnesota, 1909–10* (St. Paul, 1910); "Minnesota Leads," *Survey*, XXV (March 25, 1911), 1052–1055.

30. MBT, January 26, March 6, December 3, 1906, June 4, 1907.

CHAPTER 4

1. Committee on Educational Policy of Hamline University, *Hamline Studies* (St. Paul, 1944), 4; Samuel F. Kerfoot to the Board of Trustees, June 11, 1918; Samuel F. Kerfoot, "Seventh Annual Report of the President to the Board of Trustees of Hamline University;" *AQ,* XXI (Summer, 1924), 14; MBT, June 10, 1929; *Oracle*, March 25, 1927; HUC, 1912–13 through 1935–36.

2. Laws of Minnesota, Ch. 43, 1854; Special Laws of Minnesota for 1871, Ch. CXII; General Laws of Minnesota for 1877, Ch. 38; *HUB,* XLIII (October, 1953).

3. MBT, April 26, 1912; HUC, 1883–84; *AQ,* IX (July, 1912), 24; *Samuel Fletcher Kerfoot: In Memorium* ([St. Paul], 1930).

4. Samuel F. Kerfoot, "The Dynamic of the Christian College," *AQ,* X (July, 1913), 3–7.

5. *Ibid.*, 8–9.

6. FM, January 8 through February 23, 1914, March 20, 1919; HUC, 1911–12, pp. 14–19, 1913–14, pp. 16–18, 1918–19, pp. 22–23,1926–27, pp. 25–26; Frederick Rudolph, *The American College and University, A History* (New York, 1962), 304–305.

7. In her manuscript history of the University, Grace Lee Nute presents a detailed discussion of efforts to secure a Phi Beta Kappa chapter. See Nute, 260–263.

8. The General Education Board, Annual Report, 1928–1929, 7; *The General Education Board: An Account of Its Activities, 1902–1914* (New York, 1915), 17, 143, 147, 158. Between 1902 and 1914, Hamline received $50,000 from the Board, Carleton received $100,000, Macalester, $125,000, and St. Thomas, $75,000.

9. "Report of a Survey of Hamline University Under the Auspices of The Commission on Survey of Educational Institutions of the Methodist Episcopal Church, February, 1930," mimeographed volume in HUA, 31; FM, April 29, 1925.

10. HUC, 1911–12 through 1926–27; *Hamline Studies*, 4; MBT, November 12,

1920; "President S. F. Kerfoot's First Annual Report to the Board of Trustees of Hamline University, June, 1913;" "President S. F. Kerfoot's Eighth Annual Report to the Board of Trustees of Hamline University, 1920."

11. HUC, 1912–13 through 1926–27.

12. MBT, April 11, 1916; *Oracle,* April 27, 1916, May 16, 1918, December 17, 1920, April 28, 1922; John D. Hicks, *The Constitution of the Northwest* (Lincoln, 1923); "Six Constitutions of the Far Northwest," *Mississippi Valley Historical Review*, V (May, 1919), supp., 360–379; "The Political Career of Ignatius Donnelly," *Mississippi Valley Historical Review*, VIII (June, 1921), 80–132; "The Origin and Early History of the Farmers' Alliance in Minnesota, *Mississippi Valley Historical Review*, IX (December, 1922), 203–226; "My Six Years at Hamline," *Minnesota History*, XXXIX (Summer, 1965), 213–226; "My Nine Years at the University of Nebraska," *Nebraska History,* XLVI (March, 1965), 1–27.

13. Harold Scott Quigley, "The Immunity of Private Property from Capture at Sea," *American Journal of International Law,* II (January, 1917), 22–45; "Legal Phases of the Shantung Question," *Minnesota Law Review* (April, 1922), 380–394; "The Political System of Imperial China," *American Political Science Review,* XVII (November, 1923), 551–566. A representative selection of Quigley's later publications is on file in the University Archives.

14. Among Blegen's publications during his Hamline career were "Early Norwegian Press in America," *Minnesota History Bulletin,* III (November, 1920), 506–518; "Cleng Peerson and Norwegian Immigration," *Mississippi Valley Historical Review*, VII (March, 1921), 303–331; "The Norwegian Government and the Early Norwegian Emigration," *Minnesota History*, VI (June, 1925), 115–140; and "Minnesota Pioneer Life as Revealed in Newspaper Advertisements," *Minnesota History*, VII (June, 1926), 99–121.

15. Grace Lee Nute, *Caesars of the Wilderness: Medard Chouart, sieur des Groseilliers, and Pierre Esprit Radisson, 1618–1710* (New York, 1943). Other representative examples of Nute's scholarship are *The Voyageur* (New York, 1931); *Documents Relating to Northwest Missions, 1815–1827* (St. Paul, 1942); and *Lake Superior* (New York, 1944).

16. Ryder file, HUA; Dorothy M. McGhee, "Voltairian Narrative Devices as Considered in the Author's Contes Philosophique" (unpublished Ph.D. thesis, Ohio State University, 1930); "Voltaire's *Candide* and Gracian's *El Criticon,*" *PMLA*, LII (September, 1937), 778–784; "The 'Conte Philosophique' Bridging a Century," *PMLA*, LVIII (June, 1943), 438–449.

17. Charles Byron Kuhlmann, *The Development of the Flour-Milling Industry in the United States, with Special Reference to the Industry in Minneapolis* (Boston, 1929).

18. Rysgaard discussed the purpose of physics in an article published by the *Oracle* on February 7, 1918. An example of Muhleman's writing is "An Efficient Fume Hood," *Journal of Chemical Education,* XII (1935), 591.

19. Walter A. Kenyon, "Digestive Enzymes in Poikilothermal Vertebrates: An Investigation of Enzymes in Fishes, with Comparative Studies on Those of Amphibians, Reptiles and Mammals," *Bulletin of the Bureau of Fisheries,* XLI (1925), 181–200; "Who Shall Inherit the Earth?" *Bios*, XI (March, 1940), 19–31.

20. Charles Horswell, "Insight and Integrity," *The Hamline Review*, II (June, 1922), 2–5; *Oracle*, December 12, 1924.

21. MBT, December 14, 1915.

22. *AQ*, XXI (June, 1925), 5–6.

23. Among the monographs which deal effectively with postwar social, political, economic, and religious issues are David A. Shannon, *Between the Wars: America, 1919–1941* (Boston, 1965); Paul Carter, *The Twenties in America* (New York, 1968); Harold Cruse, *The Crisis of the Negro Intellectual* (New York, 1967); G. Louis Joughin and Edmund M. Morgan, *The Legacy of Sacco & Vanzetti* (New York, 1948); Irving Bernstein, *The Lean Years: A History of the American Worker, 1920–1933* (Boston, 1960); Joseph R. Gusfeld, *Symbolic Crusade: Status Politics and the American Temperance Movement* (Urbana, 1963); and David M. Chalmers, *Hooded Americanism: The First Century of the Ku Klux Klan, 1865–1965* (New York, 1965). Two superb scholarly articles are Stanley Coben, "A Study in Nativism: The American Red Scare of 1919–20," *Political Science Quarterly*, LXXIX (March, 1964), 52–75; and Paul L. Murphy, "Sources and Nature of Intolerance in the 1920's," *Journal of American History*, LI (June, 1964), 60–76.

24. Samuel F. Kerfoot to Rev. William J. Ferris, July 8, 1920, Kerfoot papers, HUA; "President S. F. Kerfoot's Eighth Annual Report to the Board of Trustees of Hamline University, 1920;" "Minutes of Conference on 'Our College,' Held at Hamline University April 30th and May 1st, 1925," HUA; *Oracle*, April 24, 1925, January 21, 1927. Kerfoot first proposed the idea of a Church-college conference. See FM, January 21, April 21, 1925.

25. "Conference on 'Our College,'" 2–3.

26. *Ibid.*, 5–6.

27. *Ibid.*, 4, 6–7.

28. *AQ*, XVIII (April, 1921), 9–10, XX (Winter, 1924), 3. In June, 1925, Twin City alumni issued a report which questioned Hamline's scholastic standards, the condition and serviceability of the physical plant, and the President's physical ability to promote the college aggressively. It reiterated the concerns expressed by Quigley and Richardson, and suggested that if Hamline honestly desired to raise the academic stature of its instructional staff, it must realize that money and time to do creative work were the crucial ingredients. It then recommended that entrance requirements and course expectations be raised, that trustees be chosen with greater care, that the college should strive to publicize itself effectively, that the Methodists of the state increase their giving, that the physical plant receive immediate attention, and that President Kerfoot resign, thus paving the way for the robust and "virile" leadership the college required. See "Report of Committee on Hamline Matters (June 3, 1925), Presented to Twin City Hamline Alumni at a meeting held at the Minneapolis Y.M.C.A.," mimeographed document in HUA, 1–5.

29. HUC, 1912–13 through 1926–27.

30. *Oracle*, December 5, 1924.

31. *Loc. cit.*

32. MBT, June 8, December 14, 1915, February 7, 1916, January 8, 1917, June 11, 1918; "President S. F. Kerfoot's Fifth Annual Report to the Board of Trustees of Hamline University, June, 1917;" St. Paul *Dispatch*, June 21, 1912. The Caleb Door Pool, constructed in 1915 with funds supplied by Door, a Minneapolis

pioneer and University benefactor, received notice in the *Oracle,* November 17, 1915.

33. "President S. F. Kerfoot's Third Annual Report to the Board of Trustees of Hamline University, June, 1915;" "President S. F. Kerfoot's Fourth Annual Report to the Board of Trustees of Hamline University, June, 1916."

34. MBT, June 5, December 3, 1917; "President S. F. Kerfoot's Fifth Annual Report to the Board of Trustees of Hamline University, June, 1917."

35. MBT, February 27, 1918, August 13, September 3, 12, 29, 30, October 2, 21, December 26, 1919, November 12, 1920, January 17, 1921; Samuel F. Kerfoot to W. H. Gold, October 4, December 12, 1919, W. H. Gold to Samuel F. Kerfoot, January 24, 1920, Samuel F. Kerfoot to W. H. Gold, January 28, 1920, Kerfoot papers, HUA; "President S. F. Kerfoot's Eighth Annual Report to the Board of Trustees of Hamline University, 1920;" FM, March 27, April 17, 1917; *Oracle,* March 29, May 17, 1917, October 2, 1919; *AQ,* XVI (October, 1919), 7–8, XVI (January, 1920), 1; Hicks, "My Six Years at Hamline," 219; Henry L. Osborn, *Hamline University in the World War* (St. Paul, 1920). A report issued in 1920 by the Board of Education of the Methodist Church gave support to Kerfoot's conviction that the Midway campus presented serious obstacles. It concluded that while the campus was not beyond redemption, nearby industrial developments and "the change in the character of the population which is sure to occur" made a move desirable. Such a course of action would be expensive, the document acknowledged, but University officials should take the long-range view. See MBT, November 12, 1920.

36. "President S. F. Kerfoot's Ninth Annual Report to the Board of Trustees of Hamline University, June, 1921;" *AQ,* XVII (January, 1921), 5.

37. HUC, 1905–06, pp. 58–59, 1921–22, p. 81, 1922–23, p. 84.

38. *Oracle,* March 10, 1922.

39. MBT, November 15, December 29, 1921, December 28, 1922, January 26, May 9, June 8, 1923; "President S. F. Kerfoot's Ninth Annual Report to the Board of Trustees of Hamline University, June, 1921;" Doniver A. Lund, *Gustavus Adolphus College. A Centennial History 1862–1962* (Minneapolis, 1963), 116–117.

40. James J. Hill to Samuel F. Kerfoot, January 14, 1915, Kerfoot papers, HUA; "President S. F. Kerfoot's Fourth Annual Report to the Board of Trustees of Hamline University, June, 1916;" *AQ,* XIV (July, 1917), 13; [Paul H. Giddens], "The Nortons of Winona," *HUB,* LIII (January, 1963), 8–9. The Norton article was one of several essays on prominent benefactors which President Paul H. Giddens wrote anonymously for the *Bulletin.* Noted alumni then signed their names to the articles. Paul H. Giddens to author, March 2, 1978.

41. MBT, August 2, October 10, 1924, January 15, February 26, 1925, April 23, June 25, October 19, 1926, March 26, October 31, 1927, April 11, December 7, 1928, June 10, 24, 1929; Samuel F. Kerfoot to the Board of Trustees, March 4, 1924, Kerfoot papers, HUA; "President S. F. Kerfoot's Ninth Annual Report to the Board of Trustees of Hamline University, June, 1921." Even in the midst of the 1924 Advance difficulties, the trustees inexplicably agreed to launch yet another capital campaign — this for $400,000 to finance construction projects. Predictably, it never left the drawing board. Parker College, the preparatory school in question, was founded by the Free Baptist Church as the Northwestern Free Baptist College

in 1888. It changed its name in 1891 when benefactor L. D. Parker of Minneapolis gave property valued at $40,000 to the college endowment fund. In 1911, the Minnesota Annual Conference of the Methodist Church acquired the college, which had for years been on the verge of bankruptcy. By 1924, cumulative indebtedness stood at more than $30,000, and in 1925, the Methodists magnanimously returned the college to the Baptists! But they also agreed, as part of the transfer, to assist in defraying the institution's debts.

42. MBT, December 28, 1922, January 26, 1923.

43. MBT, August 23, September 18, 1923.

44. MBT, November 5, 22, 1926, September 15, 1927, June 11, 1928, June 10, 1929.

45. MBT, May 9, November 13, 1923, March 26, August 8, September 8, 1924; Laws of Minnesota, Ch. 43, 1854; *County of Nobles v. Hamline University, St. Paul,* 46 Minn. 316, 48 N. W. 1119 (1891); *State of Minnesota v. W. L. Harris Realty Company,* 148 Minn. 20, 180 N. W. 776 (1922).

46. MBT, March 18, June 7, July 8, 1927, April 11, 1928; *AQ,* XXIV (Summer, 1927), 18; Ralph Olmsted, *From Institute to University* (Evansville, 1973), 103–107.

47. Olmsted, *loc. cit.*

48. *HUB*, n.s., I (December, 1927), 10–12.

49. *Ibid.,* 16–21.

50. United States Department of the Interior, Office of Education, *Bulletin,* 1930, *Biennial Survey of Education, 1926–1928* (Washington, 1930), 698–703; United States Department of the Interior, Bureau of Education, *Bulletin,* 1919, *Biennial Survey of Education, 1916–18,* III (Washington, 1921), 680, 682, 727; United States Department of the Interior, Bureau of Education, *Bulletin,* 1926, *Biennial Survey of Education, 1922–1924* (Washington, 1926), 578. Hereafter, the above sources are cited as *USBE, 1919, USBE, 1926,* and *USOE, 1930.*

51. *USBE, 1919,* 723–724, 789–791; *USBE, 1926,* 599, 604, 618–619; *USOE, 1930,* 721, 727, 745; United States Department of the Interior, Bureau of Education, *Bulletin,* 1923, *Biennial Survey of Education, 1918–20* (Washington, 1923), 291–292, 340–341; United States Department of the Interior, Bureau of Education, *Bulletin,* 1924, *Biennial Survey of Education, 1920–22,* II (Washington, 1925), 324, 329, 342; United States Department of the Interior, Bureau of Education, *Bulletin,* 1928, *Biennial Survey of Education, 1924–1926* (Washington, 1928), 826, 831, 846. Hereafter, the latter three sources are cited in abbreviated form also.

52. *Hamline Studies,* 4; HUC, 1917–18, p. 109, 1919–20, p. 104; *USBE, 1919,* 863; *USBE, 1923,* 392; *USBE, 1924,* 425–426; *USBE, 1926,* 705; *USBE, 1928,* 936–937; *USOE, 1930,* 799, 846–847. For a view quite different from that of Hughes, see Donald J. Cowling, "A Plea to Save the Old-Fashioned College," *Current History,* XXVII (January, 1928), 489–498. Cowling, then President of Carleton College, urged that American educators reject momentary educational fads and defend the classic arguments advanced in favor of liberal arts education. Among the worst of the offenders, Cowling charged, was former president William Rainey Harper of the University of Chicago, who had encouraged the growth of the junior college movement "by driving a wedge between the sophomore and junior years." The junior-senior college distinction, of course, was a distinction enthusiastically promoted by President Hughes and certain of his administrative as-

sociates. Chief among the latter was Milton C. Towner, who came to Hamline in 1931 from the University of Chicago, where he had become enamored of the Harper viewpoint. But the more immediate cause of Hughes' decision to advance his junior-senior college plan was the 1930 Methodist survey. This fact, set in contradistinction to the views advanced by Donald Cowling, provides vivid implicit commentary on Hamline's distress and Carleton's success — both then and in subsequent decades.

53. MBT, July 8, 1927, June 11, 1928; *AQ,* XXIV (Summer, 1927), 18.

54. MBT, June 8, 1920; "President S. F. Kerfoot's Eighth Annual Report to the Board of Trustees of Hamline University, 1920."

55. Walcott file, HUA; Gregory D. Walcott to alumni, July 5, 1928, in *AM,* XXV (July, 1928), 9; Gregory D. Walcott to Henry L. Osborn, April 29, July 23, 1928, Osborn file, HUA; MBT, September 11, 1928; H. W. Taylor to Alfred F. Hughes, December 14, 1928, and all Hughes correspondence both with Walcott and with the A.A.U.P., Walcott file, HUA; *AM,* XXV (September, 1928), 6; New York *World-Telegram,* September 18, 1951; New York *Times,* September 28, 1952. Walcott proved benevolent and forgiving. On February 17, 1960, President Paul H. Giddens announced that the former professor had designated Hamline a beneficiary in his will. See FM, February 17, 1960.

56. "Report of a Survey of Hamline University . . . 1930," 1–3, 9, 40, 45, 49–51, 165. Only 30 per cent of the student body came from the Twin Cities during the 1929–30 academic year.

57. "Report of a Survey of Hamline University . . . 1930," 10.

58. *HUB,* III (May, 1930), *passim,* III (June, 1930), *passim; Oracle,* December 9, 1927, January 20, 1928.

59. MBT, March 5, June 10, 1929, May 22, 27, June 9, 1930, September 17, 1931; *HUB,* III (June, 1930); unidentified faculty to Henry L. Osborn, pencilled Ms., undated, in Hughes file; unsigned student Ms. notes, from a meeting held by Hughes with students, May 29, 1930, and containing notations by Henry Osborn, Hughes file; notes of a meeting between Hamline faculty and University of Minnesota officials, May 31, 1930, Hughes file; St. Paul and Minneapolis newspapers for April and May, 1930, MHSN; MMC, 1894, pp. 27–33.

60. "Report of a Survey of Hamline University . . . 1930," 3, 7, 11–12, 20–21, 23–26, 53–55, 57, 62–63, 66–68, 292–297, 362–403.

61. *Ibid.,* 11; MBT, June 11, 1928, November 26, 1929, November 3, 1931, January 12, April 19, 1932.

62. MBT, September 24, November 24, 1930, May 1, September 17, 1931, January 12, 15, February 18, March 31, April 2, 7, 1932; St. Paul *Dispatch,* August 28, 1930; Minneapolis *Star,* August 28, 1930.

63. "Report of the President of Hamline University to the Board of Trustees, April 7, 1932," Hughes file, HUA; St. Paul *Pioneer Press,* April 8, 1932; St. Paul *Dispatch,* April 9, 1932.

64. MBT, June 6, 1932; "Report of the Committee of Five to the Board of Trustees of Hamline University, June 2, 1932," Hughes file, HUA.

65. MBT, June 6, November 29, December 15, 1932, April 27, June 5, 27, September 14, October 19, December 29, 1933, February 15, 1934.

66. In all, five individuals have become Rhodes Scholars. They include Harold S. Quigley, Henry Allen Moe, Lynn Beyer, Carlyle Beyer, and Judson Sheridan.

CHAPTER 5

1. *AM,* XXVIII (April, 1932), 3; *Oracle,* April 15, 1932.

2. James S. King to Alfred F. Hughes, January 15, 1932 (copy), in FM, II, 301; FM, January 27, 1932; Alfred F. Hughes to staff, January 30, 1932, Hughes file, HUA; MBT, April 19, May 19, October 20, 1932.

3. MBT, April 19, June 6, July 21, 1932.

4. MBT, November 29, 1932.

5. MBT, July 21, 1932, June 5, 1933; Grace Lee Nute, manuscript history of Hamline University, 284, 290–291; *AM,* XXIX (October–November, 1932), 12; Thomas P. Beyer in *Oracle,* September 23, 1932; FM, December 14, 1932, January 11, 1933; HUC, 1932–33 through 1939–40; Committee on Educational Policy of Hamline University, *Hamline Studies* (St. Paul, 1944), 4.

6. FM, April 24, 1933; MBT, April 27, June 27, 1933; *Oracle,* April 28, 1933; *AB,* XXX (Summer, 1933), 4. Hutton interviewed 80 students, 85 per cent of whom had no direct interest in athletics. Of the total amount of aid granted, 23 per cent went to athletes. Basketball players received an average credit of $140, which was just $35 under the $175 tuition charge. And the proportionate amount of aid to athletes was higher than that granted to non-athletes.

7. *Oracle,* May 5, 19, 26, 1933; FM, July 1, 1933; MBT, June 27, 1933.

8. MBT, July 13, September 14, 1933; *AB,* XXX (Summer, 1933); FM, January 14, July 1, 1933.

9. MBT, September 14, October 19, December 29, 1933, February 15, March 23, 1934.

10. *Oracle,* April 21, 1934; Charles N. Pace to the Board of Trustees, February 4, 1936.

11. Charles Nelson Pace papers, HUA.

12. Charles Nelson Pace, "The Contemporaneous Scene," Pace papers, HUA.

13. MBT, February 5, July 30, October 1, 1935, February 4, June 6, October 27, 1936; FM, February 8, 1935; *Oracle,* February 8, 1935.

14. "Librarian's Report, 1923–1924" and Library file, HUA; MBT, April 30, May 8, June 10, July 30, August 10, 1935, February 4, March 25, June 6, 1936, December 22, 1939, June 8, July 29, October 29, 1940, November 4, 1941, March 9, 1943; *Oracle,* January 8, May 7, 1937, February 17, November 3, 1939, September 27, 1940, January 10, 1941; *AB,* XXXV (October, 1939), 2; Charles S. Templer to Charles N. Pace, August 19, 1938, in Pace to the Board of Trustees, October 25, 1938. In 1978, Bridgman Hall was once again restored, and in March, 1979, soprano Neva Stevens Pilgrim, a 1960 graduate of the University, presented a dedicatory recital with The Musical Offering, an instrumental chamber group headed by Professor of Music Rees Allison.

15. *County of Nobles v. Hamline University,* 46 Minn. 316, 48 N. W. 1119 (1891); *State of Minnesota v. W. L. Harris Realty Company,* 148 Minn. 20, 180 N. W. 776 (1922); *State of Minnesota v. Trustees of Pillsbury Academy,* 204 Minn. 365 (1939); Charles N. Pace to the Board of Trustees, February 2, 1937, February 7, 1939; William P. Westfall to the Board of Trustees, October 31, 1944; MBT, June 10, 1935. For a succinct discussion of the *Pillsbury* case and its relationship to Hamline's circumstance, see Nute, chapter 12, footnote 21.

16. *Trustees of Hamline University of Minnesota v. H. I. Peacock et al,* and *State of Minnesota v. Trustees of Hamline University of Minnesota,* 217 Minn. 399

(1944); William P. Westfall to the Board of Trustees, October 31, 1944; *Oracle,* October 13, 1944; St. Paul *Dispatch,* June 4, July 9, 10, 1942, May 19, October 10, 1944.

17. *In re Hamline* (1944) and *In re County of Ramsey* (1944); *State of Minnesota v. Bishop Seabury Mission,* 90 Minn. 92, 95 N. W. 882; Charles N. Pace to the Board of Trustees, June 3, 1944.

18. Paul H. Giddens to the Board of Trustees, September 29, 1967, April 24, 1968.

19. *Oracle,* October 25, 1929, March 7, 1930, March 22, May 3, December 6, 1935, April 24, 1936, November 19, December 10, 1937.

20. *Oracle,* February 16, March 16, April 13, October 26, November 2, 9, 1934, January 18, 25, October 11, 1935.

21. *Oracle,* February 15, May 31, November 1, 8, December 6, 1935.

22. *Oracle,* September 29, 1939; FM, September 18, 1939, March 1, April 26, September 27, October 18, November 16, 1940.

23. *Oracle,* January 10, February 7, March 7, May 2, 1941.

24. FM, June 9, December 12, 16, 1941, January 14, 28, 30, February 6, May 27, 29, 1942. In January, 1941, Professor of Physics Kent Bracewell became campus coordinator of the C.A.A. student pilot training program. The faculty authorized a two-year program in occupational therapy in 1942, created many special, technical, accelerated, and revised courses, and approved an X-Ray Technology sequence in 1943. See FM, January 22, 1941, May 30, 1942, January 15, March 12, 1943.

25. Charles N. Pace to the Board of Trustees, March 9, 1943.

26. *Oracle,* March 19, 1943.

27. *Ibid.,* September 24, 1943. Although the University expected to secure an army or navy training unit, two circumstances — excessive cost and the absence of dormitory quarters — prohibited that occurrence. Even so, the college trained 110 men in the C.A.A. program, continued to graduate nurses, and ultimately saw hundreds of its men and women off to war, 31 of whom gave their lives in service to country. See MBT, June 15, August 2, 1943; Charles N. Pace to the Board of Trustees, March 9, October 26, 1943.

CHAPTER 6

1. William P. Tolley quoted by Charles N. Pace in Pace to the Board of Trustees, March 14, 1944.

2. Charles N. Pace to the Board of Trustees, October 26, 1943, June 3, 1944; Committee on Educational Policy of Hamline University, *Hamline Studies* (St. Paul, 1944); Miron A. Morrill to the Educational Policies Committee, October 15, 1943.

3. *Hamline Studies,* 77.

4. *Loc. cit.*

5. *Ibid.,* 78–79.

6. Charles N. Pace to the Board of Trustees, June 3, 1944; ''Message to the Congress on Education of War Veterans, October 27, 1943,'' in Samuel I. Rosenman, comp., *Public Papers and Addresses of Franklin D. Roosevelt* (13 vols., New York, 1938–50), XII, 449–455; David R. B. Ross, *Preparing for Ulysses. Politics*

and Veterans During World War II (New York, 1969), 89–124; Charles Hurd, *The Veterans' Program. A Complete Guide to its Benefits, Rights and Options* (New York, 1946), 2–4; FM, October 6, November 17, 1943; MEPC, December 7, 1943; *Hamline Studies*, 88–92; *Oracle*, September 29, 1944.

7. Sub-Committee on Higher Education and National Rehabilitation to the Educational Policies Committee [1945], EPC files, HUA; HUC, 1944–45, p. 129, 1945–46, p. 132, 1946–47, p. 142, 1948–49, p. 146, 1974–76, p. 133; *Oracle*, January 18, February 8, October 24, December 5, 1946; MBT, March 30, 1946; Lyle Koch to Charles N. Pace, in Pace to the Board of Trustees, June 7, 1947; *AB*, XLI (October, 1946), 9.

8. HUC, 1945–46, pp. 30–31; FM, January 5, 1945.

9. MBT, March 17, June 3, 1944; *Oracle,* May 19, 1944; Charles N. Pace to the Board of Trustees, June 3, 1944.

10. Charles N. Pace to the Board of Trustees, October 29, 1946; Paul H. Giddens to the Board of Trustees, April 24, 1968; Hurst R. Anderson to author, April 11, 1978; *HUB, L* (January, 1960), 5.

11. MBT, March 13, August 21, October 15, November 6, 1945, March 12, April 15, June 1, 1946, August 7, 1947; Charles N. Pace to the Board of Trustees, March 13, June 3, 1945; *Oracle,* November 10, 1944, April 27, 1945, March 14, April 4, 1946, January 16, February 20, March 20, April 17, 1947; *AB, XLI* (October, 1946), 2.

12. Charles N. Pace to the Board of Trustees, October 29, 1946; Arthur S. Williamson to faculty, September 12, 1947; Hurst R. Anderson to author, April 11, 1978; *Oracle,* December 18, 1947.

13. Charles N. Pace to the Board of Trustees, June 1, 1946; Miron A. Morrill to Arthur S. Williamson [Summer, 1946], in Charles N. Pace to the Board of Trustees, October 29, 1946.

14. Arthur S. Williamson to Charles N. Pace, in Pace to the Board of Trustees, October 29, 1946.

15. *Ibid.*

16. Miron A. Morrill to faculty, April 18, 1944, Morrill file, HUA.

17. *Ibid.*

18. MMC, 1935, p. 411, 1947, p. 43, 1948, p. 89. See also the financial statistics in MMC, 1895 through 1948.

19. Charles N. Pace to the Board of Trustees, June 7, 1947, June 5, 1948; MBT, June 7, 1947, March 9, 1948; *AB,* XLIV (October 1947), 1.

20. Hurst R. Anderson to author, April 11, 1978; MBT, May 25, 1948. Treasurer John E. Bowes argued vociferously against the selection of a non-ministerial candidate; see Bowes to Walter C. Coffey, April 17, 1948. Hurst R. Anderson, *An Educational Journey* (Lakeside, Ohio, 1977), is a series of light, informative, and enormously revealing autobiographical essays.

21. Hurst R. Anderson to author, April 11, 1978; *HUB,* XXXVIII (October, 1948), 7–10.

22. Hurst R. Anderson to author, April 11, 1978; Hurst R. Anderson to the Educational Policies Committee, September 29, 1948; Hurst R. Anderson to the Board of Trustees, October 26, 1948; EPC minutes, 1948–49, *passim,* and especially November 12, 19, 1948; FM, March 5, 1934; Fred B. Millett, *The Rebirth of Liberal Education* (New York, 1945), v, 23, 49, 126–128.

23. FM, March 13, 1947; Hurst R. Anderson to the Educational Policies Committee, November 16, 1949.

24. HUC, 1949–50, pp. 33 ff; *Oracle*, April 1, 1949; Hurst R. Anderson to the Board of Trustees, June 11, 1949.

25. MEPC, February 16, March 22, 29, 1950; FM, April 4, 26, 1950; Hurst R. Anderson to the Board of Trustees, June 3, 1950; HUC, 1951–53, pp. 29–30; *Oracle,* May 5, 1950.

26. Hurst R. Anderson to author, April 11, 1978; FM, April 29, 1935, November 19, 1947; Hurst R. Anderson to the Board of Trustees, March 14, 1950.

27. Hurst R. Anderson to author, April 11, 1978; Carl Billman to Grace Lee Nute, February 12, 1952, in MBT, March 11, 1952; Hurst R. Anderson to the Board of Trustees, March 11, 1952; FM, March 19, 1952; *Oracle,* September 14, 1973; Grace Lee Nute, manuscript history of Hamline University, 331, HUA.

28. Hurst R. Anderson to the Board of Trustees, October 31, 1950, March 13, June 2, 1951; MBT, November 27, 1950, March 13, 1951.

29. Hurst R. Anderson to the Board of Trustees, June 9, 1952; MBT, June 12, 1952.

CHAPTER 7

1. Laws of Minnesota, Chapter 43, 1854.

2. HUC, 1857–58, 1858–59.

3. HUC, 1862–63, pp. 14–16, 1865–66, p. 15; Henry L. Osborn, ed., *Alumni Record of Hamline University* (St. Paul, 1924), 6–9.

4. Grace Lee Nute, manuscript history of Hamline University, 80–82, HUA; Alumni Association of Hamline University, *History of the Hamline University of Minnesota When Located at Red Wing, Minnesota from 1854 to 1869* (St. Paul, 1907), 46; Theodore C. Blegen, *Minnesota, A History of the State* (Minneapolis, 1963), 159–165, 186–187, 409–413; MMC, 1856–1870, *passim.*

5. Nute, 80–82; *Red Wing History,* 46; MMC, 1858–1859, *passim.*

6. "The Contribution of J. A. Vandyke [*sic*] to Professor Innis' Course in Education at Hamline University in 1895 and 1896," in Osborn papers, HUA; Osborn, *Alumni Record*, 9–39; HUC, 1891–92, p. 17, 1865–96, p. 28, 1901–02, p. 25; Blegen, 411–412.

7. HUC, 1905–06, pp. 36–37, 1915–16, pp. 31–32, 1919–20, pp. 40–41; Samuel F. Kerfoot, "Seventh Annual Report of the President to the Board of Trustees of Hamline University;" Charles R. Richardson in *AQ,* XVII (July, 1920), 5; Blegen, 412.

8. *Oracle,* February 10, 1928. For a description of state requirements, see HUC, 1928–29, p. 77.

9. Nute, 268.

10. *HUB,* n.s., I (December, 1927), 20; Charles N. Pace to the Board of Trustees, June 8, 1940.

11. Hurst R. Anderson to the Board of Trustees, June 11, 1949; Kenneth R. Doane, "A Study of the Professional Curriculum Requirements for the Preparation of High School Teachers in the United States," *Journal of Experimental Education*, XVI (September, 1947), 66–9. For an account of the St. Paul Teacher Recruitment Project, see Doane and W. J. Scanlan, "Future Teachers Are Recruited and Plans Made for a Teacher-Trainee Group in the St. Paul, Minnesota, Schools," *National Association of Secondary School Principals Bulletin,* XLII

(January, 1958), 94–114. The University Archives also contains a file on the history and evolution of the project.

12. MEPC, September 28, October 12, November 2, 9, 1949; FM, November 16, 1949, February 27, 1957; Blegen, 412–413; HUC, 1950–51, pp. 103–104.

13. *HUB,* LVII (October, 1967), 5; "Institutional Profile, Hamline University, Saint Paul, Minnesota, Prepared for the Membership Review to be conducted by The North Central Association of College and Secondary Schools, April 25 and 26, 1968," 35; MAPC, January 28, 1970; FM, February 3, 1970, October 6, 1971.

14. *Prospectus of Hamline University* (Mankato, 1880), 14; HUC, 1880–81, p. 22, 1881–82, p. 19; Arthur S. Williamson Ms. notes, May 22, 1967, HUA; *HUB,* LII (April, 1962), 3.

15. HUC, 1895–96, pp. 63–65, 1896–97, pp. 53–55, 1897–98, p. 53; *Oracle,* January, 1896; MBT, June 3, 12, 1891, November 4, December 16, 1895, June 6, 1905. President Bridgman made the medical school affiliation announcement on December 16, 1895.

16. *Oracle,* December, 1897, January 15, 1903; MBT, March 3, June 9, 1908; *AQ,* IV (January–April, 1908), 1, 3–4; Williamson Ms. notes; Leo M. Crafts to George H. Bridgman, May 23, 1923, HUA; *HUB,* LII (April, 1962), 3; St. Paul *Dispatch,* October 20, 1900.

17. MBT, June 8, 1940; FM, April 24, 1940, May 15, 1944; HUC, 1940–41, pp. 110–111; Robert R. Martin to Mildred Montag, December 12, 1941 (copy), HUA.

18. Robert R. Martin to Charles N. Pace, January 13, 1941; FM, October 25, 1939, February 21, 1940, January 22, 1941.

19. Nursing file, HUA.

20. *Oracle,* May 4, 1945; Alice B. Brethorst, *Methods of Teaching in Schools of Nursing* (Philadelphia, 1949).

21. Nursing file, HUA; FM, December 12, 1945, September 16, 1946. During the 1943–44 academic year alone, the federal government contributed $86,656.50 to Hamline, especially for the training of cadet nurses. See Charles N. Pace to the Board of Trustees, October 26, 1943.

22. Hurst R. Anderson to the Board of Trustees, June 11, 1949; FM, September 20, 1948, November 16, 1949, December 16, 1953; HUC, 1949–50, p. 141, 1950–51, pp. 142–144; St. Paul *Pioneer Press*, February 11, 1949.

23. FM, February 15, October 17, 1956; MEPC, May 24, 1956; Paul H. Giddens to the Board of Trustees, February 21, 1956; MBT, October 28, 1958.

24. Paul H. Giddens to the Board of Trustees, May 7, October 24, 1957.

25. Paul H. Giddens to the Board of Trustees, October 24, 1957, March 5, 1958; FM, September 10, November 20, 1957; MBT, October 29, 1957.

26. Paul H. Giddens to the Board of Trustees, March 5, 1958; Educational Policies Committee to Giddens, April 29, 1958; Giddens to the Board of Trustees, May 6, 1958.

27. Paul H. Giddens to the Board of Trustees, October 22, 1958; Daphne Rolfe to Charles R. Wimmer, April 28, 1959, in EPC file, HUA; Giddens to the Board of Trustees, May 4, 1959; MBT, October 28, 1958, January 14, 1959; MEPC, November 5, 1958; *HUB,* XLIX (April, 1959), 5.

28. MBT, December 16, 1895, April 7, June 3, 1896; HUC, 1895–96, pp. 83–94, 1896–97, pp. 77–86, 1897–98, p. 46, 1898–99, p. 46, 1899–1900, p. 46,

1921–22, pp. 48–49; *AQ*, XVIII (Summer–Fall, 1921), 5–6, XIX (Summer, 1922), 22; *HUB,* XI (October, 1921), 9.

29. FM, April 9, June 9, 1941, May 30, November 20, 1942, March 12, 1943, May 2, 1945, March 13, 1947; Archer W. Hurd to Charles N. Pace, in Pace to the Board of Trustees, June 7, 1941; HUC, 1943–44, p. 57.

30. FM, April 18, November 22, December 6, 13, 1894, January 25 through March 8, 1899, November 7, 1906, March 27, 1913; HUC, 1883–84, p. 33, 1888–89, p. 40, 1893–94, p. 47.

31. FM, February 14, 21, 1934; HUC, 1934–35, p. 45; "Report of a Survey of Hamline University Under the Auspices of The Commission on Survey of Educational Institutions of the Methodist Episcopal Church, February, 1930," mimeographed volume in HUA, 16.

32. HUC, 1917–1953; commencement programs, 1917–1953.

33. Committee on Graduate Studies to Educational Policies Committee, February 8, 1945, EPC file; FM, February 8, 9, 1945; Charles N. Pace to the Board of Trustees, March 13, 1945; HUC, 1948–49, p. 46.

34. FM, February 22, April 26, 1950, November 18, 1953; *Oracle,* September 28, 1950; HUC, 1953–54, p. 168, 1958–60, pp. 57–62, 1960–62, p. 65, 1962–64, p. 63, 1964–66, p. 59; National Council for Accreditation of Teacher Education, "Hamline University Evaluation Report" [1957], 56, HUA.

35. Charles U. Walker to Graduate Studies Committee [December, 1964], in Graduate Studies Committee file, HUA.

36. David M. Pletcher to Charles U. Walker, December 11, 1964, in Graduate Studies Committee file, HUA.

37. Graduate Studies Committee to faculty, January 11, 1965; FM, January 20, 1965, May 17, December 13, 1972, February 4, 1976; *Oracle,* December 15, 1972; Continuing Education Committee to faculty, December 8, 1972, in FM.

38. FM, April 3, May 15, September 3, December 4, 1974, March 5, 1975, March 3, May 5, 1976, March 9, 1977; MBT, June 3, 17, 19, 1974, March 20, April 9, May 5, May 2, 1977; interview with Richard P. Bailey, September 28, 1977; *Oracle,* February 22, September 6, December 6, 1974, February 7, 28, 1975.

CHAPTER 8

1. *Oracle*, 1893–1913, *passim*. The issue of October 15, 1905 contained the reference to the band.

2. *Oracle,* April 18, 25, May 9, 1913, October 29, 1920, November 19, December 3, 1926, January 14, 1927; conversation with Robert Holliday, January 19, 1977.

3. *Oracle,* April 23, 28, October 1, 8, 1926.

4. *Ibid.,* May 31, 1929; conversation with Robert Holliday, January 19, 1977; Joseph M. Shaw, *History of St. Olaf College, 1874–1974* (Northfield, 1974), 217. Simson had most recently been choirmaster of St. Mary's Episcopal Church, St. Paul.

5. *Oracle,* November 8, December 6, 1929, February 28, 1930; MBT, June 8, 1931; Florence Fitzgerald quoted in *Liner*, 1931, p. 93.

6. MFC, April 18, 25, June 6, 1932; FM, October 14, 1932.

7. *Oracle,* September 23, October 21, 1932, January 25, 1935.

8. John K. Sherman and Frances Boardman quoted in *Oracle,* April 12, 1935; Boardman column reprinted in *Oracle,* April 15, 1938.

9. Hamline University A Cappella Choir programs, 1934–1939, HUA.

10. Charles N. Pace to the Board of Trustees, October 30, 1934.

11. *Oracle,* May 22, 1942; Charles N. Pace to the Board of Trustees, in MBT, June 7, 1941.

12. Conversation with Robert Holliday, January 19, 1977; Ernst Krenek, "Teaching Composition in America: Reminiscences," *American Music Teacher,* XXIV (February–March, 1975), 6, 8; *HUB,* XXXII (July, 1942), 9; Eric Blom, ed., *Grove's Dictionary of Music and Musicians* (5th ed., London and New York, 1954), IV, 844; *Oracle,* May 22, 1942.

13. Conversation with Robert Holliday, January 19, 1977; Krenek, "Teaching Composition in America."

14. *HUB,* XXXIII (July, 1943), 13; St. Paul *Pioneer Press,* May 21, 1942; Ernst Krenek, *Music Here and Now* (New York, 1939); Robert C. Erickson, "Krenek's Later Music" (unpublished M. A. thesis, Hamline University, 1946).

15. Krenek, "Teaching Composition in America," 8–9; *AB,* XXXVI (April, 1943), 8; FM, May 7, September 13, 1943; *Oracle,* May 14, October 8, 1943, April 28, 1944, September 28, 1945, November 7, 1946, March 6, 1947; Charles N. Pace to the Board of Trustees, June 15, October 26, 1943.

16. Blom, 847–848; New York *Times,* November 30, 1947; *Oracle,* November 7, 1946.

17. Ernst Krenek, "Self-Analysis," *New Mexico Quarterly,* XXIII (Spring, 1953), 34–36; Ernst Krenek, ed., *Hamline Studies in Musicology* (2 vols., Minneapolis, 1945), i.

18. *Oracle,* January 15, 1948; *AB,* XLV (February, 1948), 3.

19. *Oracle,* March 11, 1948, October 24, 1958; conversation with Robert Holliday, January 19, 1977.

20. *Oracle,* September 24, October 29, 1943, March 24, 1944; *HUB,* LX (October, 1970), 39.

21. *Oracle,* April 17, 1959, February 19, 1960, April 13, 1962, January 24, 1964; Hamline University A Cappella Choir programs, HUA.

22. *HUB,* LVII (October, 1967), 26; conversation with Robert Holliday, January 18, 1977; *Oracle,* February 25, 1966, January 13, 1967.

23. *Liner,* 1946–1975.

24. *Oracle,* February 21, 1936, December 4, 1947; *AM,* XXVIII (April, 1932), 5; *HUB,* XLVIII (November, 1958), 4–5.

25. *Oracle,* February 27, 1947, February 9, October 9, 20, 1955, October 24, 1958, April 17, 1959; *HUB,* XLVI (March, 1956), 2; *Liner,* 1947–1964, *passim.*

26. *Oracle,* March 25, April 1, 1949, March 27, April 10, May 8, 1953.

27. Reprinted in *HUB,* LII (July, 1962), 12.

28. *Oracle,* November 22, 1963.

CHAPTER 9

1. *HUB,* XLIII (October, 1953).

2. *Ibid.*

3. For a complete list of Giddens' publications, see the Giddens papers, HUA.

Books and articles cited in the text include *The Birth of the Oil Industry* (New York, 1938), *Beginnings of the Petroleum Industry: Sources and Bibliography* (Harrisburg, 1941), *Pennsylvania Petroleum 1750–1872: A Documentary History* (Harrisburg, 1947), *Early Days of Oil* (Princeton, 1948), *Standard Oil Company (Indiana): Oil Pioneer of the Middle West* (New York, 1956), and "A Visit to the Oil Regions of Pennsylvania in 1865," *Western Pennsylvania Historical Magazine,* XVIII (September, 1935). See also *Oracle,* January 16, 1953.

4. *Oracle,* January 16, 1953; MBT, October 7, 1963; Paul H. Giddens to author, March 2, 1978.

5. Hurst R. Anderson to the Board of Trustees, June 11, 1949; Paul H. Giddens to the Board of Trustees, March 5, 1958; Arthur S. Williamson, "The Giddens Years, 1953–1968," *HUB,* LVIII (April, 1968), 4–6.

6. Williamson, "Giddens Years," 4–6; copy of memo on sources of Ph.D. in "Survey of Hamline University" file, HUA; *HUB,* LXI (April 1971), 23.

7. Paul H. Giddens to the Board of Trustees, October 23, 1956, March 5, 1958, March 14, 1961; *HUB,* LXI (October, 1971), 5; HUC, 1978–80, pp. 134–139.

8. *Oracle,* April 9, 1965.

9. HUC, 1954–56.

10. HUC, 1954–56; MBT, May 11, 1956.

11. Robert R. Martin, "Village Changes in the Pacific Northwest," *Social Forces,* XV (May, 1937), 536–542; "Integration in the Inland Empire Region of the Pacific Northwest," *Social Forces,* XVII (October, 1938), 29–40; "Economic Resources in Relation to Regional Growth and Integration in the Inland Empire Region," *Social Forces,* XVII (March, 1939), 309–323.

12. Leland R. Cooper, *Indian Mounds Park Archaeological Site, Rice Lake, Wisconsin* (*Bulletin* of the Science Museum of the St. Paul Institute, No. 6, 1959); "A Preliminary Report on the Excavation of Two Late Middle Woodland Mounds in Northwestern Wisconsin," *Journal of the Minnesota Academy of Science,* XXXII (1964); *Oracle,* November 10, 1944; *HUB,* LI (July, 1961), 3, LIII (October, 1963), 7.

13. The Methodist Episcopal Church, *Minutes of the Annual Conferences of the Methodist Episcopal Church, Spring Conferences, 1939* (Nashville, 1939), 62, 64; *HUB,* XLIII (July, 1953), 5–6; *Oracle,* October 9, 1953.

14. Thurman L. Coss, *Secrets from the Caves: A Layman's Guide to the Dead Sea Scrolls* (New York, 1963); *HUB,* LIII (January, 1963), 10–11; *Oracle,* October 9, 1953; Eugene D. Tate in *HUB,* LX (April, 1970), 25–26.

15. David M. Pletcher, "Prospecting Expedition Across Central Mexico, 1856–1857," *Pacific Historical Review,* XXI (February, 1952), 21–41; "General William S. Rosecrans and the Mexican Transcontinental Railroad Project," *Mississippi Valley Historical Review,* XXXVIII (March, 1952), 657–678; "Inter-American Shipping in the 1880's: A Loosening Tie," *Inter American Economic Review,* X (Winter, 1956), 14–41; "Fall of Silver in Mexico, 1870–1910, and its Effect on American Investments," *Journal of Economic History,* XVIII (March, 1958), 33–55; *Rails, Mines, and Progress: Seven American Promoters in Mexico, 1867–1911* (Ithaca, 1958); *The Awkward Years: American Foreign Policy under Garfield and Arthur* (Columbia, Missouri, 1962); MBT, January 8, 1958.

16. F. James Davis, "The Iowa Juvenile Court Judge: A Study in Role Conception and Definition" (unpublished Ph.D. thesis, State University of Iowa, 1949);

"The Treatment of Law in American Sociology," *Sociology and Social Research,* XLII (December, 1957), 99–105; "American Minorities as Seen by Turkish Students in the United States," *Sociology and Social Research,* XLVI (October, 1961), 48–54; *Society and the Law: New Meanings for an Old Profession* (New York, 1962); *Oracle,* October 13, 1961; *HUB,* LII (January, 1962), 8–9.

17. Benjamin M. Lewis, *An Introduction to American Magazines, 1800–1810* (Ann Arbor, 1961); *Oracle,* October 20, 1955; FM, March 21, 1956; *HUB,* LII (January, 1962), 3.

18. Williamson, "Giddens Years;" HUC, 1953–68; interview with Richard P. Bailey, September 20, 1977.

19. FM, 1932–1946, *passim;* MBT, June 6, 1936, February 2, June 5, 1937, June 8, 1940, November 4, 1941, June 3, 1944, March 13, 1945, March 12, 1946; Faculty Committee on Salaries to Charles N. Pace, February 21, 1946; Pace to faculty, March 7, 1946; Hurst R. Anderson to the Board of Trustees, June 11, 1949, October 30, 1951. By 1948, salary ranges were $2,200 to $3,200 for instructors, $2,800 to $4,000 for assistant professors, $3,400 to $4,800 for associate professors, and $4,200 to $6,500 for professors.

20. Paul H. Giddens to the Board of Trustees, October 28, 1958, December 22, 1965, December 27, 1966; MBT, May 11, 1956, March 12, 1957, September 18, 1964, October 8, 1965, April 24, 1968; *HUB,* XLVI (July, 1956), 1, LIV (January, 1964), 5, LVI (January, 1966), 2, LVI (October, 1966), 6, LVII (October, 1967), 32; *Oracle,* January 19, May 24, 1956; Williamson, "Giddens Years," 4–6; "Consumer Price Index for Urban Wage Earners and Clerical Workers," data compiled from U.S. Department of Commerce Reports by Minneapolis Public Library.

21. Paul H. Giddens to author, March 2, 1978; Giddens to John D. Hicks, October 6, 1964 (copy), Hicks file, HUA; Giddens to the Board of Trustees, February 21, 1956, March 3, 1959, February 26, 1960, October 16, 1961, March 8, 1962, April 27, 1964, September 29, 1967; MBT, May 8, 1958, October 13, 1967, January 5, 1968; MEPC, March 1, 8, 22, 1961; MAPC, January 10, 1968, May 9, 1972; FM, April 19, 1961, May 17, 1972; Educational Policies Committee-Phi Beta Kappa Joint Committee to Educational Policies Committee, January 21, 1955, EPC file, HUA; *Oracle,* September 14, 1973, April 19, 26, 1974; *HUB,* LI (October, 1961), 2. The University installed the chapter on April 19, 1974. Historian Peter Gay was speaker for the occasion.

22. FM, September 9, 1958; *HUB,* L (July, 1960), 2, L (October, 1960), 2.

23. *HUB,* LI (January, 1961), 2.

24. FM, November 9, 1934, February 8, 1935, March 17, May 27, 1948, September 17, 1953, December 11, 1957, May 16, 1962, October 20, 1964, October 2, 1968, April 14, November 17, 1971, December 5, 1973, February 4, 1976, May 11, 1977; MEPC, May 2, 1962; MAPC, March 24, November 11, 1971, February 22, 1972, November 28, 1973, November 12, 25, December 10, 1975, January 14, 1976, May 4, 1977; Paul H. Giddens to the Board of Trustees, October 23, 1956, October 20, 1962; *Oracle,* September 22, October 19, 1950, April 19, 1968; *HUB,* LVII (July, 1967), 10–11.

25. Ad Hoc Committee on International Programs to Academic Policies Committee, June 4, 1968; MAPC, September 18, 1968; FM, October 2, 1968, December 5, 1973.

26. FM, March 29, 1963, May 12, 1969. See faculty minutes from October 24, 1962 through March 29, 1963, along with the minutes and report of the Summer, 1962, Curriculum Study Committee; and faculty minutes from May 18, 1966 through May 12, 1969. See, in addition, EPC and APC minutes for the same periods.

27. MBT, October 24, 1961; FM, March 3, 1910, October 17, December 5, 1916, October 1, 1919; HUC, 1916–17, pp. 87–88; *Oracle*, November 11, 1909.

28. Vernon Kellogg to Samuel F. Kerfoot, June 17, 1921, in Kerfoot papers, HUA; FM, February 9, 13, 15, May 24, June 7, 1926, May 1, November 22, December 11, 1940, January 22, 1941, September 10, 1958, February 27, 28, 1959; MFC, January 8, February 17, 18, 26, March 6, 1931, April 18, 1932; *Oracle*, April 12, 1940; Hurst R. Anderson to the Board of Trustees, May 31, 1952; "Report of the Activity of the Team from Hamline University at the Danforth Foundation Campus Community Workshop, June 23–July 12, 1958," in FM, September 10, 1958. See also Charles R. Wimmer to faculty, August 26, 1958, and "Individualized Study Committee 1964 and Prior" file, HUA.

29. Minneapolis *Tribune*, February 22, 1960; Paul H. Giddens to the Board of Trustees, February 26, 1960; MBT, October 24, 1961; Donald E. Bridgman, "An Honors Program for Hamline University," HUA.

30. "Honors Program Preliminary Report, March 5, 1962," HUA; "A Recommended Curriculum for Hamline University, St. Paul, Minnesota, August 4, 1962," i–iv, 2–7, 10–11, in FM, April 15, 1964; MBT, March 13, 1962; FM, March 21, October 24, December 12, 1962; MEPC, October 17, 22, December 5, 1962.

31. Educational Policies Committee to faculty, May 28, 1965; Academic Policies Committee to faculty, March 17, 1966; FM, March 28, May 18, 25, 1966, September 14, 1967; APC minutes, 1966–67, *passim; Oracle,* May 29, 1964.

32. Academic Policies Committee to faculty, December 11, 1968; Quay Grigg to faculty, May 9, 1969; FM, May 12, 1969, February 3, 26, 1970, February 13, 1974, April 27, 1977; *Oracle,* January 24, February 14, April 18, November 21, 1969, February 27, 1970, April 29, 1977; HUC, 1976–78, pp. 11–14.

33. *HUB*, LVIII (January, 1968), 10–11.

34. *Ibid.*

CHAPTER 10

1. Paul H. Giddens, "The Scramble for College Athletes," *Atlantic Monthly*, CCXVI (December, 1965), 49–52.

2. Frederick Rudolph, *The American College and University, A History* (New York, 1962), 373–377.

3. Alumni Association of Hamline University, *History of the Hamline University of Minnesota When Located at Red Wing, Minnesota from 1854 to 1869* (St. Paul, 1907), 231; Leonard J. Dobner to Henry L. Osborn, November 23, 1935, Osborn papers, HUA.

4. *Oracle,* October, 1888, October, 1894, February, 1895; Raymond P. Kaighn to Henry L. Osborn, February 5, 1936, Athletics file, HUA; FM, September 13, 1899.

5. Raymond P. Kaighn to Henry L. Osborn, February 5, 1936, Athletics file, HUA.

6. *Oracle*, October 15, 1904; *AQ*, I (October, 1904), 8–9.

7. *Oracle*, May 15, 1905; *AQ*, III (July, 1906), 2.

8. *Oracle*, December 15, 1905; *AQ*, III (October, 1906), 5–6.

9. *Oracle*, February 10, 1910, March 8, 1912, October 17, 24, 31, November 7, 14, 1913, February 13, March 6, 27, May 1, 1914.

10. FM, January 9, 1913, March 11, 18, October 7, 1915, February 24, 1916; *Oracle*, March 3, 24, 1915, March 15, 1916, February 15, 1917.

11. *Oracle*, February 21, March 8, December 6, 1917; *AQ*, XVI (April, 1920), 21; FM, January 19, 1921.

12. *AQ*, XX (Summer, 1923), 13–14; undated Samuel F. Kerfoot memorandum [1924], Kerfoot file, HUA.

13. FM, April 5, November 22, December 6, 1922, January 31, May 25, November 6, 1923; *Oracle*, November 21, 1924.

14. *AQ*, XXI (June, 1925), 6; *Oracle*, November 8, 1929.

15. Arthur S. Williamson, ed., *Alumni Directory Hamline University 1854–1966* (St. Paul, 1966), 48; Arthur S. Williamson memorandum, January 6, 1965, Athletics file, HUA; *Oracle*, November 21, 1930, February 6, November 28, 1931; December 8, 1954; "A Salute to Joe Hutton," printed pamphlet in HUA.

16. FM, March 4, 1946; *Oracle*, March 7, 14, 21, 1946.

17. *Oracle*, March 7, 14, 1946.

18. I am indebted to Professor Philip A. Nordquist of Pacific Lutheran University for the information in this paragraph.

19. HUC, 1948–49 through 1950–51.

20. *Oracle*, January 18, 1946, February 17, March 18, 1948, March 10, 1950; FM, February 20, 1952.

21. *HUB*, XLIII (October, 1953); *Oracle*, February 20, 1953; Paul H. Giddens to author, March 2, 1978.

22. St. Paul *Pioneer Press*, July 15, 1955; St. Paul *Dispatch*, July 15, 1955; Hamline University, *Official Directory*, 1952 through 1956.

23. Paul H. Giddens to the Board of Trustees, March 13, 1956, summarizes the troubles from June, 1955, onward. The problem first surfaced in the minutes of the Board of Trustees on October 25, 1955.

24. Paul H. Giddens to the Board of Trustees, March 13, 1956; MBT, March 13, 1956.

25. *Oracle*, February 28, March 14, 1958; FM, January 15, February 28, April 16, 1958; MBT, March 11, 1958; *HUB*, XLVIII (April, 1958), 2, 5.

26. Paul H. Giddens to the Board of Trustees, May 4, October 19, 1959; MBT, May 8, 1959; FM, October 21, 28, 1959; *Oracle*, October 30, 1959, November 13, 20, December 4, 11, 1962, January 15, 1963; *HUB*, L (January, 1960), 2.

27. Paul H. Giddens to the Board of Trustees, October 24, 1957; *Oracle*, November 3, 1961; Paul H. Giddens, "Anatomy of a Football Team," *Minnesota Journal of Education* (September, 1967), 11–12.

28. *HUB*, LVII (January, 1967), 8–12.

29. Giddens, "Anatomy," 11–12.

30. Paul H. Giddens to the Board of Trustees, December 27, 1966.

CHAPTER 11

1. *Oracle*, February 11, 1921.

2. Information in this paragraph is based upon data drawn from the University

Catalog, 1921–1976. See also Paul H. Giddens to the Board of Trustees, October 20, 1962.

3. *Oracle,* December, 1896, March 4, 1909, May 20, 1920, November 11, 1932, November 1, 1940, November 5, 1948, October 31, 1952, April 26, 1956, November 11, 1960, October 30, 1964, November 1, 1968. The mock political convention was the brainchild of Professor Scott D. Johnston, and was first held in 1952.

4. *Prospectus of Hamline University* (Mankato, 1880), 11; "Hamline University Rules," a three-page printed pamphlet, undated, HUA.

5. FM, October 17, 1881, February 7, March 2, November 16, 27, 28, 29, December 13, 1882, May 24, 1883.

6. *Oracle,* December, 1888, March 1, 1907.

7. *Ibid.,* February, 1889, February 15, 1902.

8. *Ibid.,* February 27, 1908, March 17, 1915.

9. *Ibid.,* October, 1888, October, 1897, January, 1900, June 1, 1903, October 31, 1913; *AQ,* XIV (April, 1918), 16.

10. *Oracle,* June 16, 1910, January 20, 1915, March 15, 1917, April 22, 1920; HUC, 1880 ff.; FM, November 16, 1938, May 16, 1951.

11. *Oracle,* December, 1888, November 12, 1926; FM, September 23, November 11, 1925; "Organized Groups" file, HUA.

12. *Oracle,* December 12, 1913, January 23, 1914.

13. "Minutes of Conference on 'Our College,' Held at Hamline University April 30th and May 1st, 1925," HUA.

14. *Ibid.*

15. *AQ,* XXI (June, 1925), 6.

16. MBT, June 11, 1928; Alfred F. Hughes to Louise B. More, April 5, 1929, Hughes file, HUA; *Oracle,* October 28, 1927.

17. *AQ,* XV (January, 1919), 14; Grace Lee Nute, manuscript history of Hamline University, 217–218, HUA.

18. Nute, 219–220; *Oracle,* May 2, 1913, February 20, 1914.

19. FM, October 19, November 2, 1921, January 30, September 21, 1922, April 12, 1926; Nute, 222; HUC, 1927–28.

20. *Oracle,* June 16, 1908, December 6, 1912, January 17, 1913, May 14, November 18, 1914; FM, November 7, December 19, 1912.

21. *Oracle,* November 16, December 7, 1923; Charles N. Pace to the Board of Trustees, June 5, 1948.

22. *Oracle,* October 31, 1941.

23. *Ibid.,* February 5, 1965, January 13, 20, 1967; FM, March 3, April 28, May 19, 1965; January 19, 1966.

24. *HUB,* LIX (January, 1969), 16–17; interview with Richard P. Bailey, September 20, 1977; Paul H. Giddens to the Board of Trustees, April 24, 1968.

25. FM, February 12, 1969, January 7, 1970; *Oracle,* March 21, 1969, January 9, 30, 1970, April 30, 1971; MBT, May 5, 1969. The sole remaining committee on which students did not yet vote was the Curriculum Committee.

26. *Oracle,* May 2, November 7, 1969, February 6, 1970, February 12, 1971; FM, February 22, 1967, April 17, 1968, May 5, 27, 1970.

27. MBT, May 4, 1970, May 3, 1971, May 20, 1972; FM, April 5, 1972; *Oracle,* April 7, 1972; interview with Richard P. Bailey, September 28, 1977.

28. *Oracle,* March, 1889, February, 1891, February, 1896.

29. *Ibid.,* January 20, 1895, May 1, 1899, March 15, May 15, October 1, 1905, February 17, October 20, 1910, February 23, April 20, 1911, April 19, May 3, October 11, November 8, 1912, February 27, March 6, 1914.

30. *Ibid.,* 1924–1926, *passim,* especially Peterson's editorials of November 14 and December 5, 1924, and March 19 and April 16, 1926.

31. Carlyle Beyer to author, March 4, 1978; *Oracle,* April 21, May 25, 1934, February 14, 1936.

32. *Ibid.,* October 19, 1934, February 16, 1945.

33. *Ibid.,* June, 1892, March 1, 1904, June 16, 1910, December 2, 1932.

34. *Ibid.,* December 13, 1968, January 10, 17, 1969, November 5, 1971, September 19, 26, 1975; FM, May 12, 1971; interview with Richard P. Bailey, September 28, 1977.

35. Student Publications files, HUA.

36. Student Publications files, HUA.

37. Student Publications files, HUA; *Oracle,* December 6, 1968.

CHAPTER 12

1. Interview with Richard P. Bailey, September 20, 1977.

2. FM, January 19, 1949; *AB,* XLVI (October, 1949), 2; *Oracle,* November, 12, 1948; Hurst R. Anderson to author, April 11, 1978; "Report on the Physical Plant and a Comprehensive Plan for the Campus of Hamline University, Prepared by Holabird and Root and Burgee, June 1, 1949," Physical Plant file, HUA.

3. MBT, June 22, 1949; *Oracle,* September 30, 1949, October 18, November 2, 1950.

4. MBT, October 25, November 18, 1949, January 5, March 14, June 3, September 7, 1950, October 27, 1953; *Oracle,* September 22, 1950, September 26, October 17, 1952; "Science Hall Dedication" file, HUA; Hurst R. Anderson to author, April 11, 1978.

5. MBT, March 9, 1954, May 24, October 25, 1955, January 20, 30, March 13, December 14, 1956, January 3, April 24, November 6, 13, 1957, February 12, March 11, May 9, June 7, October 17, 28, 1958, July 13, October 23, 1959, May 24, December 8, 1961, January 19, 1962; Paul H. Giddens to the Board of Trustees, March 5, 1958; *Oracle,* August 15, October 10, November 7, 1958, April 16, 1963; *HUB,* LIII (January, 1963), 6.

6. MBT, April 16, October 8, 27, 1953; FM, May 20, December 16, 1953; Marts and Lundy, Inc., "Fund Raising Survey Report Made for Hamline University, St. Paul, Minnesota," *passim,* HUA.

7. Marts and Lundy Report, 31–48, 54–55; MBT, October 8, 1953, June 4, 1955, June 2, 1956; FM, September 10, 1957; Paul H. Giddens to the Board of Trustees, February 21, 1956; *Oracle,* September 26, 1957.

8. Paul H. Giddens to the Board of Trustees, October 23, 1956, October 22, 1958, April 10, 1968; "Historical Data on Hamline University," HUA; Richard P. Bailey, "If I Had Three Wishes" (Honors Day Address, May 2, 1974), HUA; Muriel McEachern to author, August 14, 1978.

9. Paul H. Giddens to the Board of Trustees, March 5, 1958, October 16, 1961; *HUB,* XLVIII (July, 1958), 2, 12, LIII (July, 1963), 13; Arthur S. Williamson, "The Giddens Years, 1953–1968," *HUB,* LVIII (April, 1968), 10; FM, November

15, 1956, April 20, September 14, 1960, September 13, 1961; Olaf Runquist, "The Hamline University Class Plan for St. Paul Developmental Program Students: A Report of a Three-year Experiment in College Classes for Talented High School Students in Mathematics and Science" [1963], HUA. Doane published his research as "Our Alumni: A Century of Achievements and Activities," *HUB*, XLVI (June, 1956).

10. MBT, May 12, June 14, 1961, January 4, March 17, May 3, 1965.

11. University Senate of the Methodist Church, "Survey Report to the President and the Board of Trustees of Hamline University, March, 1965," HUA; FM, January 4, March 3, 24, May 19, 1965.

12. MBT, June 5, July 28, October 8, 1965.

13. Long Range Planning Committee to Faculty and Administration, December 6, 1965, Office of Development file, HUA.

14. *Ibid.*

15. MBT, January 7, 1966.

16. John Price Jones Company, Inc., "Fund Raising Potentialities at Hamline University: An Analysis and a Plan, May, 1966," 1–3, 6–7, 19, Office of Development file, HUA.

17. *Ibid.*, 27, 31, 33–34.

18. *Ibid.*, 36.

19. Interview with Richard P. Bailey, September 20, 1977; FM, March 28, 1966, March 29, April 19, 1967; Long Range Planning Committee documents, Office of Development file, HUA; *Oracle,* January 29, 1971.

20. MBT, August 10, 1967; interview with Richard P. Bailey, September 20, 1977.

21. MBT, August 10, 1967; interview with Richard P. Bailey, September 20, 1977.

22. *Oracle,* November 15, December 6, 13, 1968, January 9, 1970, May 7, 1971; MBT, October 13, 1967, December 11, 1968; *HUB,* LIX (January, 1969), 2–7; "Announcing a Program of Renewal for Hamline University," [1969], Office of Development file, HUA.

23. MBT, March 29, 1969, May 4, 1970; *Oracle,* December 6, 1968, May 23, 1969, May 1, 8, 1970, April 25, 1975; *HUB,* LXI (November, 1971), *passim*; FM, November 6, 1968.

24. MBT, May 31, August 13, 1969, May 22, 1971; *HUB,* LXI (October, 1971), 4; *Oracle,* September 15, 1972.

25. MBT, October 19, 1974; FM, October 13, 1976; *HUB,* LVIII (April, 1968), 9; University Senate of the Methodist Church, "Survey Report," 155.

26. FM, October 1, 1975, September 6, 1976; *HUB*, LXI (July, 1971), 15–16, LXI (October, 1971), 1; *Oracle,* October 9, 1970, April 7, 1972, October 1, 1975, October 29, 1976. In the autumn of 1970, Edgar Carlson, Executive Director of the Minnesota Private College Council, reported that only two private colleges in the state were currently operating on a balanced budget. See MBT, December 9, 1970.

27. MBT, March 10, 1971, September 18, October 19, 1974, May 5, 14, 27, 1975; FM, October 4, 1972, May 7, 9, 1975; *HUB,* LXI (July, 1971), 15.

28. A recent reprint of the 1940 AAUP *Statement of Principles on Academic Freedom and Tenure* appeared in the *AAUP Bulletin*, LXIV (May, 1978), 108–110. The 1940 document was actually a restatement of principles set forth in the

1925 *Conference Statement on Academic Freedom and Tenure,* subsequently revised between 1934 and 1940 by the AAUP and the Association of American Colleges.

29. MBT, June 11, November 14, 1949, June 3, 1950; Hurst R. Anderson to faculty, September 19, 1950; FM, June 4, 1934, January 17, 1940, May 11, 13, 1949, September 27, 1950, November 6, 1968; Faculty Institutional Relations Committee to faculty, May 11, 1949; University Senate of the Methodist Church, "Survey Report," 53; *Statement of Principles on Academic Freedom and Tenure, loc. cit.,* 109. There were minor modifications between 1950 and 1968. See FM, May 28, 1957, MBT, December 12, 1962; Paul H. Giddens to the Board of Trustees, June 1, 1957.

30. MBT, June 18, 1975, January 10, May 3, 1976; FM, October 1, November 5, 1975, February 4, April 7, 14, 21, 1976; *Oracle,* October 3, November 21, 1975, April 23, 1976.

31. MBT, October 25, November 12, 24, 1969, January 14, April 8, May 13, 21, August 19, November 11, 1970, December 13, 1972, April 11, May 7, June 13, 1973; Muriel McEachern to author, August 14, 1978; Barbara Flanagan, *Ovation: A Partnership Between A Great Orchestra and a Great Audience* (Minneapolis, 1977), 112.

32. Laws of Minnesota, Ch. 43, 1854; Special Laws of Minnesota for 1871, Ch. CXII; Hurst R. Anderson to author, April 11, 1978; Hurst R. Anderson to the Board of Trustees, March 15, June 11, 1949, May 31, 1952; MBT, June 11, 1949.

33. MBT, April 28, 1954; Harry A. Bullis papers, MHSA; *HUB,* LII (July, 1962), 2, LVI (April, 1966), 2, LVII (July, 1967), 1, LIX (April, 1969), 5, LXVII (February, 1977), 19; Paul H. Giddens to author, March 2, 1978.

34. *HUB,* LIII (July, 1963), 2, 14; MBT, May 10, 23, 1963; Paul H. Giddens to author, March 2, 1978.

35. MMC, 1963, pp. 30, 84–85; MBT, October 7, November 13, 1963.

36. Paul H. Giddens to author, March 2, 1978; *HUB,* LIII (July, 1963), 2, 14, LIV (January, 1964), 2–3.

37. MMC, 1964, pp. 26–27, 29, 1974, p. 42; Paul H. Giddens to author, March 2, 1978; MBT, October 7, 1963, November 13, 1963, January 3, 1964; Special Charter Committee, minutes, December 12, 1963; *HUB,* LIV (July, 1964), 11, LV (October, 1965), 2; Paul H. Giddens to John D. Hicks, October 6, 1964 (copy), Hicks file, HUA.

38. "Report of the Conferences Visitors to Hamline University," in MMC, 1962, p. 93.

39. MMC, 1963, pp. 104–106.

40. Paul H. Giddens to the Board of Trustees, September 13, 1963. The University and the Church eventually resolved the controversy. See Paul H. Giddens to the Board of Trustees, April 27, 1964.

41. Paul H. Giddens to the Board of Trustees, September 13, 1963.

42. MBT, October 25, 1955, March 13, 1956; Special Committee to Report on Responsibility of College to Church, memorandum to the Board of Trustees, May 11, 1956; Paul H. Giddens to the Board of Trustees, October 16, 1961, April 10, 1968; *HUB,* XLVII (Fall, 1957), 4; interview with Richard P. Bailey, September 20, 1977.

43. *HUB,* LXII (January, 1972), 1.

INDEX